THE HISTORY
OF
Shipwrecks

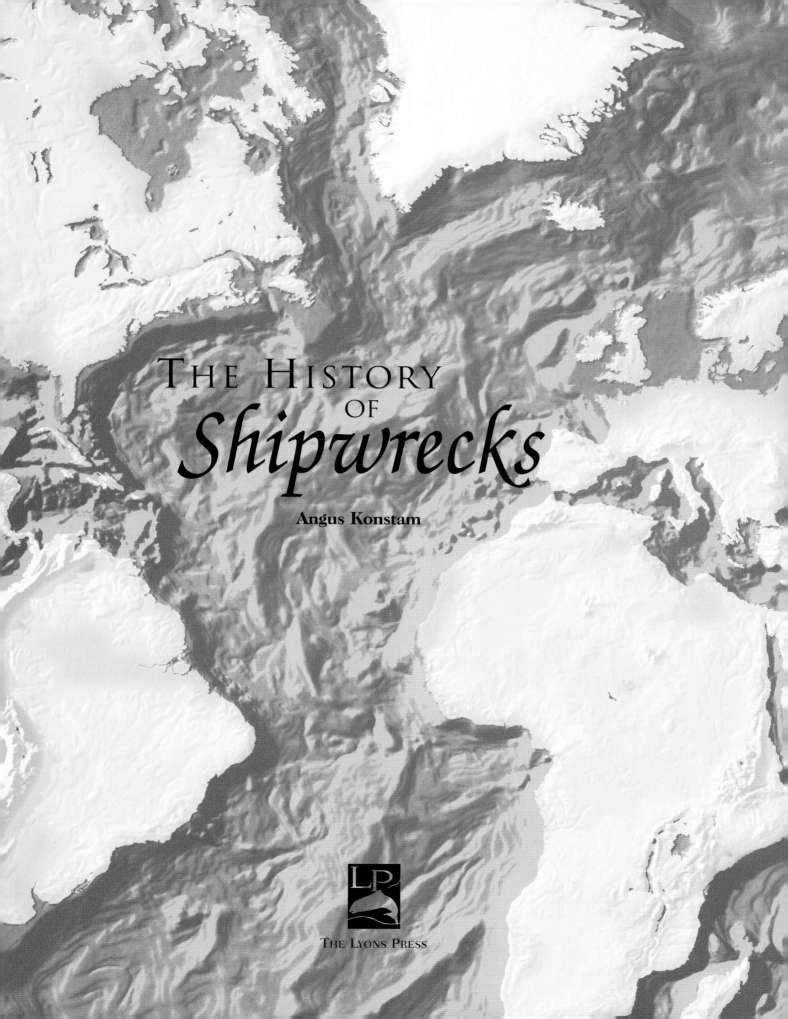

THE HISTORY
OF
Shipwrecks

Angus Konstam

THE LYONS PRESS

ISBN-13: 978-1-58574-620-0
ISBN-10: 1-58574-620-7

Library of Congress Cataloging-in-Publication data is available on file.

Picture Credits:
John Adams: 94, 130, 131; AKG London: 22 bottom, 47; Ancient Art & Architecture Collection, London: 46, 54, 55, 65; The British Library: 63, 122; The British Museum: 48; John Broomhead: 154; Colonial Williamsburg, Virginia: 166; Colorific: 41; Nicholas Dean: 169; Delaware State Archaeologist's Office: 156; Delaware State Museums, Delaware: 157; Deutsches Schiffahrtsmuseum, Bremerhaven: 72, 73; Draeger Limited: 40; Florida Bureau of Archaeological Research: 82, 83; Gary Gentile Productions: 172, 173, 182, 183 top, 185; Hamilton-Scourge Foundation: 159 Hamilton-Scourge Foundation and Ian Morgan: 158; The Hispanic Society of America: 106, 107; Imperial War Museum: 186, 187, 188; The Institute of Nautical Archaeology: 2, 50, 51, 57, 76, 79; Jamestown-Yorktown Educational Trust, Williamsburg, Virginia: 167; Kälmar Läns Museum/Kronan Project: 152, 153; Michael L. Katzev: 18, 52, 53; L'Invincible Society, Portsmouth: 155 top; Abraham Lopez: 80, 81; Rod MacDonald: 189; Mariners' Museum, Newport News, Virginia: 164, 165, 178, 183 bottom, 184; Colin Martin: 17 bottom, 96, 97, 128, 129; Edward Martin: 101; Mary Evans Picture Library: 15 left, 30, 134; The Mary Rose Trust: 10, 11, 22 top, 36, 66, 67, 95; Mel Fisher Maritime Museum, USA: 29, 126; Mel Fisher Maritime Museum, USA/Pat Clyne 27, 116 top, 117; Mel Fisher Maritime Museum, USA/Dylan Kibler: 8, 14 top, 15 right, 17 top, 20, 21, 26, 28, 38, 84, 85, 111 top, 112, 113 top, 140, 141; Mel Fisher Maritime Museum, USA/Scott Nierling 9, 16, 105, 110, 111 bottom, 116 bottom, 127 top; Estate of Keith Muckelroy: 100; Robert Muir: 189 bottom; Musée Archeologique de Beyrouth: 49; The Museum of London: 62, 68, 69; National Geographic Society/Jonathan Blair: 114, 115; National Geographic Society/Sisse Brimberg: 127 (bottom); National Geographic Society/Robert Goodman: 59; National Geographic Society/Emory Kristof: 39; National Geographic Society/Davis Meltzer: 56; National Geographic Society/J. Baylor Roberts: 24 bottom; National Geographic Society/Lloyd Townsend: 58 bottom; National Maritime Museum, London: 1, 5, 6, 7, 12, 14 bottom, 31, 32, 34, 35, 64, 77, 90, 92, 93, 104, 105 top, 120, 121, 135, 136, 149, 150, 155 bottom, 162, 163, 170 top, 179, 180, 181; National Park Service, U.S. Dept. of Interior: 167 top; North Carolina Archives and History/Julep Gillman-Bryan 145; North Carolina Archives and History/Alan Westmoreland 144; Parks Canada/Denis Pagé: 138, 139; Peabody Essex Museum, Salem, Massachusetts: 168; Pepys Library, Magdalene College, Cambridge: 12 bottom, 91; Prima Editions: 24 top; Prima Editions/Oliver Frey: 171 top; Rijksmuseum, Amsterdam: 19, 78; The Sea Venture Trust: 87; The Sea Venture Trust/Bank of Bermuda: 86; Texas Historical Commission: 38 bottom; Texas Historical Commission and the Corpus Christi Museum of Science and History 108, 109, 113; Thames and Hudson Limited: 58 top; Vasa Museum, Sweden: 98, 99; The Viking Ship Museum, Roskilde: 70, 71; Western Australia Maritime Museum/Patrick Baker 125; Western Australia Maritime Museum/Jeremy Green 124; The Whydah Society/Barry Clifford/City Arts Centre, Edinburgh: 142, 143; Woods Hole Oceanographic Institution: 39, 170 bottom, 171 bottom left and right, 174, 175

title page: *"The loss of HMS Magnificent, March 1801." Oil painting by John Christian Schetky.*

previous page, inset: *The Highborn Cay shipwreck. A diver surveys the wreck in 1986, noting the design of the mast step-up.*

opposite page: *An East Indiaman comes to grief during a heavy gale. "The wreck of the Amsterdam." Oil painting by Cornelius Wieringen.*

CONTENTS

FOREWORD

Why the interest in the discovery of ships lost at sea? Why the fascination with events that happened so long ago, or conversely, so recently that they are the subject of the evening news? Is the tragedy of losing a ship, her crew, and cargo more significant after divers discover it and begin to reclaim those objects from the sea floor? Why does a shipwreck seem more important than the ship itself?

For some, these recovery efforts and archæological studies document something more human than history alone can relate, because the story of the ship was never completed. These objects were not passed down through the ages, touched by countless hands, used and discarded. To others, the discovery of a shipwreck collapses time. The years between the wreck and the subsequent recovery disappear, and readers are connected directly to the people whose lives were lost, whose stories were so abruptly ended.

Or perhaps it is the mysterious transformation that the sea brings to anything man has made. When the sea has time to work its changes, the ordinary vase or the most common tool takes on an unearthly essence. Coral encrusts, the water erodes, and the worms have their way. The shipwreck is at once familiar, and yet unlike anything known. Shakespeare recognized this when, in *The Tempest*, he wrote:

> *Full fathom five thy father lies;*
> *Of his bones are coral made;*
> *Those are pearls that were his eyes:*
> *Nothing of his that doth fade*
> *But doth suffer a sea-change*
> *Into something rich and strange*

Whatever their reasons, people of all ages and backgrounds seem to fall under the enchantment of shipwrecks. A ship on the ocean floor represents something rich and strange. Whether in a book or a museum exhibition, the detective work that brings it to light and the humanity of the objects discovered fascinates and stirs the imagination.

The discovery of lost ships is increasing dramatically. Each new shipwreck brought to light reveals the rich world from our past. As we come to understand these wrecks and know the people lost so many years ago, the stories of the ships will finally be completed.

Claudia L. Pennington

CLAUDIA PENNINGTON
Director, Mariners Museum, Newport News, Virginia, USA

below: *"The Wreck of the East Indiaman Dutton at Plymouth Sound, January 26th, 1796," by Thomas Luny. Survivors and onlookers stand on the shore, helplessly watching the tragedy of a shipwreck unfold, while others try to rescue the crew.*

SHIPWRECKS

The fascination of shipwrecks is in the tales they produce of treasure and tragedy. They also give us a unique window into our past, the rare opportunity to understand the mariners of days gone by and the ships in which they sailed.

Shipwrecks are fascinating things. From childhood, they conjure up images of beautiful sailing ships cast against a rocky shore, of tragedy and terror, of daring rescues and lost treasures. This book describes 40 of the world's most fascinating shipwrecks and tells the story of how the ships were lost, and, equally important, of their subsequent discovery. Although the romantic image of sunken treasure is a powerful one, only a handful of these shipwrecks produced treasures in the conventional sense. The rewards they produced were equally priceless: information about the past, the ships themselves, the cargoes they carried, and the people who sailed on them. Treasure can mean many things to many people. To a treasure hunter (salvor), it is embodied in the gold and silver bars and precious jewelry recovered from the remains of a Spanish galleon; to an underwater archæologist, treasure can mean knowledge of how ancient ships were built, or how the cargo of, say, wine jars fitted into the economy of its day.

One of the topics covered by this book is the resulting conflict between archæologists and treasure hunters. The development of underwater archæology and the skills and techniques it draws upon are revealed in the following pages.

Two generations ago, this book could not have been produced. Until the 1940s there was no way ordinary people could have explored the underwater world, seeking to uncover the past. Jacques Cousteau's invention of the Aqua-lung in 1942 changed all of that. At last mankind had the key to

above: *"Catching a Mermaid." Oil painting by James Clark Hook. The aftermath of a human tragedy. Children scour the shore after a storm for the flotsam and jetsam of a shipwreck. Coastal communities saw the debris of a shipwreck as a rare windfall.*

unlock the vast hoard of information lying on the seabed. There has been an amazing leap forward in our knowledge of historic ships in the last 50 years, mainly through the discovery of shipwrecks. I hope to give the reader an idea of what information can be gleaned from a historic shipwreck, if it is approached properly.

The shipwrecks covered in this book have been divided into ten sections, each giving insight into a particular period of maritime activity. Most of the fascination of learning from wrecks lies in answering questions. These can range from determining how ships were built, through explaining how they fought, to answering why they were there to begin with. These sections of the book piece together the information gathered from shipwrecks and show how each one has helped to answer some of the main questions about the vessel's period.

Shipwrecks and diving is about people as much as ships and underwater techniques. The book is sprinkled with short outlines describing four characters who have contributed to the story in one way or the other, for good or otherwise. Choosing a pioneer, a deep-sea explorer, an archæologist, and a treasure hunter was a conscious move. It is important to understand what drove these people to do what they did, and why, from designing the first diving equipment to finding the *Titanic*.

Unless the reader is a diver, they may find the notion of working in the alien environment beneath the sea a strange one. While everything has to be adapted for use underwater, many archæology techniques used on land can also be applied underwater. However, the constraints of visibility, time spent on the bottom, and the influence of sea conditions are like nothing ever encountered on land. This lends an aura of romance to underwater exploration and archæology, rolling back the world's last great frontier. The rewards are well worth the effort, as shipwrecks give us the chance to visit the past in a way that is impossible on land. This book explains why.

right: *Underwater archæologists Corey Malcolm and David Moore working on the St. John's Wreck in the Bahamas, the site of a 16th-century Spanish "ship of discovery." The jumble of "concreted" objects and ballast stones in the foreground will be methodically plotted, recovered, and conserved by the archæological team.*

UNDERWATER ARCHÆOLOGY

The science of underwater archæology allows us to investigate shipwrecks and reveal the secrets they contain. The development of scuba diving over the past 50 years has made this fascinating scientific discipline possible, and fresh and valuable information is constantly being produced by diving archæologists.

Although Cousteau investigated classical wrecks in the Mediterranean during the 1950s, the first professional archæological excavation was in 1960. An American team led by George Bass excavated an ancient shipwreck off Cape Gelidonya, Turkey, which was over 3,500 years old (*see page 50*). This proved that archæologists could work underwater. The following year the warship *Vasa* was raised intact from the mud of Stockholm harbor in Sweden, a maritime salvage feat that brought the potential of shipwrecks to the world's attention (*page 98*).

As the number of sports divers increased during the 1960s and 70s, new historic wreck sites were discovered, mainly in America, Europe, and Australia. The number of diving archæologists slowly increased, and the projects they undertook included the mapping of sunken harbors and lake dwellings, as well as investigating ships. By the 1980s the underwater techniques and methods had become established, and training programs were introduced in universities in Europe and North America.

What does underwater archæology involve? By definition, archæology involves the identification and inter-

pretation of the remains of past ways of life. Rather like detectives, archæologists piece together the past from the evidence they uncover. Underwater archæologists do the same job, only in a different medium. As an archæological specialization, it encompasses the investigation of the submerged remains of shipwrecks, but it can just as easily involve the excavation of submerged buildings or even cities.

Archæological work is rigorous and labor-intensive, on land or underwater. However, underwater archæologists have to be competent at diving and working in their environment before they can begin their job. The archæologist can spend far less time per day working than his colleagues on land. Limited by decompression time, tide, weather conditions, air supply, and often temperature, the aquatic archæologist has to spend as much time battling with his alien environment as he does uncovering the past.

Underwater archæological skills

Other problems that are not encountered on land are poor visibility and lack of communication with colleagues, which means working in semi-isolation. They have to be competent archæologists and divers, and also need to be adept in a whole battery of other skills, such as being a technician, mechanic, fabricator, photographer, and surveyor. Although the aim is to work to the same exacting standards as expected on a land site, achieving this underwater is far more demanding and problematic. For many, that is part of the challenge.

Today, numerous diving archæologists can be found in federal or state employment, working for universities, museums, commercial companies, or operating freelance. Some even work with commercial salvage or treasure-hunting groups, trying to instill a degree of archæological recording into their operations. An archæological purist may deride their activities, saying they are assisting in the "looting" of an historic site. In reply, archæologists working with salvors might counter that the salvage work cannot be stopped, and it is better to learn something than nothing. For more on the conflict between archæology and salvage, see pages 26–28.

Of the 40 shipwrecks covered in this book, all but a handful were surveyed and excavated in an archæological manner, with scientific standards applied to the work. Two of the wrecks—the *Andrea Dorea* and the *Titanic*—are deemed too modern or too deep for archæological investigation. Others, such as three of the wrecks covered in the Spanish treasure fleets section, were not the subject of archæological work at all.

A number of shipwrecks subject to salvage by treasure hunters or commercial companies have been included by way of contrast. Their inclusion is not in any way a sign that the author or publisher condones treasure hunting, but serves to highlight some of the problems created by commercial salvage. Our past is too important a legacy for us to cause it harm simply for transitory financial gain.

above: *These silver "eight real" Spanish coins from a 17th-century shipwreck are not the only kind of treasure on the seabed. Archæology can reveal the vast treasure of information about our past that shipwrecks contain.*

below: *A bronze astrolabe recovered from the shipwreck of an early 17th-century Spanish galleon. This rare instrument was a navigational tool, used to determine the latitude of the observer. Mariners were unable to determine longitude until the mid-18th century.*

SHIPS AS TIME CAPSULES

Shipwrecks take place at a specific point in history, and represent the progress of mankind at the instant of sinking. Thus, they act as a time capsule, allowing us to look at the past in a unique way, an opportunity usually not provided by terrestrial archæology.

Each vessel lost during a shipwreck sank at a particular moment in our past. Everything onboard dates from that moment or earlier. One important benefit of excavating a shipwreck, rather than a land site, stems from this. Unlike a land site, which could have been occupied for centuries or intruded upon by modern objects, a shipwreck is like a photograph; a moment frozen in time. It as if the wreck is a time capsule, waiting for us to discover it and learn what life was like at that point in our past.

Each historic shipwreck has its own story to tell and adds to our picture of what life was like in the year it sank. It can show how ships of that time were designed and built, how they were armed, how they were sailed, and what cargo they carried. Although human remains are extremely rare on wrecks over 60 years old, the objects that once belonged to the passengers and crew can tell us a lot about the people who once owned them. Like the ship, their possessions were frozen at one historical moment, free of the fashions and styles of later generations. Everything on the wreck was used at the same time, and dates from the time of the shipwreck or earlier.

Sometimes these objects can date from much earlier. Although it is uncommon, antiquities and historic novelties have been lost in shipwrecks, many dating from as much as several centuries before the loss of the vessel. An example of this is the wreck of *HMS Colossus*, a late 18th-century warship that was lost off the Scilly Islands, in the western approach to the English Channel. When the wreck was discovered in 1974, as well as the usual finds associated with a warship from the age of fighting sail, it contained thousands of pottery fragments, some dating from the fourth century BC! The *Colossus* sank while carrying a consignment of Italo-Greek antiquities from Naples to London, which shows how documentary research can resolve apparently inexplicable shipwreck evidence.

above: *The spoked wheel of a gun carriage protrudes from the silt covering the remains of the after gundeck of the Tudor warship Mary Rose, which sank in 1545. Given the right conditions, artifacts on underwater sites can be amazingly well preserved.*

Mud preserves the 16th century

A ship that settled on an area of seabed with good preservative qualities has an excellent chance of retaining much of the historical information it originally contained. Ships like the *Mary Rose* (*see pages 94–95*) or the *Vasa* (*pages 98–99*) were both rapidly covered by the anærobic mud and silt of harbors in which each sank. This meant that the objects they contained, as well as much of the hull structure, was protected until the vessels were found and excavated, centuries later.

These big "time capsules" are of unique historical importance, sources of well-preserved information that can be the next best thing to traveling back in time to the moments before the sinking. Research into the finds recovered from the *Mary Rose*, where the rare conditions meant that some human bones survived intact, provided medical evidence about the health of working men of the mid-16th century. A sufficiently representative sample was recovered to show that bone deformities were common, as was dental decay. The remains of bedding and clothing had traces of lice infestation, and the remains of foodstuffs showed that the ship was plagued by rats. This kind of information would be impossible to obtain from a land site of the same period, and that is what makes shipwrecks a unique historical resource.

Even poorly preserved shipwrecks provide priceless information. For example, the vessel of the St John's wreck (*pages 84–85*) sank off the Bahamas in an exposed area that precluded the survival of extensive organic remains or ship timbers. Despite this, intact ceramic storage jars ("olive jars") and fragments of delicate glass vials, together with animal remains, show that even sites lacking a preserving layer of mud can provide vital clues about what life was like onboard Spanish ships of the era. One of the small bones, identified as that of a baby alligator, indicated the presence of a pet on board, probably carried to Spain as a souvenir of the New World. The hull structure and artillery finds can be compared with other, similar time capsules of Spanish ships from the "Age of Discovery," building up a more complete picture of how these vessels looked and how they were armed. This last example stresses the value of comparative collection, where material from similar sites can be compared, and linked to existing collections or information in the world's museums and archives.

below: A reconstruction of the same after gundeck region of the Mary Rose shown in the picture opposite. Careful study of the physical remains has allowed archæologists to understand exactly what conditions were like inside a 16th-century warship, and how shipborne artillery was used in this transitory period of naval warfare.

The diligent Spanish

The information gathered from the wrecks themselves can be augmented by documentary information. For instance, the administrators who equipped the artillery carried on Spanish Armada ships in 1588 were meticulous record-keepers. Each roundshot carried on each ship was recorded, and if the vessel managed to return to Spain after the campaign, they accounted for the shot it expended. This means that if a Spanish Armada wreck such as *La Trinidad Valencera* (*pages 96–97*) is thoroughly excavated, the

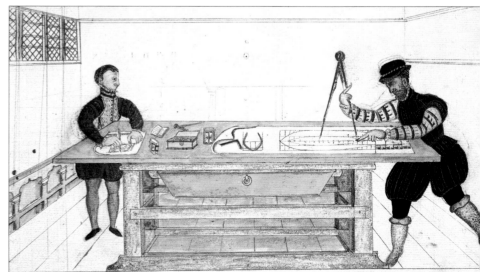

right: *Tudor shipwrights at work on the designs for a new vessel—it may even have been the ill-fated Mary Rose.*

archæologist can complete the record-keeping task of the long-dead Spanish clerks.

By comparing the roundshot recovered with those loaded before the ship left Spain, researchers can work out how many were fired during the Armada battles as the ships fought their way up the English Channel. This can reveal which guns were fired most frequently, and therefore give us an insight into Spanish tactics. It became clear that they hardly fired their big guns at all, probably because they were too time-consuming to reload. By comparison, they fired off prodigious quantities of shot for small, close-range guns, squashing the myth that the English fleet used long-range gunnery to fight the Spanish ships. This insight into an important naval campaign was only possible through a combination of archæology and archival research, taking the time capsule value of shipwrecks a stage further.

Recording the fragile past

There are only a limited number of historic wrecks lying beneath the oceans of the world. An unknown but finite number of ships sank throughout human history. Although we're aware of many, others still await discovery. New historic shipwrecks are constantly being discovered, and new deep-water search technology means that even the wrecks far beyond the reach of divers can be revealed.

Unfortunately, there are already too many known historic shipwrecks for archæologists to survey and excavate. These wrecks can all provide some historic information, however badly their remains have been preserved over the centuries. As wrecks are a finite resource, it is important that we gather information from them. As a finite resource, failing to accurately record information from any historic shipwreck is

above: *For all the poor souls aboard a sinking ship, the event is terrifying and probably fatal. George Cruikshank's "An interesting scene on board an East-Indiaman, showing the effects of a heavy Lurch," demonstrates all too well how fragile the lives of those on board could be.*

highly regrettable. It represents the loss of a time capsule and the erosion of knowledge available from this unique underwater resource.

Commercial salvage and treasure hunting have been major causes of the loss of this information, but dredging work, harbor construction, and other human actions have contributed to the process in the past. This is why the presence of archæologists working alongside treasure-hunting groups is controversial but a lesser evil than letting the material go unrecorded. On the other hand, a full recovery of archæological data from a commercial salvage operation is all but impossible.

If ships are time capsules, offering us a window through which we can look at our past, they are a resource worth treasuring. The information they contain is worth more than all the treasures ever carried by ships and lost at sea.

above: *Underwater archæologists working on the St. John's Wreck in the Bahamas.*

below: *The excavation of the North Ferriby boat was conducted in mudflats in a northern English estuary. This reconstruction shows how the remains of this 3,000-year-old craft were uncovered.*

THE LANDSCAPE OF A SHIPWRECK

Unlike fictional shipwrecks, real historic wrecks are rarely found intact; most often they contain a scattered assemblage of artifacts, with little visible hull structure. This scatter needs to be thoroughly examined in order to reveal the secrets the shipwreck contains.

For centuries, a ship was one of the most complex technological structures of its time, reflecting the latest technical achievements and built using the most modern tools. This applied to ships of the Bronze Age as much as it did to the warships of the 18th century. It was certainly true of ships built until the outbreak of the Industrial Revolution. Ships, especially under sail, were also objects of great beauty. Whether used as floating gun platforms or to transport cargo, sailing ships had a certain grace that seemed to elude many ships of the steam age.

When it wrecks, the beauty is lost. The image of the once-proud ship as a coherent object is lost with it, either during the shipwrecking or over the following decades. The notion that a ship stays on the seabed, with mast upright and tattered sails billowing, is a romantic but completely inaccurate one. The process of wrecking often breaks the ship beyond recognition.

After the first few days on the seabed, the breakdown of the hull begins, much like that of any manmade structure left out in the elements for any length of time. With time, hull structures collapse, spilling artifacts over the seabed. Silt may pile up on the wreck, and in some cases even bury it. Frequently, exposed timbers rot away or are eaten by the *Teredo* worm, and storms and seabed movement can grind up the remains of exposed sites and leave little to indicate that a ship was ever wrecked on the spot.

Semi-intact hulls are extremely rare. The usual indication of a sailing-era wrecksite is a pile of ballast stones and scattered artillery pieces. The archæologist has to use visible evidence not only to try to work out what the ship was but, if possible, also how and why she wrecked, why the artifacts scattered the way they did, and how they relate to the original ship structure. Wrecks often resemble a war zone rather than the site of a once-coherent construction.

Preserving the past

To the underwater archæologist, a wreck is a form of giant puzzle, where the information before him has to be fully understood before the answers are found. Every artifact or piece of structure may hold the clue he is

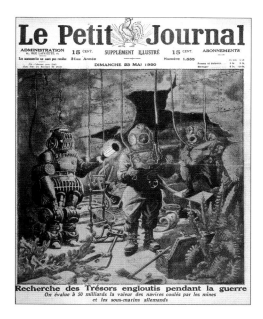

looking for, so the task ahead can be an extremely complex and laborious one. On land an archæological site may have been plowed over, built over, or looted, so finding one untouched is a rarity. Underwater, man could only swim or use grapples and dredges in limited areas. Until the invention of the Aqua-lung, wrecks were, therefore, well protected from man. Even after we could dive easily, wrecks have been protected by poor visibility, depth, and the sheer size of the seabed.

If archæology involves the study of a society through its material remains, everything depends on finding remains to study. Different conditions help or hinder the survival of material on a shipwreck. Their survival also influences what we can learn from the wreck itself. If something has rotted away, there is nothing left to recover. For instance, we know more about 17th-century Spanish artillery than the construction of Spanish galleons of that period, because far more guns survive on the seabed than ship timbers. Certain materials fare better on the seabed than others.

One significant property of an underwater site is that in the right conditions delicate objects made from wood, leather, skin, or other organic material can survive. Lack of oxygen in still water or sediments is the key to survival, so potentially large timber structures such as ships can survive well in deep silt. This happened with the *Mary Rose*, Henry VIII of England's flagship that sank in the English Channel in 1546. When excavated, over half of the vessel's hull remained intact and was subsequently raised (*see page 94*). The wealth of material that can be found on well-preserved sites is one of the best features of investigating historic shipwrecks.

top left: *The romantic view of shipwrecks and their exploration. This French journal dating from the 1920s depicts a shipwreck strewn with chests of sunken treasure, and hard-hatted divers recover the cargo aided by an underwater robot!*

above: *The reality of a shipwreck. The scattered remains of the 16th-century Spanish ship known as the St. John's Wreck show how the hull has rotted away, leaving only a few remaining timbers buried under a pile of ballast stones.*

FINDING A SHIPWRECK

The remains of a shipwreck are often hard to locate. The artifacts are often covered by sand, and can only be located by using sophisticated electronic search equipment. Once found, the remains need to be surveyed so that the shipwreck can be understood.

above: *A shipwreck hunter uses a magnetometer to search the seabed for the physical remains of a shipwreck. He is examining a paper trace for signs of magnetic anomalies that may betray the presence of metal shipwreck artifacts.*

Shipwrecks are often found by accident—fishermen catch their nets in timbers, sports divers see newly exposed timbers, and beachcombers discover remains washed up on the shore. Other people deliberately look for a wreck, either searching a general area as part of an underwater survey or hunting for a particular ship. The Emanuel Point Wreck was discovered in the first way (*see pages 82–83*), and the *Kronan* was found after a specific search for her remains (*pages 152–153*).

Searching for a wreck is a difficult business, as so many factors affect the hunt: equipment, the nature of the underwater terrain, weather conditions, and the proximity of land, among numerous others. While divers can search visually, electronic aids can achieve the task faster and more efficiently.

Magnetometers read the strength of a magnetic field. When towed behind a boat, its sensor picks up metallic contacts (or "hits"). The size of the hit indicates the size of the object on the ocean floor.

Echo sounders or sonar can identify a shipwreck by producing an image of what the seabed looks like below the boat carrying the device. Sub-bottom profilers work like echo sounders but use a lower frequency pulse to penetrate the seabed. A wreck covered by several feet of sand or silt can be detected, even if there is no trace of it on the seabed. Sidescan sonar sweeps out echoes at an angle, so wrecks poking up from the seabed will stand out, almost like a side elevation of the sunken craft.

Accurate position fixing using satellite navigation equipment (sat nav) or a global positioning system (GPS) help the searcher to comb the seabed in a logical pattern and eliminate areas that have already been covered. Searching for wrecks is often a process of elimination—you have to know where the vessel isn't!

One of the best search aids is information. Historical records can contain information about contemporary salvage, the ship's log, or even eyewitness reports of the sinking. Knowing where to look can pinpoint a specific area, but the sources aren't infallible. Even well-documented wrecks, with detailed positions of where the sinking or wrecking took place, can be off by several miles.

Surveying a shipwreck's remains

Although treasure hunters may not want or need to survey a wreck once they find it, a survey is a vital starting point to archæologists. With a completed survey, an archæologist could detect features of the wreck that weren't previously apparent. The survey acts as a map on which to plot the finds recovered; without one, any excavation would be destroying information to little purpose. Only by accurate plotting and measurement on the plan can the full story of the wreck be revealed. A number of survey tools can aid the process.

Photography is an essential part of archæology, on land or underwater. It can record the process of excavation, celebrate the discovery of finds, or even fill in details of a survey. A photo-mosaic (or photogrammetry) is a form of survey where a series of overlapping photographs are taken, building up a picture of the entire site. A photo-mosaic is sometimes the only practical way to record a large site in deep, clear water where divers cannot spend the time needed for a full survey.

To plot finds before they are raised, their position needs to be recorded in three dimensions. The basic method is to establish a baseline running through the wreck site, anchored at both ends by fixed points (datum points). Then, either by triangulation or using a grid system, measurements can be taken and the results plotted. Computers can help. With Direct Survey Method (DSM), a web of datum points throughout the site allows measurements of the objects, and the computer calculates an accurate 3-D position. A development of this is Electronic Distance Measuring (EDM), where readings are taken by handheld sonic measuring devices, greatly speeding up the process of surveying a shipwreck's artifacts.

above: Each anomaly revealed by a magnetometer search needs to be examined. Here a shipwreck hunter sweeps the seabed with a metal detector in an attempt to find evidence of artifacts buried under the seabed.

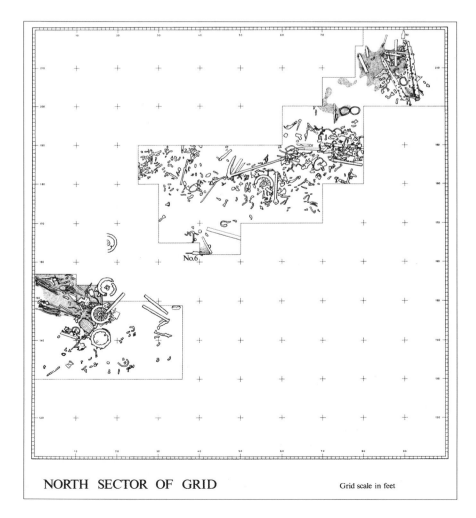

No.6

NORTH SECTOR OF GRID

Grid scale in feet

left: The archæological survey drawing of the shipwreck of the Spanish Armada vessel La Trinidad Valancera, lost off the Irish coast in 1588. Archæologists have uncovered areas of the wreck by removing the overburden of sand, revealing the scatter of artifacts beneath.

SHIPS AND TRADE

Throughout history, ships fall into three main groups: warships, merchant ships, and pleasure craft. Shipwrecks provide us with information on the last group, from Ancient Egyptian processional barges to yachts. The development of warships can be traced through shipwreck evidence from the time of the Romans until the 20th century, and they were frequently described or illustrated by contemporary observers.

Merchant ships, on the other hand, were the unsung heroes of the maritime world. Vessels carrying the humble commodities needed to feed and clothe humanity were rarely depicted in artwork or in detailed ships' plans. Evidence supplied by underwater archæology allows us to learn more about these vessels, ranging from the craft that supplied the needs of ancient civilizations to the sailing ships of the 18th and 19th centuries. Equally fascinating is the unique opportunity to find out about their cargo, and to see what it can tell us about trade in their respective eras.

Underwater archæological evidence of ships and trade is particularly important in the ancient world of the Mediterranean Sea, where documentary evidence is not prolific. The earliest known shipwreck in the world was a Bronze Age trading ship, and it provides us with a unique insight into business conducted in the eastern Mediterranean in that period. Maritime trade flourished during the Pax Romana, when Roman merchant ships could sail across the Mediterranean without fear of attack. Their only risk was from shipwreck, and the large quantity of ships that operated during the Roman period is reflected by the equally large number of known and excavated Roman wrecks. A study of these shows us how Roman traders conducted their affairs.

below: *The remains of the Kyrenia shipwreck (see page 52). A seaworthy reconstruction has been made from the remarkably well preserved timbers of this vessel. The wreck provided invaluable information about Mediterranean trading during the fourth century BC; its shell-first construction method remained in use until the 16th century.*

Wine trade from water

In 1945, only a handful of ancient Roman shipwrecks had been discovered. The invention of the Aqua-lung changed that and today over 600 Roman wrecks have been located and identified, plus hundreds belonging to other Mediterranean peoples. Work conducted by Dr. Toby Parker of Bristol University in England has shown how information from these wrecks can further our understanding of the Roman wine trade of the second century BC. A large number of wrecks contained amphoras, used to transport wine or other valuable substances. The amphora has been referred to as "the jerrycan of antiquity," and the quantity of "amphora shipwrecks" indicates the extent of Roman maritime trade.

Wrecks such as the trading vessel lost off Madrague de Giens in southern France reveal that amphora cargoes can be linked to specific suppliers through owners' markings on the containers themselves. Seals could be linked with individual vineyards, so it was even possible to see if the wine came from the quality vineyards of southern Italy or less well-regarded ones, such as those in Gaul (now France).

Based on the evidence from amphora wrecks, we know that wine from southern Italy was exported throughout the Mediterranean by the second century BC. By the mid-first century BC, the period of Julius Caesar, it appears that the Italian wine trade was in decline, probably a result of the devastation caused by numerous military campaigns fought in southern Italy during that period. Evidence from wine amphoras shows us that by the beginning of the first century AD, Spanish wine dominated the Mediterranean market, followed by wine produced in other areas, such as North Africa, by the start of the third century. This kind of evidence based on the analysis of shipwreck material is a unique and relatively new tool for classical scholars.

Other cargoes were shipped in amphoras, such as fish or fish paste, and research has identified the point of origin of many of these, helping us to understand something about the Mediterranean fish trade. It appears that the best fish paste came from southern Spain, and it was widely exported. Other similar analysis on Roman cargo such as marble has produced other useful information. Thanks to underwater archæology and the evidence of ancient shipwrecks, we now know a lot more about the economy and trade of the long-distant past than was ever thought possible 50 years ago.

above: *The major European ports became congested with trading ships from all parts of the world. This engraving of Amsterdam was drawn by Laes Jansz Visscher in 1611.*

The map on pages 42 and 43 shows the most-used routes around the world for modern shipping.

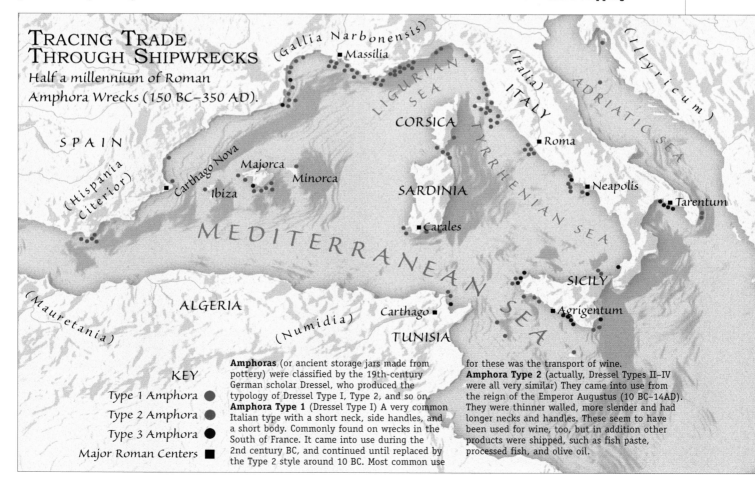

TRACING TRADE THROUGH SHIPWRECKS
Half a millennium of Roman Amphora Wrecks (150 BC–350 AD).

KEY

Type 1 Amphora ●
Type 2 Amphora ●
Type 3 Amphora ●
Major Roman Centers ■

Amphoras (or ancient storage jars made from pottery) were classified by the 19th-century German scholar Dressel, who produced the typology of Dressel Type I, Type 2, and so on. **Amphora Type 1** (Dressel Type I) A very common Italian type with a short neck, side handles, and a short body. Commonly found on wrecks in the South of France. It came into use during the 2nd century BC, and continued until replaced by the Type 2 style around 10 BC. Most common use for these was the transport of wine.
Amphora Type 2 (actually, Dressel Types II–IV were all very similar) They came into use from the reign of the Emperor Augustus (10 BC–14AD). They were thinner walled, more slender and had longer necks and handles. These seem to have been used for wine, too, but in addition other products were shipped, such as fish paste, processed fish, and olive oil.

EXCAVATING A SHIPWRECK

Archæology underwater is much like archæology on land, except different tools are used to excavate the remains. Archæologists have also adapted their techniques to suit the underwater environment, allowing them to meet the challenges facing them.

Each wreck site is different; the archæologist has to decide what degree of excavation is needed, if any. They need to know where to dig and what tools are required to complete the job. Any excavation will disrupt or destroy part of the wreck site, and in some cases it may be decided that excavation is not appropriate.

Once the pre-disturbance survey has been carried out and the decision is made to dig, the archæologist needs to use his skill and the information gathered by the survey to plan an excavation strategy. This strategy includes objectives, such as recovering all evidence from the wreck or answering specific questions.

One of two main approaches can be adopted: excavate large areas layer by layer, or work on one small section at a time, repeating the process across the site. Information gathered during the pre-disturbance survey plays an important part in this decision. Unlike land sites, shipwrecks aren't always laid out in a regular manner, as wrecking is a destructive process. The archæologist has to know roughly what to expect and how to deal with the results of the excavation as work progresses.

below: *An archæologist using a water dredge to excavate a portion of the St. John's Wreck. Water is pumped down the hose on the top of the dredge to create a suction effect.*

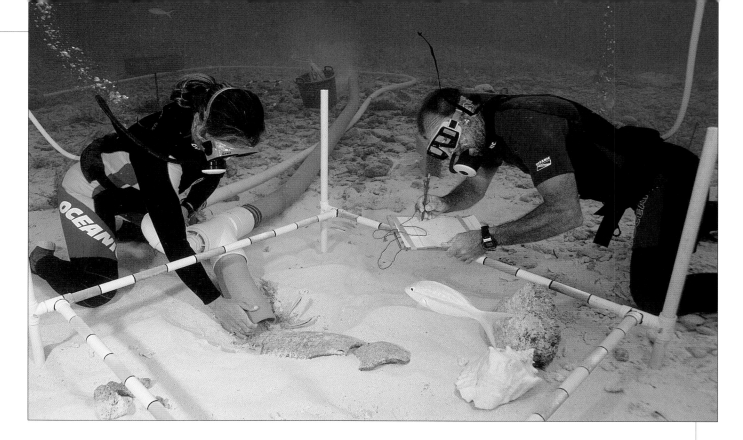

When you dig a hole underwater, the deeper you get, the greater the build-up of sand or silt removed. This "overburden" falls back into the hole, however fast you dig. Because of this "doggy hole" effect, the removal of overburden is vital for excavation. Archæologists use a range of devices to help remove the overburden from the excavation area, including water dredges, airlifts, water jets, and even buckets and spades! Different sites may require different tools.

Eliminating the overburden

On land, archæologists use a masonry trowel to scrape away the earth, but underwater the best tool is the diver's hand. By gently fanning the water over the seabed, a gentle current removes the overburden of silt or sand without damaging any artifacts or deposits within it. The force of the hand-fanning can be varied from just wafting a finger in very delicate areas to vigorously waving a hand or paddle to move large quantities of overburden. This silt or sand overburden hangs in the water and needs to be removed by a water dredge or airlift, otherwise it falls back where it came from. These tools move it clear of the excavated area.

The water dredge is the most versatile excavation tool used in underwater archæology. It consists of a long tube with a bend (nozzle) at one end. High-pressure water is pumped down a hose and injected into a tube at the bend. Standing water in the bend is picked up as the water moves up the tube and replacement water enters the nozzle, creating a suction effect—essentially an underwater vacuum cleaner. The longer the pipe, the less effective the suction, so excavated overburden can only be moved a short distance from the site.

The water dredge can work effectively in shallow or deep water. Apart from the short-range removal of overburden, its main drawback is that it works best horizontally—a dredge's efficiency decreases if it's pointed upward, so it doesn't perform well when excavating a vertical face or digging in a steep gully.

above: Excavation is often conducted in one small area at a time. Here, archæologists are using a water dredge to excavate a three-foot square, marked by the grid. The grid frame also serves as a survey tool, and the second archæologist is recording the location of the ceramic shards revealed by the excavation.

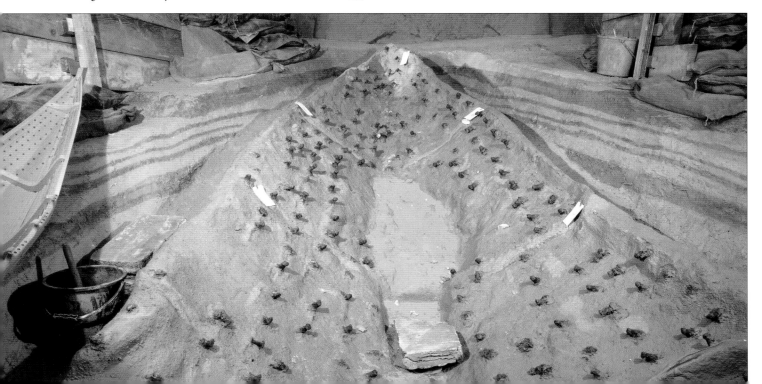

above: *This reconstruction of the gundeck of the Mary Rose shows the daunting task facing archæologists on a major excavation project. Each portion of the wreck had to be excavated inch by inch, revealing the complex structure shown here.*

below: *Shipwreck evidence can sometimes come in unlikely forms. This reconstruction of the land excavation of the Dark Age Sutton Hoo boat in England shows how discoloration of the sand revealed the location of planking and hull fasteners, where the physical remains had long since eroded away.*

Industrial vacuum

An airlift operates by pumping air into the bottom of a rigid tube that creates suction in the same manner as the water dredge. As more water is sucked in and up, a vortex is created, speeding ascent. Because the airlift works using air pressure and buoyancy, the shallower the water, the less efficient it becomes. Its optimum depth is 20–80 feet.

As the airlift works vertically, in theory the overburden would fall back onto the operator, so it has to be angled slightly and the whole device anchored to the seabed. In practice, water current usually floats the overburden away from the airlift area and off the site.

The airlift can remove large amounts of overburden so it's a powerful tool, but its main drawback is a lack of mobility. It can only be moved small distances before it has to be re-anchored, so a flexible hose is often fitted to the working end, which allows it to be directed to where it is needed. In simple terms, if the water dredge acts like a household vacuum cleaner, the airlift resembles an industrial-sized version.

Treasure hunters have a different set of priorities from archæologists—the need for controlled excavation is not usually considered necessary. Often their aim is to remove any overburden of sand or silt as quickly as possible and decide whether an area contains objects of commercial value.

The propwash deflection system was invented by Mel Fisher and is used extensively by treasure hunters and some archæologists to remove large overburdens of sand. Also known as a "mailbox" or "blaster," it involves large right-angled deflector cowlings fitted over the propellers of the investigator's boat. These direct the anchored vessel's propwash to the seabed, which can dig substantial holes in the sand. The more powerful the thrust, the greater the depth at which it can work effectively, and the bigger the hole.

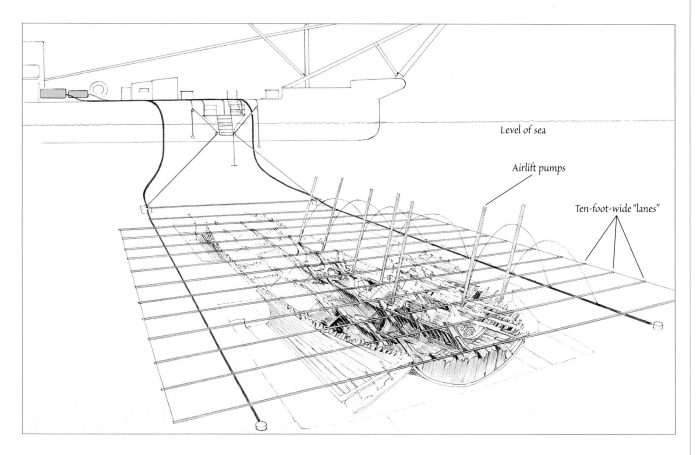

Level of sea

Airlift pumps

Ten-foot-wide "lanes"

The risks of excavation

The propwash deflection system is mainly used as a search tool and to uncover debris and artifact trails found on highly scattered wrecksites. Used carefully, it's useful in the right circumstances, but used carelessly it causes untold damage. Although not a true excavation tool, many treasure hunters use the propwash directly over exposed wreck sites, hoping to minimize the effort taken to recover objects. In underwater archæology, there is still no substitute for careful, painstaking, and controlled excavation.

One of the main purposes of excavation is to recover artifacts that help us to learn more about the ship, its crew, and its cargo. Moving these artifacts from the seabed to the dive boat is a critical process, particularly if they're so fragile that they may be damaged. Large objects like cannons and anchors can be winched directly onboard a boat or, if this is impractical, lifting bags or even air-filled oil drums can be used. When filled with air, these devices float upward like a balloon. The lifting capacity of commercially available airbags ranges from a few hundred pounds to several tons.

More delicate objects can be brought to the surface in crates or even plastic boxes filled with sand to protect the structural integrity of fragile artifacts. In some cases special containers are needed. For example, on the *Mary Rose* archæologists used sand-filled semi-circular sections of plastic drainpipe to raise bundles of longbow arrows intact. The archæologist has to gauge each situation carefully and choose the best method to raise each precious find from the seabed.

above: *This reconstruction of the Mary Rose excavation shows how the excavation was conducted. A grid divided the site into ten-foot-wide lanes. These were excavated layer by layer in a series of trenches bisecting the hull. The seven airlifts were used to remove the silt from the wrecksite.*

JACQUES COUSTEAU (1910-97)

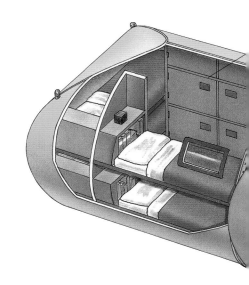

Diving through the remains of a shipwreck, free of lifelines, diving chambers, or support vessels finally became a reality in the 1940s. The figure responsible for this revolution was Jacques Yves Cousteau, who did more to reveal the mysteries of the deep than anyone before or since.

Cousteau and a group of friends began skin-diving for sport in the Mediterranean in the years just before the outbreak of the Second World War. Using homemade "underwater lungs" that stored pure oxygen, he experimented with new forms of diving equipment, including masks, fins, and fishing spears. The underwater lungs proved dangerous, so Cousteau tried to create reliable diving equipment that used compressed air.

Following the fall of France to Germany in 1940, Cousteau continued his diving experiments, which also provided a useful cover for his clandestine work for Allied naval intelligence. In Paris, late 1942, he met Émile Gagnan, an expert in industrial equipment. Cousteau explained what he needed to make a diving regulator for a tank of compressed air. Gagnan showed him a gas attachment designed for an experimental gas-powered car. Within weeks it was adapted into the world's first working regulator (or demand valve), allowing humans to breathe compressed air underwater. Initial experiments were a failure, but after a simple modification it worked—at least in a water tank.

In June 1943, Cousteau and his colleagues tested the new tank and regulator in the sea, near the French Riviera town of Bandol. As Cousteau's wife swam on the surface and friends waited to rescue him if there were problems, the French adventurer slipped beneath the surface. "I breathed sweet, effortless air," Cousteau later wrote. "There was a faint whistle while I inhaled, and a light rippling sound of bubbles when I breathed out. The regulator was adjusting pressure precisely to my needs .... The sand sloped down to a clear blue infinity ... my arms hanging at my sides, I kicked the fins languidly and traveled down. I reached the bottom in a state of excitement .... I looked up and saw the surface shining like a defective mirror." It worked! He called his invention the Aqua-lung.

below: *Jaques Cousteau receiving the National Geographic Award for achievement in 1961 from President John F. Kennedy.*

Aboard the *Calypso*

For the remainder of the war, Cousteau and his group logged thousands of dives, exploring the exciting world that the Aqua-lung opened up for them. They also discovered its limitations. They pushed as far as 240 feet before encountering serious problems. Nitrogen narcosis produced an elated, almost drunken euphoria. The Frenchmen called it "the rapture of the depths." Modern divers don't go much below 150 feet without

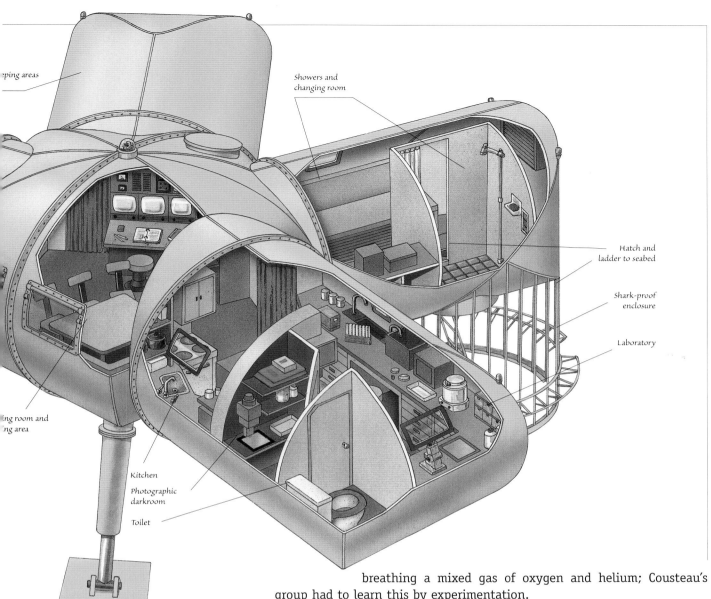

...eping areas

Showers and
changing room

Hatch and
ladder to seabed

Shark-proof
enclosure

Laboratory

...ng room and
...ng area

Kitchen

Photographic
darkroom

Toilet

above: *An artist's reconstruction of Cousteau's underwater research laboratory, Conshelf One. Cousteau pioneered the use of deep-water laboratories, capable of housing a team of several diving scientists for up to a month.*

breathing a mixed gas of oxygen and helium; Cousteau's group had to learn this by experimentation.

When the war ended, the French Ministry of Marine hired Cousteau to investigate and salvage wartime wrecks off the French coast. He founded the Undersea Research Group and combined work for the government with his own diving exploration. In 1949 he took command of the *Calypso*, which became his main research vessel for the next 25 years. In 1952 he used it to excavate a merchant ship dating from around 230 BC at Grand Conglué, a bay near Marseilles. This was the world's first glimpse of the potential of underwater archæology. Where a land site of the same age might only reveal a handful of broken pottery shards, Cousteau's wreck produced hundreds of intact ceramic containers.

He experimented with television, sending divers down with cameras for the very first time. This led to regular television programs and eventually to his own series. It was screened worldwide, bringing Cousteau's underwater expeditions to tens of millions of people. He explored the oceans' historic and natural resources throughout the remainder of his life, and developed groundbreaking technological tools, such as small manned submersibles and underwater laboratories. Long before his death in 1997, Cousteau had become a figure of international acclaim, publicly recognized for his incredible list of achievements. Today, he is probably remembered most as the man who made the mysteries of the deep accessible to ordinary people.

ARCHÆOLOGY VERSUS SALVAGE

Developments in diving technology meant that treasure hunters as well as archæologists were capable of searching for historic shipwrecks. The controversy over the ethics of treasure hunting has resulted in a long-running battle between salvors and scientists.

above: *Silver ingots and coins alongside gold "finger" bars and jewelry recovered from the wreck of the Spanish Treasure galleon Nuestra Señora de Atocha, which was lost off the Florida Keys in 1622.*

below: *Silver "eight real" coins and jewelry from the Nuestra Señora de Atocha are displayed alongside gold bars. The bars were marked to show gold purity, its owner, and the Spanish government's tax stamp.*

Commercial salvage often involves the recovery of objects from historic shipwrecks for monetary gain. Although many archæological sites have little or no financial value, there are others where the conflict between recovery for profit or for information is marked. Shipwrecks such as the *Nuestra Señora de Atocha* (1622) have resulted in the location of priceless sunken treasure, the finds from the Spanish galleon alone being valued at around $400 million. The *Atocha* search and recovery was conducted with an archæological team working alongside the treasure salvors. Despite this, the collection was dispersed between investors, and sold at international auctions and to private buyers. Only a representative sample remains in the hands of a local museum. In an archæological project such as the *Mary Rose* (1545) excavation in the 1980s, the entire collection was kept together for future generations to study. That is probably the biggest lasting difference between the two.

Treasure hunting comes in many forms. Some of the earliest "salvors" in Florida were the beachcombers who searched the shoreline with metal detectors, looking for the remains of the 1715 Spanish treasure fleet. These days, large multi-national salvage companies use the latest technology. The author knows of several such projects currently underway, in the waters of the Central Pacific, off the Bahamas, and in the Caribbean Sea.

Funding often comes from the selling of shares or investments for a specific treasure-hunting project, or for a set period. These investors are gambling that the salvors will recover treasure; at the end of the period, the finds are distributed on a share-by-share basis. Other sources of finance are the sale of objects, such as coins recovered from previous projects. Investors are often attracted by the romance of searching for sunken treasure, or by the prospect of a substantial return on their investment.

Questionable returns

Although this practice is fairly commonplace, particularly in the United States, few salvage companies have delivered the level of return that the investors may have wanted. Some

treasure hunters, such as the late Mel Fisher, were able to demonstrate a degree of success in both finding treasure and attracting investors. Many others ended in failure, unable to find the lost treasure wreck or keep the project financially viable.

One of the problems with sunken treasure is that although it may have a commercial value, turning it into hard currency is not easy. Consistently, the sales of treasure in highly publicized international auctions have not resulted in the profits that were first imagined. Others, such as the *Atocha* find, become victims of their own success. With so much silver recovered, the sale of treasure had to be conducted a small amount at a time, to avoid depressing the international market.

These cases are rare, and even valuable treasure wrecks still produce much more non-valuable material such as ship fittings, hull structure, and iron fasteners than gold or silver. Without adequate conservation, these recovered artifacts are put at risk. Although some commercial salvage operations have exemplary records, most don't conserve all the materials they recover.

Technological improvements in underwater search and recovery, especially in deep water, mean that wrecks that were once safe from the attentions of treasure hunters are now being located. The *Titanic*, *HMS Edinburgh*, and the steamer *Central America* have all been subject to salvage by commercial salvage firms in recent years. Also, as many of these deep water wrecks lie in international waters, they are not subject to protection under the law.

It appears that salvors are gradually swimming against the current of public and governmental opinion, as their activities have resulted in legal controls being placed on commercial exploitation of historic wrecks. In the United States and many European countries, government-funded underwater archæological units have been created to support this legislation. With these national controls becoming increasingly common, treasure hunters are increasingly involved in the salvage of wrecks in international waters. This in turn means that the costs involved in commercial salvage operations are prohibitive to all but a few organizations.

above: *Treasure hunters working for Mel Fisher recovering silver ingots from the wreck of the* Nuestra Señora de Atocha *using a supermarket trolley. The salvors referred to the site as "the motherlode," where the silver ingots formed a reef on the seabed. Each ingot weighs about 70 pounds.*

Two types of archæologists work with treasure hunters or commercial salvors on a regular basis. In the United States, many coastal states run State-funded archæological programs, where part of their brief is to supervise the work of commercial salvors working on historic wrecks. In many States, commercial salvage is still possible, but only if a State archæologist is present, and the State receives a portion of the finds recovered. Disliked by archæological purists for seemingly condoning commercial salvage and by salvors for inhibiting their enterprise, this procedure in itself is controversial, and the archæologist can find himself at the center of bitterness and even legal action. The ideal solution to the problem has yet to be found.

Protecting the shipwrecks

Some commercial salvors have archæological teams working with them on their projects, as discussed earlier. Archæologists who work with salvage teams, lending a veneer of respectability to a commercial operation, are often seen as "selling out" by some of their colleagues. These archæologists reply that they are recording important information that would otherwise be lost. One of the problems remains that the financial controllers of the treasure hunt often retain total control of the project, and commercial considerations outweigh archæological ones. Although at least one commercial salvage project resulted in a full site report of archæological quality, most such projects have produced no published body of information that can be used to benefit future researchers. Although collaboration may be possible, the incompatibility of archæological practice with treasure hunting makes successful teamwork all but impossible.

Legal protection of historic shipwrecks is more effective in some countries than others. After having so many antiquities looted over the past century, Greece is one of the most stringent. Museums also make life difficult for treasure hunters. Museum bodies such as the International Council of Museums (ICOM) and the American Association of Museums (AAM) have issued relevant ethical policies. These condemn the acquisition of commercially salvaged material after the cut-off date of 1991. Much as the world's national museums no longer acquire antiquities looted from Egypt or Greece, now neither does the world's main maritime museums. The author's own museum, although holding objects recovered from the *Atocha*, has incorporated its endorsement of this ethical practice into its policy.

The debate over the ethics of commercial salvage versus archæology will continue indefinitely, but in the meantime there are far more sites worldwide excavated by commercial salvors than by archæologists. There is not an infinite number of historic shipwrecks, so the logical solution is to stop commercial salvage altogether—almost impossible—or for archæologists to be encouraged to help salvors get the maximum information possible from the site, for the benefit of everyone. Neither solution seems likely at present.

EARLY DIVING

For centuries, mankind has sought ways in which to explore the bed of the ocean. Since the Renaissance, diving equipment of varying degrees of practicality has been designed and used in a quest to allow humans to breath and work underwater.

below: *17th-century Spanish salvors recovering the cargo from a shipwreck. Grappling hooks were used to tear open the hull, then swimmers went down to recover what they could. The salvage operation could take years to complete.*

The sea is not man's natural element. As even record-breaking divers can only hold their breath for a little over four minutes, the task of exploring shipwrecks requires diving equipment. Although contemporaries, using trained sponge or pearl divers, salvaged ancient and Renaissance wrecks, depth and time on the bottom were extremely limited.

Leonardo da Vinci (1452–1519) was one of the first to invent a diving aid. He designed a hard leather diving helmet, complete with glass eyepieces and even spikes to ward off sea monsters! It was fitted with a long, snorkel-like breathing tube, the open end kept above the water's surface by a cork float. Unfortunately, the water pressure at even nine feet would have made breathing through the tube all but impossible.

Another solution was to use an open-bottomed diving bell, resembling a bell or upturned tumbler. As they were lowered, the water level inside the bell rose, but air pressure ensured that there was an air pocket to breathe from. At 30 feet, the air pocket would be half the volume it was on the surface, and the water pressure on the bell would be two atmospheres (approximately 30 pounds per square inch). At 60 feet the pocket would be a third of the size, and the water pressure would be three atmospheres.

For every 30 feet a diving bell descended, the pressure would increase by one atmosphere, reducing the air pocket. At depths over 60 feet the volume of breathable air was small, limiting the duration of the dive. Despite the drawbacks, diving bells were used to salvage shallow water wrecks throughout the 17th century. With divers sitting on a bench inside the bell, trying to work while up to their necks in often freezing water, conditions were grim.

above: *A 15th-century illustration shows Alexander the Great being lowered into the sea in a glass cage. This depiction from the "Travels of Alexander the Great" shows what forms of life late-medieval mariners expected to find beneath the ocean.*

The first diving suits

A diving breakthrough came in 1690. Edmund Halley, the discoverer of Halley's Comet, developed a way to pump fresh air into a diving bell. As the volume of air inside the bell shrank inside the descending craft, it was replaced by air pumped in from casks strapped to the outside. This allowed diving bells to safely descend to 200 feet, and divers could stay down for over an hour. Halley experimented unsuccessfully with personal mini-bells, allowing divers to swim short distances from the main craft with their own air supply.

At around the same time, an experienced wreck salvager named John Lethbridge invented individual diving suits. These were improved upon during the early 18th century by another salvor, Jacob Rowe. In these, the diver wore a barrel-like suit to protect his body from the water pressure, fitted with leather sleeves and a viewing porthole. At 60 feet, divers using a Lethbridge suit could remain on the bottom for 30 minutes before they were hauled to the surface and the suit replenished with fresh air. The advantage of the suit over the bell was that it allowed freedom of movement. Lethbridge was contracted to perform salvage work on behalf of the Dutch East India Company, making him one of the earliest commercial salvors.

The first real diving helmets were being used by 1750, when a brass helmet was fixed to a leather diving suit. The problem of supplying air under pressure restricted them to a maximum depth of 30 feet, but within a decade a new suit was invented. Two English brothers, John and William Braithwaite, designed a diving helmet that allowed them to work in

60 feet of water. They used it with considerable success to salvage coins lost on an English East Indiaman vessel.

Another Englishman, John Deane, invented a diving helmet and suit in 1828 that were even better. During the early 19th century, he used his system to salvage the wrecks of the *Mary Rose* and the *Royal George*, both sunk in Portsmouth harbor, in southern England, and recorded his achievements in a series of watercolor sketches. A problem with the Deane helmet was that the diver could not lower his head for fear of it flooding with water!

Siebe's dependable suit

A German, Augustus Siebe, invented the prototype of a more modern hard-hat style of helmet. By 1837 it was augmented by a watertight rubber diving suit. These helmets relied on a supply of pressurized air pumped down from the surface. Intake and outlet valves allowed stale air to be expelled. This meant that a diver's time on the bottom was only limited by his endurance to the cold. For the first time, dives of 120 feet or more were possible.

Diving suits gradually became more commonplace as the century progressed, used by engineers and salvors. The major limitation of the helmets was their reliance on air from the surface, which limited their range and mobility. There was also a risk of the lifeline becoming tangled in an underwater obstruction.

In 1865, French engineer Benôit Rouguayrol teamed up with Auguste Denayrouze, a naval officer, to produce the first diving air tank. The diver breathed air from a cylinder of compressed air strapped to his back, while a valve regulated air intake and outlet. Although a revolutionary design, the problems of producing a tank that wouldn't crumple under pressure prevented the system from being adopted. Similar "free-diving" systems were invented by Charles Condert of the United States, although its safe use was equally fraught with problems.

The Siebe system remained the one reliable form of diving gear. Although in theory an archæologist could use a hard-hatted diving suit to explore the seabed, few did. Diving was seen as a specialist occupation, beyond the aspirations of most gentleman archæologists of the Victorian, Edwardian, or inter-war eras. No more than a handful of antiquarians or archæologists used the new technology, notably the late 19th-century surveyors of early lake-dwelling remains in Scottish and Swiss inland waters.

below: *Early forms of diving equipment, including Halley's diving bell, Rowe's early diving shell, and Klingert's diving helmet and suit. All imposed severe limitations on the ability of the diver to work underwater.*

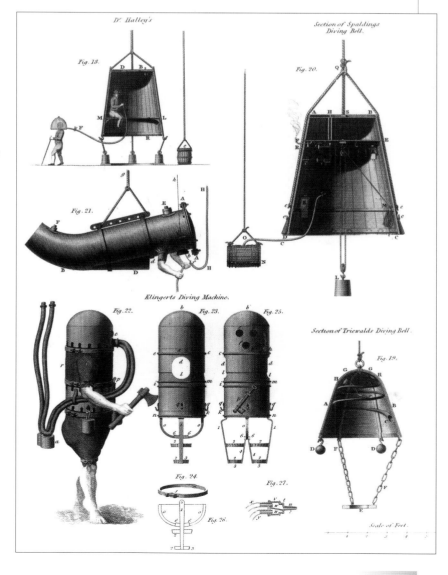

The salvage business develops

Underwater photography, now a vital archæological tool, was first attempted in 1856. William Thompson's first blurred photographs of the seabed off the English south coast were almost indecipherable, but by 1893 French photographer Louis Bouton produced a real underwater camera. Housed in a sealed copper case, his wet-plate camera used underwater flash bulbs to obtain clearer images.

Two things placed diving on the map around the end of the 19th century. Science fiction writing, such as Jules Verne's *20,000 Leagues Under the Sea*, caught the public's imagination and made diving a popular subject for the literary medium. At the same time, well-publicized construction projects and underwater inspections that used divers were widely reported in the world's newspapers. For example, divers' investigation of the shipwreck of the *USS Maine* in 1898 was conducted amid a media frenzy. Blown up in Havana harbor, the battleship's loss, resultant investigation, and the "yellow journalism" of the reporters led directly to the Spanish-American War of 1898.

By the end of the First World War, commercial salvage had become a viable industry. The work of the Cox and Danks Company in recovering the sunken German High Seas fleet during the inter-war years was probably the most ambitious diving project of its day, and showed that divers could perform complex salvage tasks underwater (*see pages 186–187*). Hard-hatted diving suits remained in use as the only safe diving system until the Second World War, when military research allowed naval "frogmen" to use self-contained breathing devices and dispense with their lifelines to the surface.

below: *The salvage divers John and Charles Deane working on the wreck of HMS Royal George, which sank off the English coast in 1782. A pump on the surface tender supplies air to the diver, who is shown wearing a hard-hat designed by the Deane brothers.*

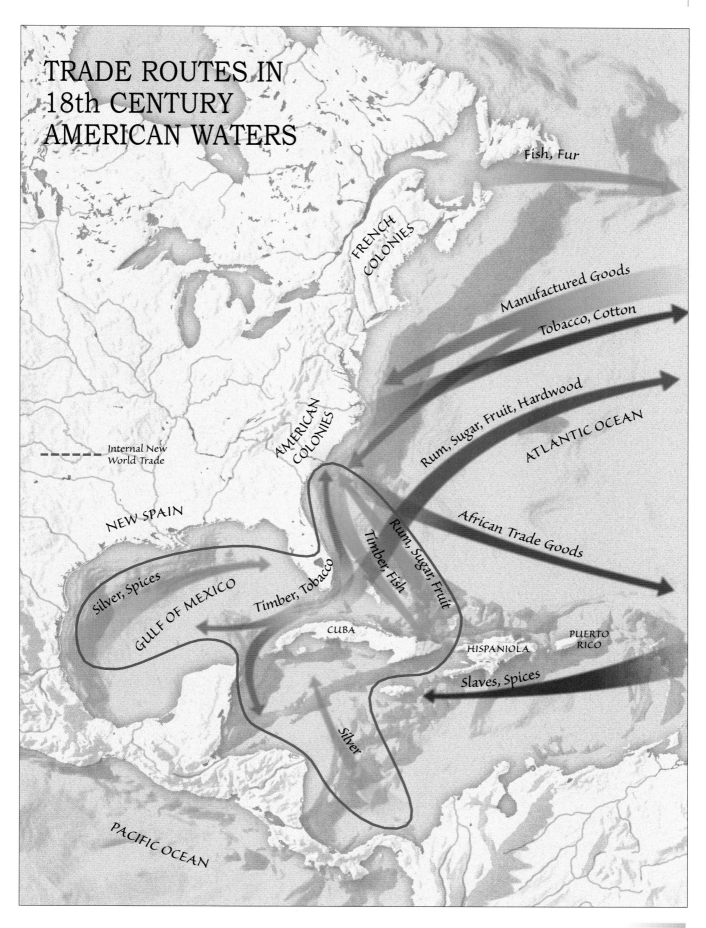

TRADE ROUTES IN 18th CENTURY AMERICAN WATERS

Fish, Fur

FRENCH COLONIES

Manufactured Goods

Tobacco, Cotton

Rum, Sugar, Fruit, Hardwood

ATLANTIC OCEAN

AMERICAN COLONIES

Internal New World Trade

NEW SPAIN

African Trade Goods

Rum, Sugar, Fruit

Timber, Fish

Silver, Spices

GULF OF MEXICO

Timber, Tobacco

CUBA

HISPANIOLA

PUERTO RICO

Slaves, Spices

Silver

PACIFIC OCEAN

WHAT HAPPENS WHEN A SHIP WRECKS?

The reasons for a wreck are varied, but in most cases the human tragedy underlying the event cries out to us. A number of contemporary accounts of shipwrecking can give us some idea of what happened.

Although archæologists speak about the "wrecking process" and other sanitized phrases to describe a tragedy, it is almost impossible to recapture the horror of a ship's final moments. Not all were lost in storms—some were beached in a badly leaking condition, others were lost through battle, while a few capsized through faulty design. The *Mary Rose* was lost in 1545 because the vessel heeled over unexpectedly, filling her gunports and making the ship capsize (*see pages 94–95*). A half-century later, a survivor of the Spanish Armada ship *La Trinidad Valencera* reported to his English captors how his ship grounded in an Irish bay in 1588 (*pages 96–97*):

"They lost sight of the Armada on the night of 12th September, during a tempest. The same night their ship sprang

main: *The horrors of a shipwreck are captured in this 17th-century view of a multiple shipwreck: "A ship and galley wrecked on a rocky coast." Oil painting by Mathieu van Plattenberg.*

inset below: *Survivors scramble ashore or take to the boats as their ship breaks apart on the rocks. "Wreck of a ship off a rocky coast." Oil painting by Samuel Walters.*

a great leak forward, and for the next two days they were at the pumps. On the 14th they brought up on the coast of Ireland, toward Blasket, and all the soldiers, except 40 who remained in the ship, and were afterward drowned when she foundered, were put on shore, with their arms, in a little boat."

Once ashore, the troubles of the survivors were far from over, as another survivor stated: "He said that as they came near the land, he saw some 20 of the savage people standing on a rock, and on landing about four or five came and did help them out of the boat and used them

courteously until the rest of the wild people that stood on the rock, and more with them to the number of 40 came together, at which time they took from them in money, gold buttons, rapiers, and apparel to the value of 7,300 ducats or thereabouts."

After surviving a robbery by local Irish, the survivors were captured and some massacred by patrols of the English army. A less hostile local reception met the survivors of the Dutch East Indiaman *Amsterdam*, wrecked off the south coast of England in 1748 (*pages 130–131*). A local gentleman recorded the event:

"She was called the *Amsterdam*, of that place, and bound for Batavia, about 700 tons and 52 guns, and had when she came out two months ago 300 men, about half of which have been lost by sickness and washed overboard, and her loaded with money, bale goods and stores of all kinds.

"She was a new ship, and had been all this time beating about and never got beyond Beachy [Head] in her way. She struck in Pevensey Bay, and lost her rudder, and has lain off Bexhill at anchor several days. Some of the Hastings people got to her, and undertook to carry her to Portsmouth when the weather would permit, but she could hold out no longer than Sunday."

Crashed on a reef

Human error was possibly the cause of the loss of the *Amsterdam*. There is no doubt that it was the cause of the wrecking of the British merchant ship *L'Athenaise*, on a reef off the east coast of Florida in 1804. This account was written by an English naval officer returning from Jamaica onboard the doomed vessel, which was carrying 184 French prisoners of war.

"We found it necessary to keep [the Master] from liquor by every means in our power, but he escaped all our vigilance, and after cutting away the foresail, took the desperate solution of getting drunk. Consequently, the ship was not wore, and, standing on, soon gained the eddy current. The first thing seen was the breakers about a mile away on the lee beam. Directly I went on deck the anchor was cut away, but before she was brought up the ship struck a coral reef with a tremendous crash.

"The scene that followed is indescribable; there were upward of 200 men crouching on the deck, naked, and most praying and confessing their sins, whilst the sea broke over her mast heads, and to heighten the confusion, the mizzen mast fell across the deck, breaking one man's ankle, and maiming several others. The sea soon threw the ship over the coral reef into deep water, and fortunately she remained afloat until she reached the beach. She was gradually sinking, and on striking the beach a few waves soon filled her."

Even if they survived the wreck, poor souls sometimes faced an uncertain future. The survivors of *L'Athenaise* had to march hundreds of miles along the Florida coast, while shipwreck victims described later in this book were stranded on the wreckage of their vessel (*pages 114–115*), faced mutiny and massacre (*124–125*), or death from hypothermia (*170–171*). The human suffering involved in shipwrecks is what gives the subject part of its fascination. Although the historic value of wreck artifacts can be inestimable, knowing that it once belonged to someone who was part of a tragedy has a terrible appeal of its own.

FINDS FROM SHIPWRECKS

Labor-intensive and painstaking conservation needs to be undertaken if the object recovered from a wreck is to be preserved. This process can often take years, and the conservation of maritime finds is a ground-breaking scientific discipline in its own right.

below: *Trade beads recovered from the wreck of the English slave ship Henrietta Marie, wrecked off the Florida Keys in 1700. The beads were designed to be exchanged for slaves on the coast of West Africa, and they each required individual conservation before they were in a stable enough condition to be displayed.*

One of the benefits of a shipwreck over a land site is that the uncovered material is often better preserved. The environment can also cause special conservation problems, beginning when finds are exposed to the air, often for the first time in centuries. In any underwater archæology project, the conservation of artifacts can cost more and take far longer than the excavation of the wreck itself. The hardest find of all to conserve is often the hull itself, where the size and scope of the work means that its recovery is frequently impossible. In these cases the timbers are reburied on the site and only the smaller finds are recovered.

Conservation is an exacting science—trained conservators are a vital part of any archæological enterprise. Their skill ensures the safe transition of objects from what was probably a stable environment, through an unstable transitory stage, to a final preserved condition. Recovering the object can trigger physical and chemical changes that in some cases destroys it. For example, cannonballs recovered from the sea eventually disintegrate if they are not conserved.

Different objects react in different ways. For example, marble statues from a Greek wreck need little treatment apart from washing, as do pottery remains, to a lesser extent. Conversely, wood or other organic material such as rope or clothing requires extensive treatment.

Waterlogged wood from a shipwreck has had its natural resin leached out and replaced with salt water. If timbers are allowed to dry, they eventually collapse, as the cell structures are only supported by water. The conservator has to replace the water with something as similar to the original wood resin as possible. In most cases, this is polyethylene glycol (PEG), a form of artificial wax.

The conservation process involves adding a weak PEG solution to a water tank containing the timber. The concentration of the solution is gradually increased until the

above: *A conservator carefully removes concretion from the remains of a musket stock found on a 17th-century Spanish shipwreck. Waterlogged wood is one of the hardest materials to conserve, and the larger the object, the longer the process takes to complete.*

wood cells are sufficiently impregnated with PEG to survive a controlled drying-out process. The whole operation is expensive to undertake, and lengthy. For extremely large wooden structures, such as the hull of the *Mary Rose* (*see pages 94–95*), the process could take up to 20 years!

Preservation by electrolysis

Other techniques used to stabilize small wooden finds include freeze-drying, where the water is removed then a wax inserted before the cells have time to collapse, or acetone coating, where acetone replaces water in the wood before the object is coated with acetone resin.

Another commonly recovered material is iron. Although all metals cause conservation problems, ferrous metals are by far the most difficult to stabilize. When a ship wrecks, iron objects corrode and attract concretion, particularly in Caribbean or Mediterranean waters. Concretion looks like a layer of concrete surrounding the object but is composed of a thick layer of calcium carbonate, magnesium hydroxide, rust, and particles of sand, shell, silt, or coral.

A lump of concretion can vary in size, from encasing a single small object to large, boulder-like conglomerates. These have to be recovered from the seabed and excavated in controlled conditions before the objects inside can be conserved. They are often X rayed first, so the conservators know what they are dealing with.

Once separated, iron objects are usually cleaned up, then stabilized by the use of electrolytic reduction (or electrolysis). This involves passing a low-voltage current through the object placed in a water tank. Over time, the corrosive products inside the metal (chloride ions) are leached out, so allowing the object to be washed and prepared for display or storage. Other metal conservation processes involve chemical reduction or even hydrogen reduction, where the object is baked, although these are far less common.

Whatever treatment is undertaken, the process of stabilization should start as soon as finds are recovered, since decay begins the moment they are removed from the sea. This is why the conservation of shipwreck artifacts is as important (and as costly) as the more glamorous processes of search and exploration.

right: *Dental tools are used to carefully remove concretion from an object in controlled laboratory conditions. The conservator uses an X ray of the concretion to guide her in the work.*

DEEP WATER SHIPWRECKS

Modern technology has allowed mankind to venture deeper into the oceans than ever before, resulting in the discovery of well-preserved deep water wrecks.

A vast archæological treasure in the form of historic wrecks lies in deep water, beyond the reach of conventionally equipped divers. It has been estimated that up to 20 percent of all shipwrecks lie in deep water, untouched by man. In depths of over 500 feet, low temperature, still water, and lack of marine life contribute to the longevity of wooden-hulled shipwrecks. Even more importantly, the lack of oxygen in certain seas and oceans means that marine borers like the *Teredo* worm cannot survive in deep water so wood cannot be eaten away, as happens at most shallow sites.

The deep-sea technology pioneered by people like Willard Bascom and Edwin Link in the 1960s and 70s, and used extensively by commercial exploration companies, has recently been applied to maritime archæology. This potential was demonstrated by Robert Ballard in 1985 when he located and explored the wreck of the *Titanic*, 13,000 feet below the surface of the Atlantic.

Submersibles and remotely operated vehicles (ROVs) can now reveal underwater archæological treasures the like of which could only have been dreamed of a generation ago. The possibilities created by recent strides in search technology mean that archæologists have the ability to search for wrecks in deep water. Historic maritime trade routes can be followed in the hunt for historic wrecks, irrespective of the ocean depth. This means that instead of the haphazard discovery of vessels in shallow waters by fishermen, divers, or treasure hunters, archæologists can search for well-preserved and untouched wrecks that answer specific questions they want to address.

High-tech discoveries

To prove the ability to find sunken ships in this manner, Ballard followed the ancient shipping route from Carthage to Rome by using deep water search and recovery equipment. He discovered well-preserved Roman shipwrecks in deep water, surveyed them, and helped fill in gaps in our knowledge of vessels that followed that course centuries ago.

During the 1950s and 60s a number of aviation and naval disasters highlighted the need for improved deep-sea search and recovery facilities by Western navies. These search and survey technologies developed by the American and British navies in the 1960s onward eventually made possible the deep-water technology used by the oil industry and oceanographic institutes from the mid-1970s.

above: *A diving technician prepares a remotely operated vehicle (ROV) for its descent. ROVs allow the exploration of shipwrecks lying hundreds of feet below the surface of the ocean. The picture* **below** *was taken by an ROV from Bob Ballard's team surveying the Titanic. Its discovery heralded an unprecedented thirst for knowledge of the most famous shipwreck in the world.*

In the 1980s a number of projects demonstrated the value of this technology when used on historic shipwrecks. Apart from Robert Ballard's world-famous exploration of the *Titanic* in 1985, deep-water archæological surveys were conducted in the Great Lakes, the Arctic, Mediterranean, Pacific, and the Caribbean. In most of these cases, the preservation of remains exceeded all expectations, particularly in the Great Lakes, where wreck decay has been minimal.

The usually prohibitive cost of these surveys has often been met by programs of cooperation between the US Navy, oceanographic centers, archæologists, commercial companies, and the media. Ballard in particular has focused on the media as a way of making this work available to schools via his broadcasts, meaning the archæology of the present is used to stimulate the archæologists of the future.

Remote viewing

ROVs have only recently been used at archæological wreck sites, often as carriers for underwater video cameras. For deep-water inspection, such as with the discovery of the *Titanic* in the mid-Atlantic or *HMS Bredalbane* off northern Canada, they were able to go where divers could not. On shallower sites such as that of the *Mary Rose* in England, ROV-mounted video cameras were used to record the ship's structure and as a briefing tool for new divers.

The big advantage of using a video camera, particularly on deeper sites, is the lack of constraints imposed by depth and pressure on human divers. Archæologists can take their time and inspect a site at their leisure without risking themselves or their colleagues. Although definition is still not as good as that obtained from black-and-white photography, developments in computer enhancement and footage quality mean that the ROV is a useful although expensive device in the underwater archæologist's toolbox.

The "Age of Fighting Sail" section of this book describes the loss of the American naval schooners *Hamilton* and *Scourge* in 1813, off Niagara in Lake Ontario (*pages 158–159*). Both wrecks were located using a magnetometer in 1973 then later identified with side-scan sonar and an ROV. The dark, icy lake meant that the two schooners were wonderfully preserved, guns in place, shot and tools stacked next to them, and boarding weapons stored ready for use. The schooners are archæological treasures of international importance, as the vessels, together with their artifacts, provide a time capsule of

below: *A diver using a Mark III deep water diving suit examines the remains of a deep water shipwreck. The Mark III suit allows divers to operate in depths previously the terrain of just manned submersibles.*

naval life of the period. Along with the *Vasa* and *Mary Rose*, it is among the most important underwater archæological projects in the world, a discovery made possible by deep-water technology. At present there are plans to raise the ships then conserve and display them in a lakeside museum. This is the kind of untouched and largely intact wreck that technology has made available.

While deep-sea gadgets can send a variety of remotely controlled vehicles to the ocean depths, the ability to allow archæologists to visit deep sites involves the use of manned submersibles. One of the most famous of these is *Alvin*, designed by the Woods Hole Oceanographic Institute. First launched in 1964 as a craft capable of carrying three people to a depth of 6,000 feet, she can now operate in more than 13,000 feet of water. Similar submersibles can recover objects from the seabed using mechanical arms or act as the control center for unmanned ROVs. The potential is there for manned exploration of deep-water wrecks.

above: Nautile, a French manned submersible, is winched out of the ocean after a deep-water dive. Mini-submarines such as this have revolutionized deep-water exploration.

21st century ideals

Unfortunately, the low level of funding for most archæological projects means that not only are the opportunities to use such expensive equipment rare, but also are more likely to be exploited by groups seeking financial rather than archæological rewards. Commercial salvage companies have utilized deep-water technology for such projects as the controversial salvage of objects from the *Titanic*. The discoverer of the *Titanic*, Dr. Robert Ballard, has observed that "this technology is now out of control," with organizations now capable of commercially exploiting historic shipwrecks which until now had been protected by their depth.

Other treasure-hunting or commercial salvage groups have used this technology in projects as diverse as the recovery of objects from a 1,300-feet-deep Spanish wreck of 1622 in the Florida Straits (known as the Tortugas wreck) and the location of the Japanese submarine *I-52*, which was sunk carrying gold from Japan to Germany in 1944.

In 1981, the highly publicized salvage of 431 gold bars from the wreck of *HMS Edinburgh*, a cruiser sunk in 1941, demonstrated the potential of this kind of equipment. Although many deep-water historic wrecks have little or no financial value, which to some degree protects them from commercial attention, other hitherto undiscovered historic wrecks, such as those of the Spanish treasure fleets, are likely targets for high-tech treasure-hunters.

The recent investigation conducted by Ballard and his team in Mediterranean waters has shown that these tools can be used constructively. Deep-water excavation is possible using robotic arms and specialist equipment, and in the future, given adequate funding, sites could be excavated within acceptable archæological parameters, all without the need for a human presence on the wrecksite! As we enter the 21st century, the likelihood is that, increasingly, deep-water archæology will help to provide the solutions to long-unanswered historic questions.

WORLD SHIPPING TRADE

Hurricanes

PACIFIC OCEAN

ATLANTIC OCEAN

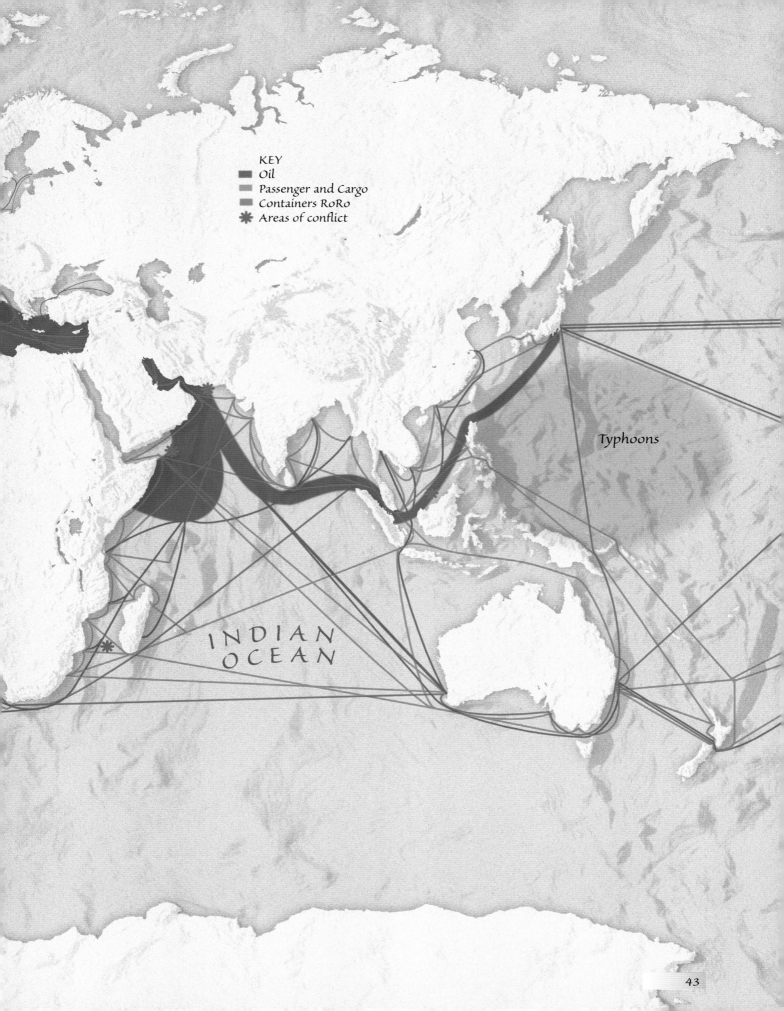

KEY
- Oil
- Passenger and Cargo
- Containers RoRo
- Areas of conflict

Typhoons

INDIAN
OCEAN

ANCIENT MARINERS

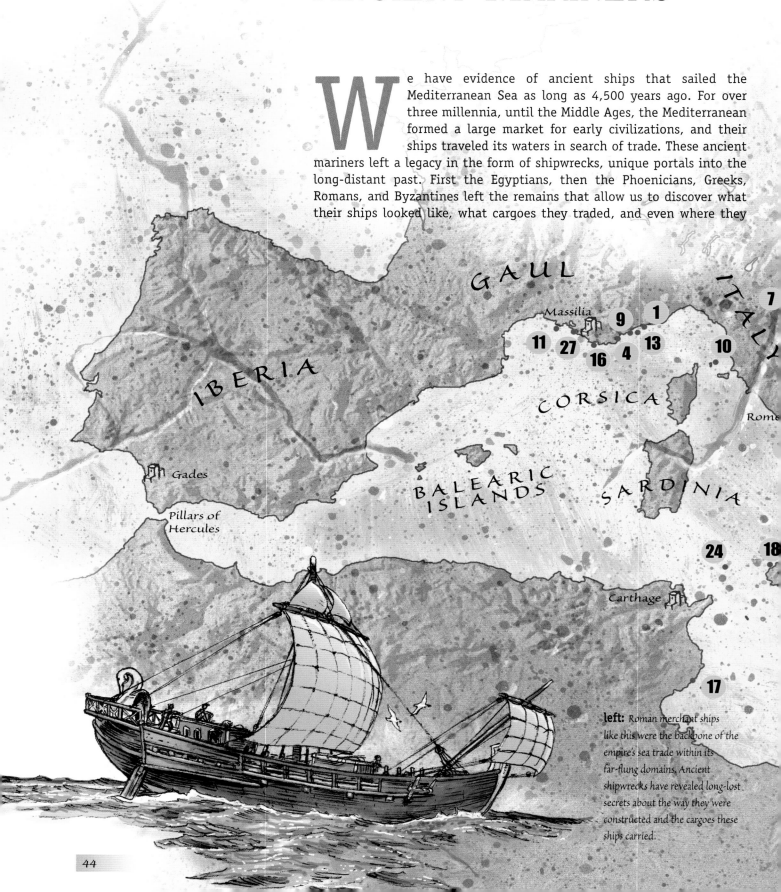

We have evidence of ancient ships that sailed the Mediterranean Sea as long as 4,500 years ago. For over three millennia, until the Middle Ages, the Mediterranean formed a large market for early civilizations, and their ships traveled its waters in search of trade. These ancient mariners left a legacy in the form of shipwrecks, unique portals into the long-distant past. First the Egyptians, then the Phoenicians, Greeks, Romans, and Byzantines left the remains that allow us to discover what their ships looked like, what cargoes they traded, and even where they

GAUL

ITALY

Massilia

9   1

11   27   13   7

16   4   10

IBERIA

CORSICA

Rome

Gades

BALEARIC
ISLANDS

SARDINIA

Pillars of
Hercules

24   18

Carthage

17

left: *Roman merchant ships like this were the backbone of the empire's sea trade within its far-flung domains. Ancient shipwrecks have revealed long-lost secrets about the way they were constructed and the cargoes these ships carried.*

were bound. Evidence supplied by underwater archæology can be combined with the writings of ancient authors and the depiction of ancient ships to give us a clear understanding of the craft. The Mediterranean Sea contains the oldest-known shipwrecks in the world, so shipwrecks give us vital information from the Bronze Age onward, almost 1,300 years before the birth of Christianity. Our understanding of these ancient ships was transformed by the discovery of ancient shipwrecks, and today archæological evidence is our main source of information about the craft of these long-lost ancient mariners.

TWO THOUSAND YEARS OF SHIPWRECKS

1   Albenga
2   Antikythera
3   Athlit Ram
4   Bon-Porté
5   Cape Gelidonya
6   Capo Rasocolmo
7   Comacchio
8   Dattilo
9   Dramont
10 Giglio
11 Grand Conglué
12 Kyrenia
13 La Chrétienne
14 Lake Nemi
15 Zaton
16 Mardague de Giens
17 Mahdia
18 Marsala Punic Wreck
19 Sea of Galilee Wreck
20 Serçe Limani
21 Sheytan Deresi
22 Straits of Messina
23 Uluburun
24 Isis Wreck
25 Yassi Adda
26 Dashur
27 Herculaneum
28 Khufu
29 Marseilles Bourse Wreck
30 Pantano Longarini
31 Marzamemi
32 Mentone

The Ancient Mariners

The Mediterranean Sea has been described as the cradle of civilization. For several thousand years, it was crossed by traders, plying their wares from port to port. For this reason, it holds a rich and varied selection of shipwrecks. From the days of the Ancient Egyptians and the various peoples mentioned in the Bible, mariners have lost ships through storm, accident, or warfare. Wrecks can help us to trace the story of the rise and fall of these ancient nations and, even more remarkably, help us understand the trade on which these nations were based.

Early Egyptian vessels and boat models found in tombs allow us to trace the early developments of Mediterranean craft. The glory that was Ancient Greece can be traced through numerous wrecks, ranging from trading vessels to warships, and these augment the evidence about shipping derived from the works of ancient writers and artists. The Roman Republic (and later Empire) is perhaps the most remarkable of these lost civilizations and, as it spanned a period of around 800 years, it is particularly well represented by shipwrecks. Following its demise, the eastern part of the Roman world became the Byzantine Empire, which continued to dominate the Mediterranean basin for a further four centuries. Through studying the available evidence, particularly that provided by wrecks, we can attempt to trace the development of the ancient mariners' ships.

The earliest evidence of shipping in the Mediterranean comes from the Egyptian Old Kingdom, c.2500 BC, the time of the building of the Great Pyramids. Inside the Pyramid of Khufu (Cheops), archæologists found the

right: *The funerary boat of King Khufu (or Cheops, 2585–2560 BC) was found hidden deep inside the Great Pyramid at Giza.*

right: *Using oars and a single sail, this wooden tomb model of a ship dates from the Egyptian 12th dynasty, c.1800 BC.*

c.2800 BC	c.2000 BC	c.1700–1400 BC	c.1550 BC	c.1500 BC	c.1482 BC	c.1400–1100 BC	c.1200 BC
Canoe-like vessels used on the Aegean Sea.	Vessels on the Aegean Sea use sails.	Height of the Cretan civilization.	Mycenaean sea traders work in the Mediterranean.	Egyptians build sailing vessels with double rudders.	Wood is carried to Egypt from Lebanon by Cretan fleet.	Height of Mycenaean civilization, dominating Mediterranean sea trade.	Date of the Cape Gelidonya wreck, a Syrian merchant's vessel.

remains of an entire reed boat, built using bundles of papyrus, with wooden fittings. This vessel was also represented by tomb paintings and described in hieroglyphic carvings. These large, almost banana-shaped river boats were powered by oars or a single sail.

The shell-first method dominates

Across the Mediterranean, the Minoans on Crete left the images of ships on pottery, their craft dubbed "frying pans" by archæologists after the distinctive shape of their prow, resembling a pan's handle. By 2000 BC, Egyptians were using wooden boats, according to evidence from ship models found in tombs. They retained the same shape as their reed predecessors, which were still used on the River Nile. It has been suggested that the wooden versions were capable of limited sea travel.

Two boats buried at Dashur show a complex form of construction, where numerous short planks were held together using mortise-and-tenon joints. This would be a widespread form of construction for much of the ancient period. Unlike the frame-first construction found in later European vessels, the mortise-and-tenon form used a shell-first method, where the outer planking basically supported itself. In frame-first construction, the frames form the ribs of the ship, with planks fastened to this structure; the standard form of ship construction used today.

During the Egyptian New Kingdom era (c.1600–1100 BC), ships are better documented. Stone carvings and written documents show that Egyptian vessels had become sturdier, and in illustrations showing them in battle with the "Sea Peoples" of the central Mediterranean, both sides have similar craft. The Sea Peoples—Syrians, Mycenaean Greeks, and Egyptians— all seemed to use the same basic design, but doubtless there are unrecorded regional variations. The traders of the Aegean were clearly different to the "black ships" mentioned in Homer's *Illiad*. Two trading vessels of this Bronze Age period provide us with our earliest evidence from shipwrecks. These wrecks, at Uluburun and Cape Gelidonya, provided vital evidence about ancient trade routes (*see pages 50–51*).

The period following the Late Bronze Age to the rise of the Greek states saw extensive maritime trade between the Phoenicians, Greeks, and the Etruscans of central Italy. Increasing amounts of evidence from

c.1000 BC	c.810 BC	c.650 BC	c.550 BC	517 BC	509 BC	c.480 BC	332 BC
Simplistic form of anchor used by Mediterranean sailors.	Carthage is established by the Phoenicians.	The first coins are made, in Lydia, Asia.	Arabs settle in Ethiopia after crossing the Red Sea.	A canal is constructed connecting the Red Sea and River Nile.	Founding of the Roman Republic.	A navy is developed at Carthage. A Greek fleet defeat the Persian navy.	Alexander the Great conquers Egypt.

documentary and archæological sources helps us understand the nature of this activity, and archæological investigation of ancient ports adds to the overall picture. Excavation of a Phoenician port provided evidence of ship cargoes, reinforced by shipwreck finds off the Israeli, Italian, and French coasts.

Wreck evidence from the fourth century BC onward forms a large part of the body of knowledge of ancient ships and shipping. The Kyrenia ship of the late fourth century BC was so well preserved that it was possible to build a full-scale working replica of the ship (*pages 52–53*). Trading vessels tended to be deep, broad craft, powered by sail rather than by oar, although there is evidence for oared Phoenician merchant ships around 700 BC.

Modifying the pattern

The continued specialization of warships is illustrated by the ram attachment to the bows of warships. These ships appear to be larger, allowing more oarsmen and hence speed, vital if the ram was to be used effectively. By the late sixth century BC, the bireme and trireme had become the warships of choice, at least in the Aegean. Illustrations show that Phoenicians continued to produce warships of the older style, allowing the Greeks a technological edge. By the fifth century BC, the trireme had become commonplace throughout the Mediterranean, although there were noticeable variations between, say, Greek and Etruscan designs. Much work has been done to reconstruct the method in which triremes operated, including a full-scale replica. The basic design remained unchanged until the second century BC, by which time the Romans and Carthaginians produced warships with four and five tiers of oars.

The Roman period began in the fourth century BC; by the second century it was the dominant power in the Mediterranean. The Romans appeared slow to discover the benefits of seapower, but during the Punic War with Carthage, beginning in 264 BC, they built a powerful navy. Based on the Greek model, this consisted mainly of quinquiremes, a larger version of the trireme, and small warships known as liburnians, used as scouts' boats. Apart from the discovery of a warship ram, there is little archaeological evidence of warships from the era of the Roman Republic and early Roman Empire. The wrecks of Roman merchant vessels, however, are numerous, and we can trace their development in considerable detail.

above: *The depiction on this Greek vase shows Odysseus tied to the mast of his vessel in order to hear the Sirens sing without being fatally seduced by their voices.*

297–280 BC	264–241 BC	146 BC	c.86 BC	72 BC	c.36 BC	26 BC	14 AD
The first ever lighthouse is built, in Alexandria.	Rome defeats Carthage in the First Punic War.	Carthage destroyed in Third Punic War.	Date of the Antikythera wreck, a vessel carrying a Roman dictator's art.	A Roman fleet off Crete is defeated by pirates.	Date of the Kyrenia wreck, a coastal trade vessel from Rhodes.	Collapse of the Roman Republic, beginning of the Roman Empire.	The Romans build an aqueduct in southern France.

There is sufficient shipwreck evidence to analyze ship construction. While earlier Mediterranean vessels had used mortise-and-tenon joints and a shell first method, the Romans developed these traditions, claiming them for their own. The first trading vessel discovered underwater was the Antikythera wreck (*pages 54–55*), followed by numerous other examples in the past 30 years. Most display the use of wooden or metal tenons to hold the planks together, as well as treenails and copper nails to attach them to the framework. In these "shell-first" constructions, the planks were joined to create the hull, then the frames added to provide strength. In some cases, copper or lead sheathing was used to protect the hull from attack by *Teredo* worms.

below: *A Roman merchant vessel from the third century AD adorns the face of this sarcophagus, which was found at Sidon.*

Following a classic design

Ships of the Roman Empire varied in size, from small coastal craft to the huge grain ships that sailed from Egypt to Rome during the empire's heyday, displacing over 1,200 tons (1,089 tonnes). The majority fall into two groups: ones of 100–130 tons (91–118 tonnes), and large merchant craft of 350 tons (318 tonnes) or more. A typical small trading ship could carry 3,000 amphoras, loaded with wine; other common cargoes included stone and grain (*see map on page 19*).

By the end of the Roman Empire and the rise of the Byzantium Empire, merchant ships had not developed greatly in terms of size, although construction methods had changed. Vessels such as the small Byzantine trading ship discovered at Yassi Adda (*pages 56–57*) and the larger one excavated off Marzamemi in Sicily show that these vessels were the size of average Roman ships. Sail types may have changed, with the lateen sail replacing the square sail, and construction methods were simplified, but the ships generally resembled earlier Roman craft. There is evidence that the ship frames were a more important part of the construction process: Although they did not seem to use true frame-first construction, the later Byzantines appear to have departed from pure shell-first construction methods occasionally.

The hundreds of ancient shipwrecks that have been discovered in the Mediterranean provide us with a remarkable resource of information with which to understand early ships, shipping, and trade. However, there are still gaps in our knowledge—with luck, there are undiscovered ancient shipwrecks out there, waiting to help us complete our understanding of the mariners' vessels.

80 AD	271 AD	455 AD	7th century AD	542 AD	605–10 AD	655 AD
The Colosseum in Rome is opened.	The Chinese use magnetic compasses.	Western Europe under attack by Attila the Hun.	Date of the most investigated Yassi Adda wreck, a vessel of the Byzantine church.	Europe is devastated by the bubonic plague.	The Grand Canal is constructed to connect the Yellow River with the Yangtze.	A Byzantine fleet off Egypt is defeated by Arabs.

THE CAPE GELIDONYA WRECK

13TH CENTURY BC

The world's oldest shipwreck?

above: *Ships are rarely wrecked in hospitable places. The rocky headland of Cape Gelidonya in Turkey marks the site of one of the world's oldest shipwrecks.*

In the late 1950s, divers searching for sponge located a shipwreck off the rocky headland of Cape Gelidonya, near Finike, on the south coast of Turkey. In 1959 they took writer and amateur archæologist Peter Throckmorton to the ship, which lay on a rocky and broken seabed at the base of a cliff, in 80–100 feet of water. Throckmorton persuaded the divers not to salvage the site. He recognized it for what it was: an incredibly old shipwreck, probably dating from the Bronze Age.

At the invitation of the Turkish government, a team led by George Bass of the University of Pennsylvania excavated the site in 1960. The techniques involved in underwater archæology were in their infancy, and Bass had to modify land-based methods for underwater use. With a little practice and a number of specialist tools such as airlifts to remove sediment, it was discovered that the same exacting standards that were imposed on a land excavation could be applied underwater.

Although the remains of the vessel had largely rotted away, enough of its cargo remained to keep the archæologists fully occupied. The few timber remains recovered suggested that the ship was built using mortise-and-tenon joints, indicating the shell-first construction that was used throughout the ancient Mediterranean. The remains suggested that the vessel was around 30 feet long, but the widely scattered cargo prevented a more precise estimation.

Much of the cargo was composed of bronze or copper ingots that were fused together on the seabed. As metal objects rust, small particles of sand or stone adhere to them, forming a layer of concretion around the object. This layer, resembling a rough concrete coating, serves to protect the object from further decay. It also makes the tasks of excavation, recovery, and conservation more problematic.

A number of pieces had fused together into huge lumps weighing as much as a ton each. Hydraulic tools, hammers, and chisels were used to separate these and allowed the concreted remains of the bronze ingots to be brought to the surface. It was found that many ingots were cast in an "ox-hide" shape, that is with four handles to make them easier to carry. These ingots, each weighing over 50 pounds, were identical to ones recorded in contemporary Egyptian tomb paintings, and several carried marks that, presumably, indicated ownership.

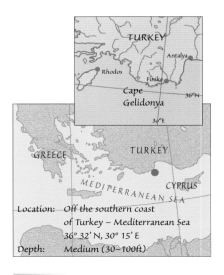

Location: Off the southern coast of Turkey – Mediterranean Sea
36° 32' N, 30° 15' E

Depth: Medium (30–100ft)

A Syrian merchant vessel?

As well as the cargo, George Bass and his team recovered hundreds of personal artifacts, including bronze weapon heads, tools, glass beads, and ceramic fragments. Almost all of the tools have been identified as being of Syrian or Cypriot origin, and this, combined with references to ox-hide ingots being produced in Syria, indicates the vessel's possible origin. All were dated to around 1200 BC. At that time the Syrian coast was settled by the forerunners of the Phoenicians, and this proto-Phoenician vessel may have been wrecked while following an ancient trade route between Syria and Mycenæan Greece.

Other recovered objects had more diverse origins. The scrap metal that formed another part of the cargo could have originated anywhere, but it has been suggested that it was loaded in Cyprus. In what was determined to be the stern of the ship, a number of specialized personal items were found, including pan weights, a clay lamp, and olive pits. Unlike the cargo, while many of the items indicated a Syrian origin, several others came from Egypt, Greece, Cyprus, or Asia Minor. It therefore seems likely that this small vessel belonged to a Syrian merchant specializing in the metal trade, and frequented the coasts and islands of the entire northeastern Mediterranean.

It appears the ship was sailing from Syria and Cyprus toward Greece when it was lost. Unfortunately, there is no indication of its destination, or what its return cargo might have been. The remains of this unique Bronze Age shipwreck are now on display in the Bodrum Museum of Underwater Archæology, on the southwest coast of Turkey.

below: *The site plan of the Cape Gelidonya wreck shows how the vessel's cargo of large "ox-hide"-shaped bronze ingots lay scattered at the foot of the cliff. The seabed is broken up by rock columns, gullies, and debris from the cliff.*

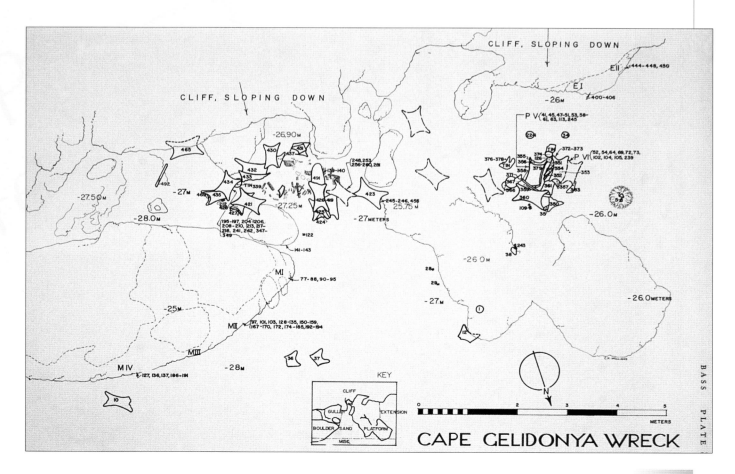

CAPE GELIDONYA WRECK

THE KYRENIA SHIP

4TH CENTURY BC

A remarkable Greek trader

above: *The Kyrenia II, a reconstruction of the original Kyrenia wreck based on the archæological evidence discovered.*

Location: Off the northern coast of Cyprus – Mediterranean
35° 20′ N, 33° 21′ E
Depth: Shallow (0–30ft)

A Greek Cypriot diver discovered the remains of a small, ancient shipwreck near Kyrenia, on the north coast of Cyprus, in the late 1960s. In 1967 he showed his discovery to American archæologist Michael Katzev, who quickly realized its importance. Located less than a mile from the shore, in almost a hundred feet of water, the formation of the wreck suggested that the remains would be well preserved.

Katzev, from the University of Pennsylvania, organized an excavation of the site in 1968, and a second one the following year. His finds were truly remarkable and gave a clear picture of what Mediterranean ships looked like, a third of a millennium before Christ. Until the discovery of the Kyrenia ship, scholars' only evidence came from pictures on vases and frescoes.

Pinned beneath the ballast mound and the remains of her cargo were the well-preserved timbers of the ship. They showed that she was 45 feet long, had a 14-foot beam, and a burden of 25 tons (22.7 tonnes). This squat little vessel was built using Lebanese pine from Aleppo in Syria, while her timbers were pinned together using oak pegs (tenons) carved in Asia Minor (modern Turkey). Oak was also used to line the inside of her hull, providing a smooth bottom to the vessel.

She was built in the manner now seen as typical for Mediterranean ships of that era: her hull planks (strakes) were joined along their edges by mortises and tenons. Two heavier strakes (wales) ran above the turn of the bilge. Frames were added to strengthen the hull, held in place by copper spikes. It appears that the lower hull was coated in pitch to make it watertight. This shell-first construction was notably different from the frame-first method used in northern European waters and described in the next chapter. As a shipbuilding method, it was used in the Mediterranean until the 16th century, two millennia later!

The Kyrenia wreck sails again

The ship was propelled by means of a single square sail—a "sail locker" excavated from the stern area produced lead rings and other rigging fittings. The step for the single mast was centrally located along the keel-line. The ship was fairly old when it sank; evidence of extensive hull repairs over a considerable period testify to her long working life. She was a cargo carrier, her hull containing the remains of over 400 amphoras (ceramic containers), most of which came from Rhodes. Over 10,000 almonds were recovered, some in the amphoras, others lying loose. The latter were probably originally stored in sacks, since rotted away. Replacing part of her usual ballast was another cargo item: 29 millstones from quarries on the Aegean island of Kos.

The remains of the ship also contained the personal possessions of her crew. Found in two groups at the bow and the stern, the crew areas must have been separated by the cargo. Jugs and tableware were found four at a time, indicating the size of her crew. All of these originated in Rhodes, so that island was probably the ship's home port. Communal cooking was performed with a large copper cauldron but, as no hearth was found, it was clear that this was a small coastal trader and that the crew would go ashore to light fires for cooking. Fishing weights hinted at what might have been prepared in the cooking pot, but small quantities of olives, nuts, fruit, herbs, and of course almonds were also recovered. Two bronze coins provided the date of the shipwreck, the latest being 306 BC.

The mass of evidence produced by the Kyrenia excavation allowed Michael Katzev to build a reconstruction of the ship. Called *Kyrenia II*, the small sailing craft is easily handled by a crew of four, and greatly adds to our understanding of ancient craft. The remains of the original ship and the finds recovered from her are on display in the Kyrenia Crusader Castle Museum, close to the spot where she sank.

below: *The wreck site of the Kyrenia ship, showing the lower hull structure overlaid by a metal grid. The grid provided stable datum points for the survey and excavation of the wreck.*

THE ANTIKYTHERA WRECK

1ST CENTURY BC

The lost loot of a Roman dictator

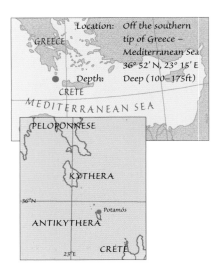

Location: Off the southern tip of Greece – Mediterranean Sea 36° 52' N, 23° 15' E
Depth: Deep (100–175ft)

opposite top: *This statue of a youth, probably intended to grace the home of the Roman dictator Sulla, was only one among a hoard of objects recovered from the wreck.*

below, left and right: *Two pieces that made up the lunar and astrological "calculator" found on the Antikythera wrecksite.*

In 1900, divers looking for sponge around the remote Greek island of Antikythera found the remains of an ancient shipwreck. It was the first such wreck ever discovered in the Mediterranean and was of immense archæological value. Hard-hatted men assisted the sponge divers, and a number of objects were recovered from the wreck, which lay in 160 feet of water. These were taken to Athens for study, but the collection raised more questions than it answered.

The site contained amphoras (ceramic containers for liquids) from the Greek islands, Roman pottery fragments, fine bronze statues dating from the fourth century BC, and delicate marble carvings. Clearly the wreck was an unusual one, and careful dating indicated that it sank some time in the middle of the first century BC. Other unusual finds included the remains of a bronze bed, gold jewelry, and a mechanical device that resembled a navigator's astrolabe (forerunner of the sextant) from the 16th century! The site seemed too puzzling to explain logically, and lacking the ability to examine the site for themselves, archæologists preferred to leave the enigma for future generations to answer.

The material was reexamined in the 1950s, when the "astrolabe" was found to be a lunar and astrological calculator, its complexity far surpassing anything previously recovered from the ancient world. It was probably made around 87 BC by a craftsman in Rhodes, and in its original form would have been mounted on a wooden pedestal, rather like a modern grandfather clock. A water-powered timepiece once completed the remarkable machine, and even the remains bear testimony to the ingenuity of ancient craftsmen. Until its examination, no documented proof of this kind of early scientific and technological sophistication existed.

Decorations for a dictator's home

The enigmatic quality of the wreck only increased. Further study was clearly needed to provide an answer. The island of Antikythera lies off the southern tip of the Greek mainland, halfway between the Peloponnesian peninsula and Crete. This put it in the middle of a busy ancient shipping lane between Greece and Italy. Could the ship have been carrying goods to Rome?

This was no ordinary cargo. The bronze statues were of superb quality; one of a nude god (or hero), another the head of a Greek "philosopher," and a further eight were of young males, although a number were only fragmentary. The 36 equestrian and human marble sculptures were of a poorer quality, and research suggests they were probably copies of earlier Greek pieces. The vessel appeared to be in the process of shipping a major art collection from Greece when it sunk. The presence of the "calculator," which was clearly a highly prized object, only strengthened this assumption.

Dating evidence from both the calculator, the amphoras, and other pottery fragments suggest that the ship sank between 80 and 70 BC. Back in 1900, a few fragments of hull timbers were recovered and recorded. These indicated that the hull was formed using mortise-and-tenon joints, where elm planks were pinned to oak tenons using copper nails. The lower portion of the hull was sheathed with lead. All this pointed to a Roman wreck.

A search of historical records suggested an answer to the mystery surrounding the wreck. In 86 BC, the Roman consul Lucius Cornelius Sulla defeated the army of Mithridates, King of Pontus (modern Turkey). Rome gained control of the Aegean region, and Sulla followed his victory by winning a civil war in Italy, over his rival, Gaius Marius.

Safely in position as the new Dictator of the Roman Republic, Sulla ordered the shipment of his art collection from Rhodes to Rome. The records show that the ship carrying it never arrived. It is highly probable that the wreck discovered off Antikythera is the remains of Sulla's ship, and its cargo was intended to grace the dictator's villas. Instead, it now forms a fascinating collection which is currently displayed in the National Archæological Museum in Athens.

THE YASSI ADDA WRECK

7TH CENTURY

Supply boat for the Byzantine Church

Yassi Adda (or Yassiada) means "flat island," and lies off the southwestern coast of Turkey, near the island of Pserimos. Situated on what was once a busy shipping route, Yassi Adda is flanked by a reef that has claimed several ships. In a series of excavations between 1961 and 1983, under the direction of the American underwater archaeologist, Dr. George Bass, the remains of three early shipwrecks were located, identified and examined.

The earliest was a fourth-century shipwreck, which was partly excavated in the late 1960s and early 1970s. It lies on a shelf, where part of the wreck has dropped into deeper water. The excavated portion contained the starboard side of the ship that used a form of mortise-and-tenon construction that was almost exclusively Roman. This late Roman merchant was carrying a large cargo of 1,100 amphoras containing wine and olive oil when she struck the reef. The Aegean origin of the cargo suggests she began her journey in Greece.

The most modern wreck dates from the 16th century, when the waters around Yassi Adda formed part of the Ottoman Turkish Empire. Excavated in the late 1960s and mid-1980s, this wreck was probably a small Turkish warship or auxiliary vessel. Dendro-chronological dating from tree rings found on the keel, along with a Spanish coin, placed the ship's origin in the late 16th century. A lack of finds suggests that there was time to salvage the ship before she sank, but a handful of musket balls, cannon balls, and boarding weapons remained to indicate its naval function.

The most thoroughly excavated wreck at Yassi Adda is the third, dating to the seventh century. The Roman Empire had been replaced by that of the Byzantines, and at the time the ship sank, the Aegean was filled with ships trading between the ports of the Byzantine Empire. The excavation conducted by George Bass between 1961 and 1964 was one of the earliest scientific excavations conducted completely underwater. New techniques

Location: Off the southwestern corner of Turkey – Mediterranean
36° 56' N, 27° 12' E
Depth: Medium (30–100ft)

had to be developed and tested, many of which remain in use today. The Yassi Adda excavation was a truly ground-breaking event in the development of underwater archæology.

A priest at the helm

Enough hull timbers remained on this site to give an indication of how the ship looked. She was 65 feet long, with a 16-foot beam. This small vessel had a sharp bow, a rounded stern, and a barrel-shaped hull, making her a good cargo carrier, with a capacity of around 60 tons (54 tonnes). She had a large galley and ample pantry facilities, an unexpected feature in a craft of her size.

Her hull differed from that of earlier ships by being lightly constructed, using mortise-and-tenon joints. This made her easy and cheap to produce, so her function was probably not a prestigious one. A steel yard measure recovered from the ship recorded that Georgios, the vessel's captain, was a priest. The ship was probably used to transport cargo and church passengers between the churches located around the Aegean and, as such, would have been owned and manned by the Byzantine church.

Her cargo consisted of 700 globular amphoras, carefully stacked in her hull. Retaining traces of the wine they originally contained, it has been suggested that the amphoras formed part of several boatloads of supplies destined for the Byzantine army, then fighting the Persians in the Near East.

Apart from the cargo, the other major group of finds related to the ship's galley. Almost two dozen pots, cauldrons, and pans were recovered, along with ceramic pitchers and jars. Silverware, tableware, and a set of brass scales were found in the ship's pantry area. This ability to feed large numbers indicates she was used to transport people, as well as supplies. Together with the lamps, fishing nets, and ship's stores associated with the vessel and crew, the finds from the seventh-century shipwreck at Yassi Adda provide us with a rare insight into the world of the Byzantine Empire.

opposite page: *A reconstruction of the Yassi Adda excavation during the early 1960s. It emphasizes the underwater technology available at the time, as well as the way in which the excavation was conducted.*

below: *Evidence supplied by the excavation allowed archæologists to attempt a reconstruction of the ship and to speculate about the way in which the cargo was stowed.*

GEORGE BASS
Underwater Archæologist

One of the pioneers of underwater archaeology, the American diving archæologist George Bass has led the way in the development of the discipline. His work on ancient shipwrecks introduced many of the techniques which are widely used today.

above: *Professor George F. Bass is currently the archæological director of the Institute of Nautical Archæology (INA), and is regarded as one of the pioneering figures in underwater archæology.*

George F. Bass is sometimes called "the father of underwater archæology." His position as one of the leading pioneers in the new field originated in 1960, when he excavated a shipwreck lost off Cape Gelidonya, on Turkey's southern coast. His mentor was Professor Young of the University of Pennsylvania, who had realized the potential offered by underwater archæology. Bass was a graduate student working for Young at the time. Peter Throckmorton, the archæologist and diver who discovered the site, worked closely with Bass in the planning and execution of the project. Throckmorton later founded a museum of maritime archæology in the nearby Turkish town of Bodrum, and today is seen as another pioneer of the field.

Nobody had tried a fully fledged underwater excavation before, and Bass learned to dive in order to take on the job. It was unknown whether the techniques of land archæology could be successfully applied underwater and, as the fieldwork continued, Bass and his team were constantly forced to adapt equipment and techniques to the new environment. It was important to him not to lower the professional archæological standards of the excavation, just because it was conducted underwater. As a result, he helped set the standards of underwater work for others to follow.

During the following 30 years of research, fieldwork, and teaching in the discipline of underwater archæology, Bass excavated a number of shipwreck sites, ranging from the Bronze Age site off Cape Gelidonya to the cluster of wrecks found off Yassi Adda in the Aegean, the most

below: *Work by Bass and his INA colleagues has helped our understanding of the ships and trade of the ancient Mediterranean. This allows historians to attempt to reconstruct the maritime environment of these long-lost civilizations.*

modern of which dates from the 16th century. This encompasses almost three millennia of Mediterranean shipwrecks!

Much of the focus of Bass and his team was directed at vessels of the Byzantine era. The first of these was a vessel sunk off the Turkish Aegean island of Yassi Adda in AD 626, or soon after. Although excavation work on the site ended in 1964, research is still being undertaken on the material remains recovered from the shipwreck.

On land and sea

At Serçe Limani, a harbor on the Turkish coast facing Rhodes, Bass examined the remains of a Byzantine wreck dating from the 11th century. The hull of this vessel is now displayed in the Bodrum museum first established by Throckmorton, as are many of the finds, which included a vast collection of glass, originally shipped as broken shards as well as complete vessels. The wreck was excavated in 1977–9, and was followed by work on a much earlier Greek wreck on the same site, dating from the time of Alexander the Great.

Most of the underwater archæological work conducted by George Bass took place in the Mediterranean, but he has conducted underwater research in other regions, including the Caribbean and the waters off Yorktown, Virginia, and in Maine, where he worked on the survey of the *Defence*, an American privateer.

Bass refused to specialize fully in underwater archæology. As a Classical archæologist, he saw underwater archæology as a tool, part of a wider discipline that included land archæology. As a result, he has directed or assisted on land, including the excavation of prehistoric sites in Greece, Turkey, and Italy.

In 1972 Bass founded the American Institute of Nautical Archæology, a research body attached to the University of Pennsylvania. Six years later it became the Institute of Nautical Archæology (INA), by which time it had relocated to Texas to join the Texas A&M University Anthropology Department. Bass used INA as a training ground for young archæologists interested in marine work. In addition to the wrecks mentioned above, INA teams have operated throughout the Mediterranean, in the Caribbean, and off East Africa. Bass remains the archæological director of the INA, as well as being its past president and founder, and teaches courses in underwater and classical archæology.

George Bass was a pioneer of underwater archæology and plays an active part in its development today. Through his work and the organization he founded, the future of underwater archæology as a science is assured.

below: *Divers suit up and prepare to enter the water during the excavation of the Yassi Adda wreck during the late 1960s. The development of scuba equipment allowed archæologists like Bass to grasp the opportunities presented by underwater excavation.*

Europe's Medieval Legacy

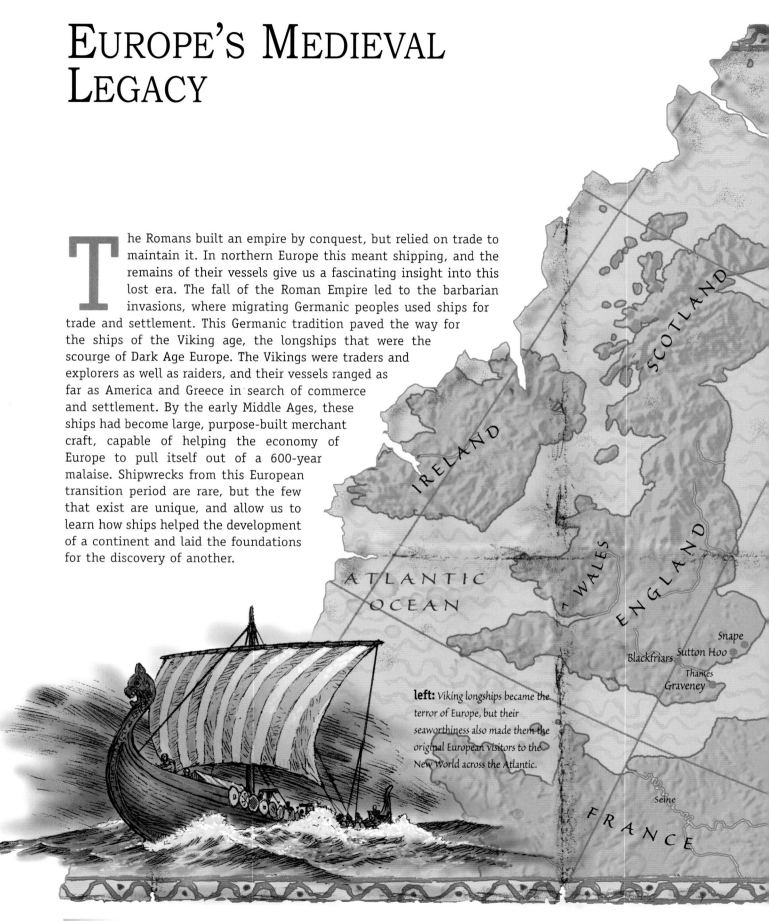

The Romans built an empire by conquest, but relied on trade to maintain it. In northern Europe this meant shipping, and the remains of their vessels give us a fascinating insight into this lost era. The fall of the Roman Empire led to the barbarian invasions, where migrating Germanic peoples used ships for trade and settlement. This Germanic tradition paved the way for the ships of the Viking age, the longships that were the scourge of Dark Age Europe. The Vikings were traders and explorers as well as raiders, and their vessels ranged as far as America and Greece in search of commerce and settlement. By the early Middle Ages, these ships had become large, purpose-built merchant craft, capable of helping the economy of Europe to pull itself out of a 600-year malaise. Shipwrecks from this European transition period are rare, but the few that exist are unique, and allow us to learn how ships helped the development of a continent and laid the foundations for the discovery of another.

SCOTLAND

IRELAND

ATLANTIC OCEAN

WALES

ENGLAND

Snape

Blackfriars Sutton Hoo

Thames Graveney

Seine

FRANCE

left: *Viking longships became the terror of Europe, but their seaworthiness also made them the original European visitors to the New World across the Atlantic.*

Kvalsund

Bryggen

NORWAY

NORTH SEA

Asker

Osberg

Gokstadt

Tune

SWEDEN

GULF
OF
BOTHNIA

FINLAND

Årby

Vendel

Valsgärde

Birka

Kollerup

Vigsø

Ellingaa

DENMARK

Kyholm

Vejby

Kalmar

Gredstenbro

Ladby

Skuldelev

Nydam

Hedeby

Hjortspring

BALTIC SEA

NETHERLANDS

Lelystadt

Bremen

Elbe

Utrecht

Gdansk

Rhine

Zwammerdam

Szczecin

Vis

LGIUM

O
der

tula

POLAND

GERMANY

Europe's Medieval Legacy

The Dark Ages cover the period of European history from the end of the Roman Empire until the Medieval era. By the time the Romans left Britain in 410 AD, a steady stream of Germanic migrants was moving into the southern portion of the British Isles. These peoples—the Saxons, Jutes, and Angles—were apparently used to sea travel; coastal traffic along the shores of northern Europe seemed to be a constant occurrence.

Further back in time, during the years of the Roman presence in Britain and Gaul (France), coastal traffic between the two countries was commonplace, as were voyages into the English Channel from the Mediterranean Sea. Many of these trading vessels were built and manned by local Celtic seafarers from France and Britain, using their own style of ship construction. This was radically different from the vessels used by the Germanic migrant peoples from 300 AD on.

Another traditional form of craft was the skin boat used on the fringes of the Celtic world, in Ireland, Wales, and western Scotland. Although not considered seaworthy for long voyages, a modern reconstruction of one such craft sailed considerable distances without serious problems.

The Germanic peoples migrating into northwest Europe brought their own tradition of boatbuilding. To some extent we can draw on pictorial records to reconstruct these craft and trace their development. Coin finds from the period have been found inscribed with boat designs, as have other remains found in excavated burial areas. Similarly, vessels of the late Roman period have been depicted on coins. Julius Caesar described the craft of the Gallic Venetii tribe as early as 53 BC, and his account

below: *A reconstruction of part of the Port of Roman London during the second century AD includes evidence supplied by the excavation of Romano-British ships found in the bank of the River Thames.*

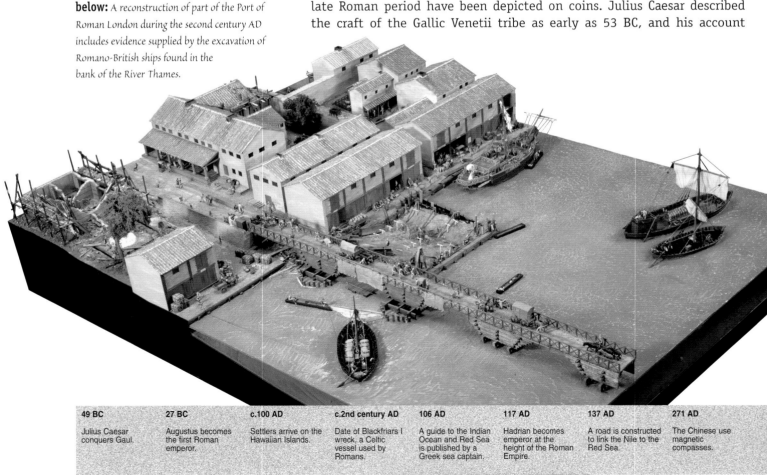

49 BC	27 BC	c.100 AD	c.2nd century AD	106 AD	117 AD	137 AD	271 AD
Julius Caesar conquers Gaul.	Augustus becomes the first Roman emperor.	Settlers arrive on the Hawaiian Islands.	Date of Blackfriars I wreck, a Celtic vessel used by Romans.	A guide to the Indian Ocean and Red Sea is published by a Greek sea captain.	Hadrian becomes emperor at the height of the Roman Empire.	A road is constructed to link the Nile to the Red Sea.	The Chinese use magnetic compasses.

matches with later pictorial evidence, clearly indicating a unique Celtic or Gallo-Roman shipbuilding tradition. Evidently, since Mediterranean designs were not entirely suitable to the different sea conditions of these northern waters, traditional Celtic techniques were not greatly modified by Roman influences. The Romans saw that these heavy Celtic ships were suited to their native environment.

A graceful craft

The craft used by the Germanic peoples in the North Sea and the Baltic were better preserved. In 1938, the discovery of a ship burial at Sutton Hoo in eastern England proved that by AD 600 these Anglo-Saxon migrants had developed fairly sophisticated open vessels. Although the timber had rotted away, archæologists revealed the detailed shape of her hull imprinted in the sand of the burial mound. It was almost as if the ghost of the ship lingered in the burial ground, a shadow image of the original craft.

Together with the priceless collection of grave relics, now housed in the British Museum, the excavators learned how these Germanic boats were constructed. The hull was almost a hundred feet long, double-ended, and with a 16-foot beam. It was built using a frame-first construction, where a series of overlapping planks were bolted to the slender frames in a technique called clinker-building. The same style of construction is used in vernacular working boats in parts of the Scandinavian and Scottish North Sea coast. The craft was therefore a slender vessel with graceful lines, powered by oars and a single mast and sail.

Other similar boat finds help to complete the picture of these Germanic craft. The remains of a second-century vessel was found south of Bergen, Norway, that suggested a link between clinker-built boats and earlier plank-sewn dugouts—a kind of maritime missing link.

Another ship, found at Nydam near the German-Danish border in 1864, was a predecessor of the Sutton Hoo ship. Dating from the late fourth century, the Nydam boat was of simpler construction but followed the same construction principles. Both the Sutton Hoo and the Nydam vessels were stoutly constructed, suitable for use in the North Sea. A fifth-century AD figurehead found in Belgium is reminiscent of those found on Viking ships, and indeed these Germanic

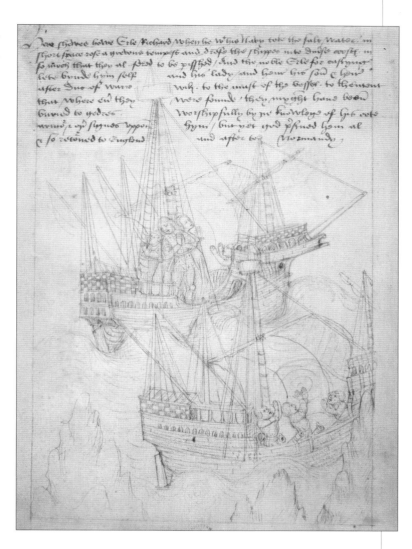

above: *Two 15th-century vessels depicted in the Warwick Roll illustrate the development of the Northern European sailing ship during the medieval period. By this stage the cog had been replaced by the more robust carrack.*

c.280 AD	c.300 AD	330 AD	c.450 AD	452 AD	593 AD	651 AD	711 AD
Date of the Guernsey wreck, a Celtic-Roman vessel.	Cargo vessels in use throughout Europe in Roman trade boom.	Constantinople, once the site of Byzantium, becomes capital of the Roman Empire.	Britain is conquered by the Saxons, Angles, and Jutes.	The Huns sack a number of cities in northern Italy.	The printing press is invented in China.	The Koran is committed to paper.	Southern Spain is invaded by Islamic armies.

craft appear to be precursors of the Scandinavian vessels of the seventh century onward.

By around AD 650, the remains of Scandinavian vessels show a development of the basic Germanic design, with tightly curving stem and sternposts, creating the sailing ships used by the northern seafarers known collectively as the Vikings. Although there is almost no pictorial evidence for these craft before the 11th century, Norse literature gives excellent descriptions of these craft, used for raiding, trading, and exploration. Archæological evidence supports these sources.

The Viking ships

The use of ships in burial mounds predates the Viking period, but Norse leaders continued the practice and it became widespread. To date, over 400 ship burials have been located and recorded in northern Europe. These provide a wealth of information about Viking craft, although only a handful were in sufficient condition to preserve the ship virtually intact.

Three boat burials near Oslo in Norway were discovered in the 19th century, and are now known as the Osberg, Gokstad, and Tune ships. The Osberg ship was excavated in 1904, found with her upper planks and beautifully carved stem and sternpost undamaged. Built around AD 800, she is 71 feet long, with a 17-foot beam. The slightly later and larger Gokstad ship (76 feet) had 32 rowing positions, two more than the Osberg ship, and was almost as well preserved.

Both ships had a marked keel structure and were designed as much for sailing as rowing. Steps for a single, square-sail mast on both vessels allowed historians to reconstruct the way Viking ships were sailed. These were the traditional longships of the Viking era, the craft that allowed the Vikings to dominate the seas of northern Europe and terrorize the coastal population.

Not all Viking ships were designed for raiding or warfare. A further development was the *knorr*, a more rounded hull form designed as a cargo-carrying sailing vessel. While longships were ideal for warfare, these craft were useful for exploration. Viking ships such as these ranged as far afield as the Mediterranean, Black Sea, and Newfoundland, carrying cargo or settlers.

Turning toward a cog

By the tenth century, Viking ships had become highly specialized, and the discovery of a trading vessel dated around AD 1200 in Kalmar, Sweden, showed that the basic *knorr* design remained in use. The Kalmar ship was a development of the basic design,

below: *A reconstruction of the hull of the fifth-century Sutton Hoo ship that formed part of a Saxon boat burial. The clinker-built form of hull construction using overlapping planks is clearly visible.*

c.790 AD	c.800 AD	839 AD	860 AD	896 AD	911 AD	c.1000 AD	11th century AD
British Isles raided by Vikings.	Western Europe's first castles are constructed.	Aethulwulf becomes King of Wessex, England, following death of Egbert.	A fleet of Rus (Russians) besiege Constantinople.	King Alfred of Wessex, England, repels a Danish invasion.	Duchy of Normandy granted to Vikings.	Greenland colonized by Vikings.	Date of the Skuldelev wrecks, vessels from the "Viking Period."

with a deeper hull and cross-beams to strengthen her hull. It was further adapted by an improved sail plan, a bowsprit, and a raised platform at the stern. Earlier boat finds at Graveney in England and in the Dutch estuaries showed that a similar but parallel form of ship construction was followed in France and parts of Britain. Clinker-built, the Graveney boat showed similarities to the Celtic boats of the late Roman period.

By the late 14th century, these trading ship designs had amalgamated into a vessel known as the cog. This was clearly designed along the principles of Viking construction, but from archæological remains it was found to incorporate significant improvements. Compared to the *knorr*, the hull was flat-bottomed and steeper sided, with a stern rudder rather than a steering oar. This also meant that the pointed stern of the *knorr* design was replaced by a square stern. Hulls became deeper, which enabled larger cargoes to be carried and improved the sea-keeping qualities of the vessels. It was decked so, unlike the earlier ships, the cargo could be protected from the weather. Finally, the use of a windlass and an improved rigging plan meant it could be handled with ease by a small crew, thereby increasing profits.

By 1450, northern European seafarers had developed well-built cargo ships, whose hulls were strong enough to endure the stresses of long voyages. As these medieval merchants traded further afield, they encountered the craft of the Mediterranean, a completely different form of vessel to the cogs of the north. An amalgam of the two styles would produce the ships of discovery that explored beyond the boundaries of the known world and ushered in a new era in history.

above: *The 9th-century Gokstad ship formed part of a boat burial, and it provides us with a rare opportunity to see exactly how a Viking ship was constructed. The hull is now preserved in a museum.*

1066 AD	1176 AD	1193 AD	1206 AD	c.1254 AD	1290 AD	14th century AD	1397 AD
Norman conquest of England.	Work begins on London Bridge; completed 1209.	Zen Buddhism founded in Japan.	The Mongols begin their conquest of Asia, led by Genghis Khan.	Birth of the explorer Marco Polo.	Spectacles invented in Italy.	Date of the Bremen cog wreck, a medieval cargo vessel.	Norway, Denmark, and Sweden united under the Kalmar Agreement.

THE GUERNSEY WRECK

3RD CENTURY AD

The burnt remains of a Celtic craft

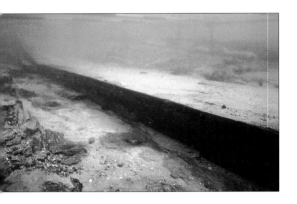

above: *The remains of this Romano-Gallic vessel were uncovered in the middle of a busy island harbor by erosion created by modern shipping. Excavation was vital in order to save this significant source of information before it was lost.*

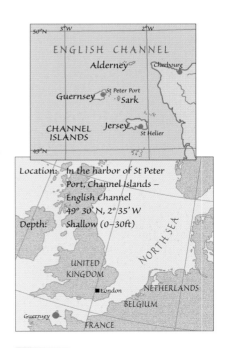

St. Peter Port is the main harbor on the island of Guernsey, one of the Channel Islands. Although lying off the French coast, it is considered a part of the United Kingdom. Guernsey diver Richard Keen is an enthusiastic amateur maritime archæologist and regularly searched for signs of historic shipwrecks. In 1982, he was diving in St Peter Port when he came across a trail of pottery fragments. He recognized these as being pre-medieval and reported his finds to the appropriate authorities.

Further examination revealed timbers that had been buried beneath silt. In recent years, bow-thrusters used by large car ferries had eroded the silt from the wreck, which lay immediately beneath the approach to their dock. Further rapid erosion was expected, so a rescue excavation was planned, led by Dr. Margaret Rule, Director of the Mary Rose Trust.

Timed to avoid the passage of ferry boats, the excavation was conducted in the poor visibility and hazardous conditions of the harbor, but what it revealed was worth the effort. The vessel was around 80 feet long, with a beam of 20 feet, and it showed evidence of being burned to the waterline immediately before it sank. Dating placed it as having been lost between AD 280 and 287, during the final centuries of the Roman occupation of Gaul and southern Britain.

What was even more remarkable was the evidence it revealed on ship design. It was a strongly built boat, based on a Celtic style. It had a thick central keel and frames, with outer and inner planks nailed to this structure. A mast step was cut into

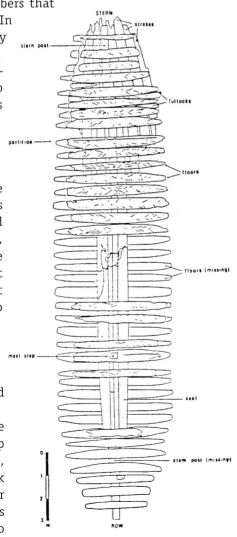

the keel about a third of the way from the bow, far further forward than in similar Roman craft. Both the mast and rudder were missing, presumably burned in the fire that consumed the ship or salvaged soon afterward.

Pine resin ballast

Similarly, there was no evidence of substantial superstructure, which was also presumably lost in the fire, although a small residue of charred timbers hinted at its construction. The seams between the outer planks were caulked using a paste of oak shavings, probably mixed with some form of glue. These were smeared on each plank before the next was fitted, rather like using mortar with bricks. Moss was used to plug a recessed hole at each nail head on the outer hull, making it remarkably watertight.

One surprising feature was the lack of ballast, which was widely used at the time, either loaded onto the floor timbers or placed in wooden pens or beneath the deck among the lower frames. The indication is that the ship carried a cargo heavy enough to act as ballast in its own right, or that it had been removed in anticipation of loading the ship. This begs the questions, what kind of cargo did she carry, and was it destroyed in the fire?

A layer of pine resin pitch was found toward the stern of the ship. Evidence suggests that this was loaded in eight blocks, which melted when the ship caught fire. Such a cargo would have been heavy enough to preclude the need for ballast. Beneath the layer of pitch, the archæologists found the crew's personal possessions. A cache of coins allowed Dr. Rule to date the wreck. Pottery fragments also hinted at the region the ship sailed. Spanish amphoras, Gallic bowls, and British drinking vessels suggested that it plied the waters of the English Channel and the Bay of Biscay.

We have no idea why the ship burned to the waterline and sank, but the owner's misfortune provides us with the opportunity to examine a Celtic-Roman boat, an ancestor of the craft described by Caesar in his Gallic Wars. It's similar enough to the boat found at Blackfriars in London to suggest that this form of Celtic vessel was a common sight in the northwestern corner of the Roman Empire.

above: *Poor visibility and constant boat traffic hampered the excavation, but the lower hull of the vessel was revealed beneath an overburden of silt. This view shows the raised keel timbers flanked by outer and inner planking.*

opposite page: *The hull structure of the Guernsey wreck revealed fresh information on the construction of coastal vessels during the period of Roman rule in Gaul and Britain.*

below: *Archæologists used their information to attempt to understand the construction of the vessel. The lack of Roman construction methods betrayed the Celtic origins of the vessel.*

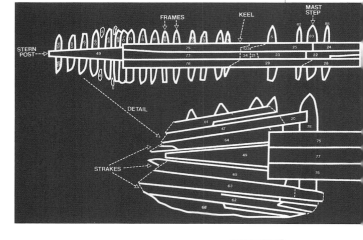

THE BLACKFRIARS BOAT

2ND CENTURY AD

A missing link in Roman ship building?

Location: London, England –
River Thames
51° 30' N, 0° 5' W

Depth: Beached (found on
river bank)

NORTH SEA

IRELAND

UNITED KINGDOM

ATLANTIC OCEAN

London

London

Blackfriars

R. Thames   Greewich

While workmen were building a new riverside wall near London's Blackfriars Bridge in 1962, they discovered ship timbers. These were examined by archæologists from the Guildhall Museum in London in an excavation directed by Peter Marsden in 1962–3; subsequent excavations during construction work revealed three more boats! The first find (Blackfriars 1) was a Roman or Romano-British vessel, dating to the second century AD.

A second vessel (Blackfriars 2), discovered in 1969, was the remains of a 17th-century river barge, complete with a cargo of bricks. Two more wrecks uncovered in 1970 (Blackfriars 3 and 4) date from the late 15th or early 16th century, and were probably lost in a collision with one another. From this range of maritime casualties spanning 1,500 years, the first vessel is probably the most fascinating.

During the winter of 1962, Marsden excavated the lower hull, stern, and collapsed port side of the Roman vessel, and removed portions for conservation and study at the Guildhall Museum. Although the starboard side was present when the ship was recovered, workmen destroyed it before its importance became apparent. While Roman craft of the period are reasonably well documented through artistic renditions and excavated remains in the Mediterranean, the Blackfriars 1 boat bore little resemblance to them. Another Roman wreck found on the River Thames at County Hall, at the turn of the century, was of decidedly Roman construction, using a shell-first hull design, secured using mortise-and-tenon joints. The Blackfriars ship was made in a completely different way.

She was built from oak, grown in the southeast of Roman Britain. Instead of a keel, she had two central planks running the full 37 feet of the hull. Naturally curved timbers formed the bow and stern, which were also used for the frames, protruding at regular intervals down the line of the central planks, like the bones of a fish. Straight timbers were laid on the lower frames to form an inner skin, and the outer skin was pinned to the frames using treenails and iron fasteners. The seams of the planks were caulked using a paste of wood shavings and pitch. A single mast step was found; in it was a votive coin, designed to be pinned in place beneath the mast.

below: *A scale model of the Blackfriars boat in the Museum of London shows how the lighter upper frames rose from the stouter keel and frames of the lower hull structure.*

Emperor Domitian's currency

The bronze coin, dating from the reign of the Emperor Domitian (AD 81–96), was minted in Rome around AD 88–89 and provided a date for the ship's construction. It is unclear how long the ship was in use, although wear on the timbers probably pushes the date of its loss into the second century AD. The ship lacked more than cursory evidence of a deck, or even any superstructure. The original structure, if it existed, was probably a flimsy affair, while Marsden postulated that the deck enclosed a hold which was less than six feet high.

When the ship sank, she was carrying a cargo of 26 tons (23.6 tonnes) of stone. This was identified as Kentish ragstone, a limestone found in the south of England, popular as building material in Roman London. Peter Marsden was able to guess that the last voyage of the ship had been from the Maidstone area in Kent, up the Thames estuary and river to the Roman port of London. Construction prevented excavation of the stern area, and few personal items were recovered; Marsden speculated that the crew's quarters were located in the stern. Her resting position suggested she was in mid-river when she sank (the river has moved since the Roman period) and was probably lost in a collision.

The Blackfriars Boat was a ground-breaking study for Roman archæologists. It provided the first evidence that Romans in Britain did not impose their own ship design. The less forgiving waters required a more robust vessel, so shipbuilders relied on their traditional Celtic designs. This theory was proved by the discovery of another, similar boat in the Channel Islands between Britain and France.

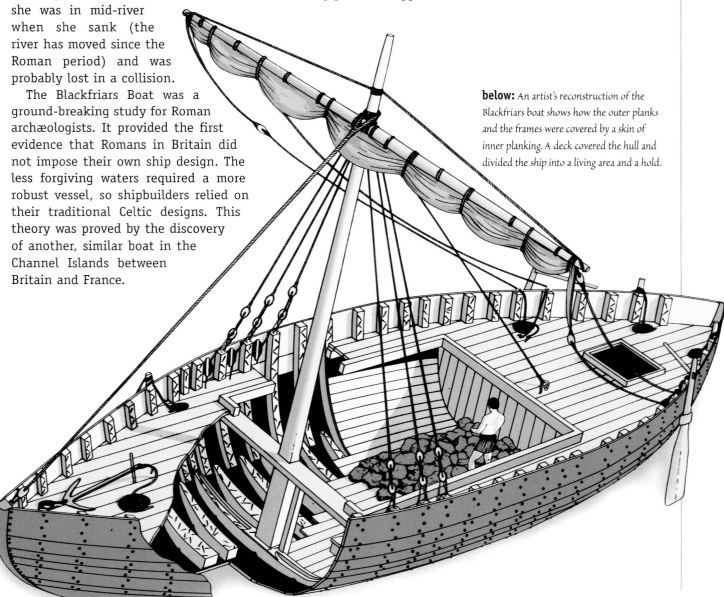

below: *An artist's reconstruction of the Blackfriars boat shows how the outer planks and the frames were covered by a skin of inner planking. A deck covered the hull and divided the ship into a living area and a hold.*

THE SKULDELEV SHIPS

11TH CENTURY AD

A sunken barrier of Viking ships

above: *A large coffer dam was constructed in the Roskilde fjord that allowed excavation of the ships to be undertaken in terrestrial conditions.*

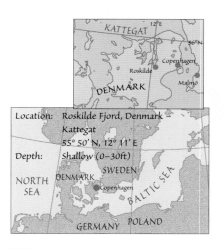

Location: Roskilde Fjord, Denmark
Kattegat
55° 50' N, 12° 11' E
Depth: Shallow (0–30ft)

At some time in the late 10th or early 11th century, a row of ships was scuttled to form a barrier. It stretched across the Roskilde fjord, guarding the sea entrance to the town of the same name. Roskilde, at that time the capital of Denmark, was surrounded by an array of marine and land defenses, incorporating ditches, watchtowers, and block-ships.

In the 1950s, Danish archæologists decided to investigate the reported remains of sunken wooden vessels, located in the narrow waterways called Peberrenden, near the town of Skuldelev. An initial investigation by divers in 1957 concluded that the vessels were of the "Viking Period," well preserved, and therefore worthy of study.

In 1962 a cofferdam surrounded the wrecks, covering an area of over 160,000 square feet. When the water was pumped out it allowed archæologists to excavate the vessels using conventional land methods, albeit in the thick, wet mud of the fjord bottom. The same anærobic mud had helped to preserve the ships' timbers, pinned beneath the cargo of rocks that was used to scuttle them and hold them in position.

Five ships were recovered during the excavation, and the timbers removed for conservation to the Danish National Museum, which organized the operation. It was found that all ships had certain similarities. They were all clinker-built, a construction style where overlapping planks were fastened to a framework by the use of iron rivets. The same construction technique was found on numerous Dark Age and early medieval ships, such as the Sutton Hoo boat and the Osberg ship. It can also be seen in many North Sea and small Scandinavian vernacular craft today.

Clinker construction can also be seen as a further development of the Celtic shipbuilding methods found at the Blackfriars and Guernsey excavations. The outer planking, which was very sturdy, allowed for a less substantial system of frames, compared to Celtic craft. Floor timbers covered the frames, these in turn covered at intervals by cross-beams. All five ships were each fitted with a single mast.

A varied flotilla

Of even greater interest were the ships' differences. They showed a construction influenced by function as much as general principles, creating a range of specialist craft. Skuldelev 1 was a *knorr*, the principal type of seagoing cargo vessel of the Viking Period. This was the type of ship used by Leif Eriksson when he discovered America, ideally suited for long voyages. It was 50 feet long, with a beam of over 15 feet, giving her a cargo capacity of 25 tons (22.7 tonnes). The rounded hull came to a sharp point at both bow and stern that allowed the fitting of a stern steering oar. The pine and oak used in her construction indicated an origin in Norway.

below: *The remains of the Skuldelev 1 vessel (or knorr) show how the wide beam gave the craft the stability and cargo capacity needed for ocean trading. This was the type of ship used by Leif Eriksson when he discovered America.*

Skuldelev 2 was poorly preserved, but enough remained to show how impressive she once was. A longship almost 100 feet long and 12 feet wide, she would have been propelled by 30 oars per side. The size indicates that it was a *draka* or dragon ship, and her oak frames show she was built in Ireland, but repaired in Denmark.

Skuldelev 3 was a small oak-built craft 45 feet long and 12 feet wide, allowing her to hold 25 tons of cargo. She was fitted to carry seven oars per side, making her a versatile craft. This was the best preserved of all the recovered vessels.

Skuldelev 5 (there was no "4") was identified as a *leidangr* or local guard ship. She was originally 56 feet long, with an 8 ½-foot beam, and bears marked constructional similarities to Skuldelev 3. Both were Danish ships, and so they may have been built in the same yard.

Skuldelev 6 was poorly preserved, but enough remained to identify her as a fishing boat or other small craft from southern Sweden. She was 38 feet long and 8 feet wide.

A unique collection of widely varied ships from all over the Viking world, the Skuldelev wrecks remain a rare resource that allows us to reconstruct the craft of that romantic but brutal age.

THE BREMEN COG

13TH CENTURY AD

Northern Europe's all-purpose ship

For two hundred years or more, the cog was the premier type of ship in Northern Europe. Descended from the Scandinavian *knorr*, by the 13th century it had developed into a highly specialized cargo carrier, capable of carrying larger loads than any other vessel. It has been widely depicted in contemporary illustrations and on objects such as city seals, but finding an almost intact example presented a rare gift to historians.

It allowed them to examine in detail the ship that plied the North Sea during the Middle Ages, and which became closely associated with the mercantile confederation known as the Hanseatic League. In 1962, the remains of a vessel were found in the harbor of Bremen, in northern Germany. Bremen was once a bustling Hanseatic port, and the craft's identification as a cog sparked intense interest, providing a direct link with the city's past.

above: *The remains of a medieval vessel were exposed in the bank of the Weser River in Bremen. This view shows an exposed portion of clinker-built hull planking, with a series of protruding frames behind it.*

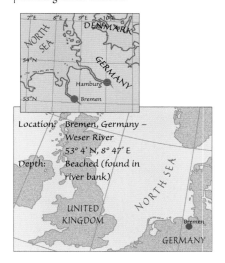

Location: Bremen, Germany – Weser River
53° 4' N, 8° 47' E

Depth: Beached (found in river bank)

The cog was excavated during the early 1960s using a variety of tools and techniques, including dredging equipment, salvage divers, and even a diving bell. By 1965 all of the timbers were recovered and taken to the Deutsches Schiffartsmuseum in nearby Bremerhaven. The find required the development of maritime archæological and conservation facilities in Germany, and the museum took the lead, acting as the catalyst for the growth of maritime archæology in Northern Europe. At a time when diving was becoming increasingly popular, unique shipwreck finds in 1960s' Sweden, Britain, and Germany caught the imagination of divers everywhere.

Over the next decade, the timbers were slowly stabilized to prevent further decay. It took over seven years to piece the ship timbers together again, but the work produced a wealth of information about her construction. The cog was 75 feet long, with a 25-foot beam, giving her a fat, rounded appearance, that matched the evidence from contemporary illustrations. With a hold almost 10 feet deep, she could carry a large cargo for her size, estimated at 130 tons (118 tonnes). Compared to earlier cargo vessels such as the *knorr*, her capacity was enormous.

The vessel had a flat bottom, with a sharp turn at the bilge, giving her hull a barrel-like cross-section. The centerpiece was the keel, in three

sections, with the bow and stern pieces curving slightly upward. These ended in almost vertical stem and stern posts, which in turn served as an anchor for the large frames of her hull.

Sea-drenched cargo

The ship was planked using the clinker method employed throughout Northern Europe. The planks or strakes were fastened to the frames by the use of a combination of treenails and iron fasteners. A series of eight large deck beams running across the ship's width supported its deck, nailed in place over them. This wasn't made watertight, so water spilling over the deck would pour into the hold. The cargo therefore needed to be in waterproof containers, such as barrels or crates.

She was fitted with one mast carrying a single square sail, similar to the ones used by the Skuldelev ships. Fittings for a large rudder were found on the sternpost, although the rudder was not recovered during the excavation. This in itself was a great improvement over earlier types of vessel, which used a steering oar. The hull was covered at the rear by a sterncastle, extending 24 feet forward from the stern, widening as it did so. A rare find was a toilet, designed to hang off the starboard side of the ship under the sterncastle. Other fittings included a well-preserved capstan and windlass, designed to handle the vessel's heavy cargoes.

It has been suggested that the Bremen cog was never finished, but broke from her moorings and sank as she was being fitted out. This would explain the lack of a rudder. The accident provided us with a virtually unused medieval vessel that can be seen in its entirety in the Deutsches Schiffartsmuseum. Two replicas have been built, and they provide us with a wealth of information about how medieval cogs sailed and handled.

above: *The conserved vessel is now displayed in Bremerhaven, and provides a unique opportunity to examine an almost complete medieval cog. The pronounced angle of the stem and stern posts is a particularly striking feature of the design.*

The San Venture

The San Pedro

BERMUDA

ATLANTIC OCEAN

FLORIDA

Emanuel
Point

St John's Wreck

BAHAMAS

Highborn Cay

Molasses Reef

GULF OF MEXICO

The Santa María

Ines de Soto

CUBA

Santa Lucia

HISPANIOL

Las Canarreos

Padre Island Wrecks

St Anne's Bay

Bahaia Mujeres

Banco Nuevo

JAMAICA

MEXICO

CARIBBEAN SEA

YUCATAN
PENINSULA

PACIFIC OCEAN

SHIPS OF DISCOVERY

LEEWARD ISLANDS

PUERTO RICO

WINDWARD ISLANDS

SOUTH AMERICA

above: *The discovery of America created a demand for the first ships capable of sustaining lengthy ocean voyages.*

During the 15th century there was a rise of artistic, cultural, and scientific interest and a thirst for knowledge that would result in the Renaissance. It also led to the age of exploration. The combination of the stout though unwieldy ship designs of Northern Europe with the sleek, fragile lines of Mediterranean ships produced a new type of vessel. The caravel and its successor, the carrack, were capable of undertaking long ocean voyages, and when Columbus discovered the New World in 1492, a new chapter in human history was ushered in. By the start of the 16th century, well-protected ships were regularly plying between the old world and the new, carrying settlers one way and treasure and other goods on the return voyage. These small but well-armed vessels helped to uncover the mysteries of a new continent, and were the precursors of the galleons used by Spain to guard her treasure fleets.

above: *In the late 1980s, a team from the Institute for Nautical Archæology (INA) excavated a mid-16th-century ship lost off Highborn Cay in the Bahamas. The central datum line crossing the site from top to bottom marks the approximate location of the keel, and the mast step is revealed below the surrounding ballast stones.*

By the Middle Ages, the standard trading ship in northern European waters was the cog. Its hull was clinker-built, composed of overlapping planks pinned to a frame. It used a single mast carrying a large square sail for propulsion, and was aided by a single rudder.

The cog design was ideal for transporting cargo, or even troops. The addition of platforms at bow and stern (forecastle and sterncastle) gave soldiers space to fight; depictions of late medieval naval battles show them in use. The cog also allowed merchants to travel further afield and, by the 13th century, North European sailors were in regular contact with their Mediterranean counterparts. During the Crusades and the Norman settlement of Italy, these sailors encountered vessels based on Arabic lines.

In the Mediterranean, ship hulls followed the old Roman tradition of shell-first construction. Shipbuilders laid planks edge to edge on a pre-constructed series of frames, and pinned them using wooden dowels or nails. The seams between the planks were caulked to provide a watertight join. Craft made with this method are known as "carvel-built," but aren't necessarily "caravels," the term for broad-bowed 15–16th-century vessels, usually with three masts (*see side panel below*).

The other main difference was in the sail. The seafarers of the Mediterranean used a large triangular sail that ran the length of the ship, supported from a single mast. This *lateen* sail allowed them to sail far closer into the wind than their square-sailed rivals, and was therefore less reliant on wind direction. Northern vessels retained certain advantages. It was easier to tack (pass across the wind direction), and their stronger hulls were better suited to rougher Atlantic conditions. It would take centuries for ship designers to amalgamate the best features of both schools of shipbuilding.

Carvel or Caravel ?

The style of ship construction known as carvel-built (probably from the Danish word *karveel* or the medieval French *carvelle*) used planks meeting flush at the seams. As a term, caravel covered a variety of types of ship, but generally meant a broad-bowed vessel with a high, narrow poop that usually carried three masts with lateen or both square and lateen sails.

The caravel of discovery

In the late 13th century the King of France ordered transport ships to be built in Venice and Genoa to transport a crusading army. These were double-masted *lateen*-sailed ships, the biggest in the Mediterranean at the time. The Italian shipbuilders copied the increased hull size of the cog and adapted it for use in carvel-built ships.

The cog developed throughout the Middle Ages, the height of superstructure and hull size steadily increasing. By the start of the 15th century, ships combined features of northern and southern Europe. The ultimate expression of the Mediterranean shipbuilding school at the time was the caravel, a design that relied heavily on northern European

1206	1242	1348	1368	1415	1429	c.1440	1492
The Mongols begin their conquest of Asia, led by Genghis Khan.	Russians repel invasion by the German Teutonic Knights.	A third of Europe's population die with the bubonic plague.	Beginning of China's Ming dynasty.	The English win the Battle of Agincourt.	The French, led by Joan of Arc, defeat the English in Orleans, France.	Malacca, southeast Asia, is established as a major commercial port.	Christopher Columbus reaches America.

features. It combined the stern rudder and flat stern of the cog with a carvel-built hull and either two or three masts carrying *lateen* sails.

At least in Spain and Portugal, caravels were also adapted to carry a square mainsail when required, which was faster when sailing with the prevailing wind and easier to handle. The result was a lightly built, speedy, responsive vessel that was easily handled by a small crew. This variant, called the caravel *redonda*, was widely used by the Portuguese during their explorations of the African coast and the Indian Ocean. Early explorers relied on them extensively—two of Christopher Columbus's three ships were caravels.

The caravel was the first of the two main types of ship used for the discoveries of the late 15th and early 16th centuries. The second was a vessel more steeply grounded in northern shipbuilding traditions. By the late 15th century the cog had developed into a vessel capable of carrying two or three masts. Ships hulls were more streamlined, and the flimsy structures at the bow and stern were replaced by more substantial features that were an integral part of the hull. These forecastles and sterncastles made the ship more resistant to severe weather and provided greater comfort for the crew.

A multitude of sails

By the end of the century, sterncastles could extend as far forward as the mainmast, which in effect provided an extra deck. There was a gradual shift from clinker-built hulls to carvel-built ones, a trend spurred on by the development of shipborne artillery. The integrity of clinker-built hulls would be compromised by cutting holes in them, so strongly armed ships needed to be carvel-built. These ships combined a strong frame with a streamlined hull, and had a much greater cargo capacity than Mediterranean ships of the same period. This type of vessel became known as a *nao* by the Spanish and Portuguese, and as a carrack by the northern Europeans.

Like the caravel, carracks used a combination of square sails and *lateen* sails, depending on sailing conditions. The standard sail plan was a square

below: *Once maritime explorers in the late 15th century discovered sea routes to India, European trading companies were quick to take advantage of the new markets they offered. By the end of the 17th century, European trade with India was big business, and ports such as Bombay, Madras, and Goa became some of the richest trading centers in the world.*

1493	1498	1500	1520	1521	1530	1541	c.1545
Founding of Hispaniola, the first Spanish settlement in the Americas.	Vasco de Gama becomes first person to make a return voyage from Europe to India.	Pedro Cabral discovers Brazil.	Ferdinand Magellan crosses the Pacific Ocean.	Beginning of the Protestant Reformation.	The Spanish treasure fleets begin their annual trading voyages.	Hernando de Soto discovers the Mississippi river.	Date of the De Soto wreck, a Spanish vessel.

sail on the mainmast, flanked by a square sail on the foremast and a *lateen* sail on the mizzen mast (if a third mast was available). This combination helped when tacking, and allowed the vessel to sail in a variety of wind conditions. By the late 15th century a sprit-sail was added to the bowsprit, and topsails were added to the fore and main masts.

In 1492, when Columbus sailed in search of a land beyond the Western Sea, his flagship was the nao *Santa Maria*. By this time the carrack was a fully rigged ship, capable of weathering long ocean voyages. The caravel remained in use for short voyages and coastal trade, but the carrack became the premier ship of discovery in the 16th century. While vessels became larger, more specialized, and better armed, the basic design would remain unchanged throughout the era of exploration and beyond.

By the early 16th century, following the initial wave of discoveries, ships sailing to the New World took on a new role. Instead of pure vessels of exploration, they had to carry colonists and their supplies, and return with produce from the Americas.

By the 1530s attacks on Spanish shipping led to increased armament on ships sailing to the New World. The use of naval artillery was in its infancy but was already having a dominant influence in ship design; its

below: *A bustling harbor scene as a late 15th-century carrack is prepared for a voyage. Christopher Columbus's flagship the* Santa Maria *probably looked much like this vessel. "The ship of St. Stonybroke." Woodcut by anonymous artist, c.1520.*

1559	1562	c.1564	1571	1581	1587	1588	1600
Date of the Emanuel Point wreck, a Spanish settlers' vessel.	John Hawkins makes his first slave trade voyage to the West Indies.	Date of the St. John's wreck, a Spanish cargo vessel.	England's Royal (Stock) Exchange is founded.	Francis Drake is knighted.	Execution of Mary Queen of Scots.	The English defeat the Spanish Armada.	The English East India Company is formed.

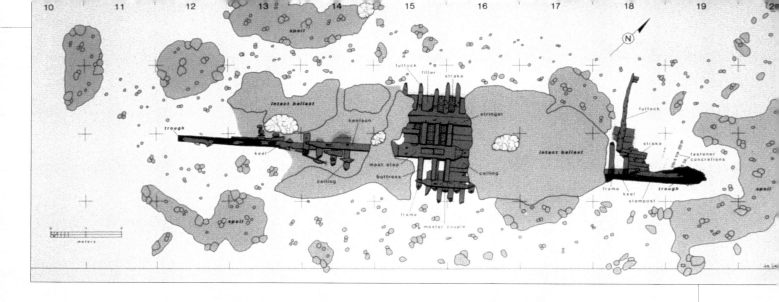

effect on clinker-built ship construction has already been noted. Ships had to be well armed, and this requirement led to the design of the galleon, a hybrid ship combining fighting power and cargo capacity.

Rediscovering the caravels and carracks

What historical records failed to clarify was how the Spanish arrived at the galleon design, whose primary purpose was to escort or transport valuable cargoes from the New World to Spain. Surely well-armed carracks and naos were used during the early and mid-16th century; their design was a precursor of the galleon. Rather than calling them ships of exploration, these vessels were really ships of exploitation. The proof of their existence came through the medium of underwater archaeology.

The Institute of Nautical Archæology (INA), a research body headed by Dr. George Bass, is based at Texas A&M University. The 500th anniversary of Columbus's first voyage approached but little was known about his ships of discovery, so INA launched a research program aimed at finding out what they looked like. After over a decade of work, ships of discovery still remain an archæological enigma, and no such shipwrecks have been positively identified. What they did find was several wrecks from the "age of exploitation," the ships forming a missing link between the ships of Columbus and the galleons of the Spanish treasure fleets.

In the early 1980s INA archæologists surveyed and excavated the remains of a small Spanish vessel lost on Molasses Reef, in the Turks and Caicos Islands lying north of Hispaniola. The ship was armed with two bombardettas (wrought-iron breech-loading guns) and 15 versos (swivel guns), the latter used for close-range defense. A similar wreck excavated at Highborn Cay in the Bahamas produced similar material. By 1992 several other vessels investigated by INA, plus others dating from the same period (1540–1610) including the St John's Wreck and Padre Island Wrecks, had produced an impressive body of information. We now know a great deal about these early ships, carrying colonists or trading goods between Europe and the New World. What still remain on the seabed, waiting to be discovered, are the shipwrecks dating from the era of Columbus.

above: *Site plan of the Highhborn Cay Wreck following INA's 1986 excavation. A test trench has been dug across the site revealing the keel, frames, strakes, and the mast step. The rest of the small vessel is still shown covered with piles of ballast stones.*

1602	1605	1607	1608	1609	1618	1636	1645
The Dutch East India Company is formed.	Construction of the Golden Temple of Amritsar is completed.	Founding of Jamestown, the first permanent English settlement in the Americas.	The French found Quebec, Canada.	Date of the *Sea Venture* wreck, an English settlers' vessel.	Beginning of the Thirty Years' War.	Founding of Harvard College, North America's first university.	Abel Tasman discovers New Zealand while circumnavigating Australia.

THE DE SOTO WRECK

1554 Cuba's earliest excavated shipwreck

above: *Archæologists from the Cuban archæological organization Carisub survey a wrought-iron breech-loading gun (bombardetta). This form of plotting work uses techniques similar to those found on land sites.*

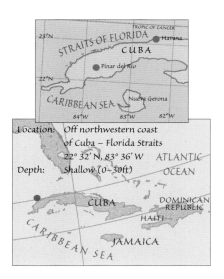

Location: Off northwestern coast of Cuba – Florida Straits
22° 32' N, 83° 36' W
Depth: Shallow (0–30ft)

In the late 1980s, the remains of a shipwreck was discovered on a reef ten miles (16km) north of Caya Ines de Soto, an island off Cuba's Pinar del Rio province. The reef and the island form part of the Archiapélago de los Colorados, a string of islands fringing Cuba's northern coastline. A team of archæologists from Carisub surveyed the site in 1992, and discovered that it contained the remains of a Spanish ship dating from the mid-16th century. Carisub is a national underwater archæological research body, founded in 1980 by the Cuban Cultural Ministry. In Cuba, legislation passed in 1977 to protect the island's cultural heritage was extended to include underwater sites within Cuban territorial waters.

Work on the site was conducted between 1992 and 1995, under the supervision of Carisub's director, José Nelson García Cejar; fieldwork was co-ordinated by Abraham Lopez Cruz. The site was surveyed using conventional means, metal detectors, and photography, before an excavation strategy was decided upon. This included a full environmental survey of the reef and any effect the wreck had on it.

The site was then divided a grid of a hundred squares, each 16 feet (4.88m) across. The grid covered the entire site, as well as much of the surrounding reef structure, where objects were expected to have scattered. The main ballast pile and largest concentration of concreted remains sat firmly astride the reef, suggesting that the ship had grounded firmly, deposited by a substantial wave, probably caused by a hurricane.

The recovered finds pointed toward it being no ordinary shipwreck. Gold finger bars and silver ingots were recovered, whose markings indicated that the ship was wrecked some time after 1554. Large numbers of gold and silver coins were recovered, the majority also dating from the mid-16th century. These were minted in Mexico or Spain, and the quantity indicated that they were part of the cargo.

In addition, personal effects such as exquisite jewelry formed from gold and precious stones, gold religious artifacts, and high-quality silver tableware suggested that the ship had carried wealthy passengers. Ceramic finds included the remains of olive jars, beakers, and bowls, all of Spanish or Spanish New World origin. Navigational equipment included two brass astrolabes and dividers. Research was needed to discover more about this mystery wreck.

Sorry fate of a rescue ship?

Archival evidence suggests that the ship may have a connection with the Padre Island shipwrecks (*see pages 108–109*). In 1554, a Spanish treasure fleet was caught in a hurricane, off the coast of what is now Texas. Three ships were lost, and the Spanish mounted a recovery operation to rescue the survivors and salvage the cargo. Almost half of the cargo of silver coins, silver ingots, and gold finger bars was recovered and transported by ship to Havana, in Cuba, ready for shipment to Spain.

It appears that one of the ships was lost *en route*, apparently off the northeastern coast of Cuba. The serial numbers on the silver ingots and gold bars recovered from the De Soto wreck match ones on the shipping manifest of the 1544 treasure fleet. Could the De Soto wreck be one of the rescue ships? More archival work needs to be done, but it is probable that some of the survivors were rescued from Padre Island, only to be shipwrecked again.

In addition to treasure, the De Soto wreck indicates a well-armed ship, carrying a complement of wrought-iron breech-loading guns (called *bombardettas* by the Spanish) and smaller swivel guns (*versos*). Given the increasing risk of hostile English and French interlopers in the Spanish Main, it appears that ships carrying valuable cargo were armed. These vessels were forerunners of the stately galleons of the late 16th and early 17th centuries.

The Cuban wreck contains many similarities to the St John's Wreck, which sank ten years later. Further information on this enigmatic Cuban wreck is eagerly awaited by archæologists and will help us to understand more about the Spanish exploitation ships.

right: *The wreck site was covered by a thick layer of coral, fused ballast stones, and rock outcrops. In order to excavate the site, archæologists first had to separate the concreted objects and ballast from the surrounding seabed using pneumatic drills.*

THE EMANUEL POINT WRECK

1559 Florida's oldest shipwreck

above: *One of the most unusual finds from the site was the wooden carving of a galleon, probably meant to depict the sunken vessel itself. The pronounced forecastle and sterncastle shown on the carving are typical features of mid-16th century Spanish naos or early galleons.*

I n 1992, state-funded archæologists from the Florida Bureau of Archæological Research chose to inventory all the shipwrecks in Pensacola Bay, near Florida's panhandle strip of land. Using a magnetometer, they found something in the middle of the bay, near Emanuel Point, and dived to examine it. The contact made by the magnetometer was a large, encrusted wrought-iron anchor, clearly dating from prior to the 19th century. Beside it, they found a small ballast mount, sticking out from the side of a shallow sandbar ridge. It was decided to dig a test excavation trench, to find out more about the site of the mysterious wreck.

After removing a portion of the ballast pile, an archæologist found the remains of ship timbers pinned beneath the stones. The construction technique unearthed was consistent with that found on Spanish shipwrecks dating from the 16th century, including the Red Bay wreck in Labrador and the St. John's wreck in the Bahamas.

In addition to timbers, the excavators found pottery shards from Spanish olive jars, as well as fragments of glazed and enameled ceramic tableware. The Bureau's archæologists had clearly stumbled across an important early Spanish ship. Looking for more information, they turned their attention to the historical archives, trying to find a likely ship that was lost in the area.

After extensive archival research, the best candidate for the wreck was one of the ships from the fleet of Tristán de Luna y Arellano, lost during a hurricane while anchored in Pensacola Bay. It was part of a large Spanish expedition that was attempting to colonize northwestern Florida.

The expedition led by de Luna consisted of a thousand settlers, 500 soldiers, and a small fleet of transports, galleons and smaller warships and sailed from Vera Cruz in Mexico in 1559. A month after their arrival, a hurricane struck from the Gulf of Mexico and most of the ships were wrecked. As many of their stores and equipment were lost in the disaster, the expedition was doomed to failure. They returned to Mexico in 1561.

Portrait of a Spanish galleon

By 1565, the Spanish had established a settlement on Florida's east coast at St. Augustine, the strategic need for a settlement at Pensacola was removed, and the project was abandoned. The remains of de Luna's fleet lay forgotten on the seabed of Pensacola Bay. The wreck was almost certainly part of that doomed expedition.

Location: Off Pensacola, Florida, USA – Gulf of Mexico 30° 29' N, 87° 10' W

Depth: Shallow (0–30ft)

The subsequent excavation of select portions of the wreck site revealed useful information about the ship. Sufficient hull timbers remained to show that the port side of her hull had been badly damaged, probably when pounded against the bay's sandbar during the hurricane. The timbers obviously belonged to a large vessel, and were consistent with those expected for a galleon.

The absence of any cargo or armament suggests that the vessel was extensively salvaged after her loss, but ship fittings and personal items were found to be well preserved in and around the timbers. Galley utensils were found toward the bow, while toward the waist and stern personal items such as Aztec-designed bowls, coins, a breastplate, and the remains of clothing revealed how the crew and passengers lived and ate.

The good preservation of organic material meant that foodstuffs were recovered, including nuts, seeds, animal, and chicken bones, as well as the remains of several rats and cockroaches. Also in the center of the ship, an array of artillery and small-arms' shot showed that the vessel was well armed. The surprising find of a small piece of wood carved into the shape of a galleon may even be an image of the ship herself.

Work is continuing on the remains of this once well-armed Spanish galleon, and despite nothing tangible that can prove conclusively that she formed part of de Luna's doomed expedition, the wreck is a vivid reminder of the period of the first attempted European settlement of mainland America.

below: *An underwater archæologist working for the State of Florida's research team uses an airlift to remove the overburden of silt covering the site. The poor water visibility is the result of the stirring up of light silt during the excavation process.*

THE ST JOHN'S WRECK

1564

The lost ship of Pedro de Menéndez?

Location: North off Grand Bahama Island,
Bahamas – Atlantic Ocean
26° 47′ N, 78° 51′ W

Depth: Shallow (0–30ft)

above: *The discovery of hull structure. Here, outer planking has been partially exposed; these would be drawn and recorded in situ before the excavation would proceed.*

The St. John's Expedition marine salvage company found a vessel's remains while searching for shipwrecks on St. John's Reef, north of the Bahamian island of Grand Bahama, in July 1991. The characteristic ballast pile and guns of an early Spanish craft were clearly visible, and after discerning that the site had little or no commercial value, they decided to turn the site over to archæologists.

The salvage company was based in Florida, so naturally they turned to the Mel Fisher Maritime Museum in Key West for help. After examining the wreck, the museum's maritime archæologist, Corey Malcom, concluded that the wreck dated from the mid-16th century. The museum and the salvors formed a partnership in conjunction with the Bahamian government, allowing Malcom and his team to excavate the wreck. From 1992 onward, five seasons of excavation were conducted on the site, providing useful information about Spanish ships of discovery.

After removing sections of the ballast pile, hull timbers pinned beneath the stones revealed that the ship was originally over 65 feet (19.8m) long, and was of the vessel type known as a *nao*—a large cargo vessel with a rounded hull. In shape and design, it was a cross between the cog of northern Europe and the caravel of the Mediterranean. The carrack, a similar ship design, is most commonly associated with the *Santa Maria*, the flagship of Christopher Columbus in 1492.

Initial investigation of the hull timbers revealed constructional similarities with other near-contemporary Spanish vessels. Although badly worn, it was discovered that the outer hull planking had been secured to now-separated frames using treenails and iron fasteners. As work continued, section by section and year by year, more information on the structure of this vessel was revealed.

A formidable warship

The St. John's wreck was well armed: the site was littered by a heavy although antiquated armament of at least three wrought-iron breech-loading guns (*bombardettas*) and seven swivel guns (*versos*). Scores of cannonballs, both iron and stone, as well as grapeshot and musket shot for the swivel guns, indicate that her armament was once more substantial. Further guns may lie undiscovered.

In addition to artillery, the ship had contained a number of soldiers for defense during boarding actions. The remains of nine crossbows were found, together with their associated goat's-foot loading levers, and the concreted remains of helmets, swords, and staff weapons (pike heads and a halberd). Dating of coins and pottery placed the loss of the ship at around 1564, when both wrought-iron guns and crossbows were considered obsolete. The find begs the question, what was a ship carrying heavy though obsolete armament doing in the waters between Florida and the Bahamas in 1564?

Dr. Eugene Lyon, a scholar of Spanish colonial history, may have provided the answer. By 1564, the French had established a base at Fort Caroline, on Florida's northeast coast. From the fort they preyed on Spanish shipping, prompting the Spanish to launch a military expedition against their enemies. Led by Pedro de Menéndez, the Spanish located the French base in 1565 and destroyed it. Menéndez owned a large fleet of ships, based in Havana, and during the French attacks he increased the armament of ships that were regularly sailing to Spain. One of these, a nao called the *Santa Clara*, was wrecked north of Grand Bahama Island in 1564.

Although it still remains to be proven, it is highly likely that the wreck is that of the *Santa Clara*. Personal items including ceramics from central America, the bones of a baby alligator, lead cloth seals, and even an enema syringe add to the fascinating range of artifacts recovered from this early colonial wreck. It is intended that everything recovered from the St. John's wreck will be displayed in a permanent gallery in the Mel Fisher Maritime Museum, in Key West, Florida.

above: *Archæologists use a water dredge to remove sand surrounding a pile of ballast stones inside a three-foot (91cm) grid. These stones would then be carefully removed to reveal what lay beneath them. In shallow sites such as this, air is supplied from a support vessel anchored over the site, so diving time is increased.*

below: *A gully crossing the wreck site is excavated a section at a time. The basket is used to remove ballast stones to a holding area just off the site itself.*

THE SEA VENTURE

1609 The shipwreck from Shakespeare's *Tempest*

above: *This reconstruction shows the Sea Venture aground on a reef. The survivors are being ferried ashore onto Bermuda and safety. Gradual shipwrecks such as this allowed the crew to rescue much of their stores and equipment before the ship sank. Painting by Deryck Foster.*

The colony at Jamestown in Virginia, founded in 1607, was England's first permanent settlement in the Americas. Funded and supplied by the Virginia Company of London, these first settlers struggled to survive their first few years, and it looked like the colony might suffer the same fate as Sir Walter Raleigh's failed settlement on Roanoke Island.

The winter of 1608–9 was particularly harsh, so the Virginia Company decided to sent a relief expedition to Jamestown, loaded with supplies, tools, and new settlers. The fleet of seven ships and two pinnaces (launches) left Plymouth in southwestern England in June 1609. The flagship of the relief fleet was the galleon *Sea Venture*, commanded by Captain Christopher Newport. She carried 150 settlers, as well as the fleet's admiral, Sir George Somers, and the new Lieutenant Governor of Virginia, Sir Thomas Gates. She would never arrive at Jamestown.

Two months into the voyage, and still eight days' sail from Virginia, the fleet was hit by a hurricane. The *Sea Venture* became separated from the other ships. Battered by the hurricane and taking in water, the small galleon was in danger of sinking. When land was sighted, Captain Newport ordered her to be beached, and she ran aground on a reef off the northeastern corner of Bermuda.

Her survivors built shelters on the island and constructed a longboat from wreckage, then sent for help from Jamestown. It never arrived. They then built two larger craft, and leaving a handful who wanted to settle on the island, the remainder sailed for Jamestown, arriving there in May 1610. By 1612, fresh settlers augmented those remaining on Bermuda, and the island developed a permanent colony. Hearing of the shipwreck, William Shakespeare was prompted to write *The Tempest*.

A crew ancestor's find

The wreck was rediscovered in 1958 by Edmund Downing, an ancestor of one of *Sea Venture*'s original crew. An initial investigation by shipwreck explorer Teddy Tucker indicated that the site might be that of the *Sea Venture*, and the project was taken up by the Bermuda Maritime Museum, under the direction of Allan Wingood. English pottery dating from the early 17th century and other personal items all pointed to a ship from the right period.

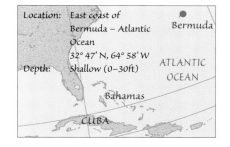

Location:	East coast of Bermuda – Atlantic Ocean 32° 47' N, 64° 58' W
Depth:	Shallow (0–30ft)

In the 1980s the Sea Venture Trust was formed, and in conjunction with the museum it organized a fully-fledged underwater excavation of the site. The work was led by a *Mary Rose* veteran, archæologist Jon Adams. Adams revealed that the ship indeed dated from the early 17th century, and was originally a vessel of around 300 tons (272.2 tonnes). The excavation revealed reasonably well-preserved layers of deposits, including organic material, as well as ship timbers.

The surviving portion of the lower hull was reasonably intact, allowing Adams and his team to record the keel, floor timbers, and frames of the vessel *in situ*. This was a revolutionary period in English ship design, and like the excavations of the *Mary Rose* and *La Trinidad Valencera*, the Bermudan wreck added greatly to our understanding of 16th-century ship construction. Personal items recovered included pottery, wooden and bone items, and clothing. Together with ship fittings that were recovered, they help us understand what life was like aboard the ships that carried America's early settlers.

It is now almost certain that the wreck is that of the *Sea Venture*. Even without its association with the colonization of America and Bermuda, and its link with Shakespeare, this ship occupies an important place in maritime history. Built during the fascinating period of the Elizabethan era and the first English colonial settlements, this vessel provides us with a rare opportunity to examine how ships of the period were built and operated. Artifacts recovered from the excavation of the *Sea Venture* now form part of a permanent display in the Bermuda Maritime Museum.

above: *The excavation of the Sea Venture in the 1980s started with a detailed survey of the exposed structure. Here an archæologist is using a three-foot (91cm) square drawing frame to record the structure. It is double-strung and, by lining up the two layers of cord, the diver can ensure he is viewing the wreck beneath the square directly from above.*

below: *The massive timbers of the Sea Venture are revealed as a complex structure of frames and underpinned strakes. Detailed recordings taken allowed archæologists to analyze how the ship was constructed.*

THE INVINCIBLE ARMADA

W hen the Spanish Armada sailed to invade England in 1588, it considered itself invincible. Its ships were the largest and best armed in the world, and the soldiers they carried were second to none in Europe. The Armada failed, battered and held at bay by a flotilla of smaller English vessels. The poor Spanish didn't know it, but they stood in the center of a century-long revolution in naval warfare. Artillery had caused the change, and the English were more advanced in the use of guns at sea than the Spanish. At the start of the era, ships relied on boarding the enemy and hand-to-hand combat. By the 1630s, warships were designed from the keel upward to use artillery as their main armament. We shall follow the path of this revolution, using shipwrecks as a guide.

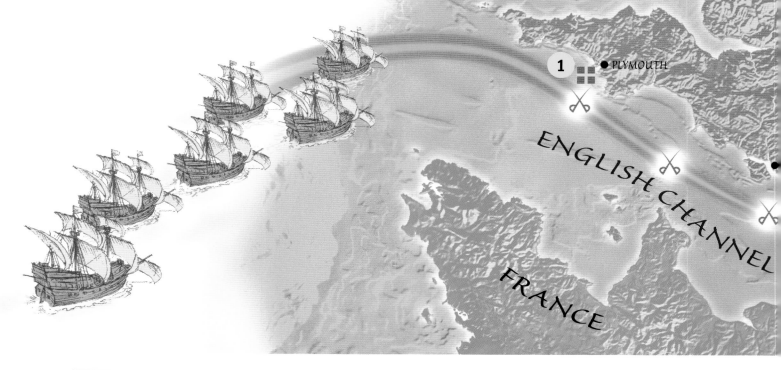

SHETLAND ISLANDS

ORKNEY ISLANDS

SCOTLAND

● EDINBURGH

NORTH SEA

ROUTE OF THE SPANISH ARMADA 1588

ENGLAND

● LONDON

● CALAIS

THE DEFEATED ARMADA

1	San Pedro
2	San Felipe
3	El Gran Grifon
4	San Juan de Sicilia
5	Girona
6	La Trinidad Valancera
7	Duquesa Santa Ana
8	Juliana
9	Lavia
10	Santa Maria de Vision
11	La Rata Encoronada
12	El Gran Grin
13	Falcon Blanco Mediano
14	San Esteban
15	Annunciada
16	Santa Mariá de la Rosa
17	San Juan Bautista

below: Spain's Armada fleet failed to conquer England through incompetence, bad weather, and superior English tactics. The outcome proved that naval artillery could be decisive in a sea battle, and changed the nature of warships forever.

The Invincible Armada

At some time in the early-to-mid 14th century, experiments with gunpowder, projectiles, and firearms finally resulted in workable artillery. While the earliest guns were considered as little more than noise-makers, they slowly developed in power and lethality.

By 1400, small guns were carried on some warships, although they were seen as little more than an auxiliary weapon, backing up the archers and crossbowmen who provided firepower at sea. These early naval artillery pieces were probably no bigger than the swivel guns found on 16th-century vessels, close-range weapons resembling large shotguns.

The warships of this 15th century were cogs, resembling the Bremen cog (*see pages 72–73*) but larger, and fitted with fighting castles or platforms fore and aft. The cog was slowly developing into the carrack, a type of vessel strong enough to take the weight of larger pieces of artillery. Archæological evidence for these early carracks is rare, but the remains of an English warship, the *Grace Dieu* launched in 1418, indicated the way these ships were slowly developing into large, specialized warships. Pictorial evidence from the mid-15th century shows that, for the first time, medium-sized wrought-iron guns were being carried, which probably led to the modification of ships' hulls to accept the extra weight.

While at the start of the century guns were seen as unimportant, there is evidence that by its end they formed a major part of a warship's

below: *In the sea battles of the late 16th century, ships fought in a loose melee, and the rival tactical schools of gunnery and boarding were tested in action. "English ships and the Spanish Armada, August 1588." Oil painting by unknown English artist.*

armament. The English warship *Sovereign*, launched in 1495, carried over 40 guns of various sizes, plus 110 hand guns or rail guns. She also carried 200 archers, since the longbow was still a vital part of naval warfare.

In 1912, the remains of the *Sovereign* were discovered in the River Thames at Woolwich, near London. It appears that the ship was refitted in 1509, and her timbers show that she was modified to carry an increased complement of artillery pieces. Her clinker-built hull was replaced by flush-fitted planking, which allowed gunports to be cut into the side of the hull. This was a major innovation, allowing heavy guns to be mounted low in the ship, where they would be less likely to hinder stability.

Superior bronze weaponry

The next piece of evidence for this transition to artillery was uncovered in 1971. The wreck of the *Mary Rose* was discovered, a major warship dating from the reign of Henry VIII. It sank in 1545, and a comparison between archæological and documentary evidence shows us that she was a true artillery-armed vessel, designed as such from the keel up. Following a refit in 1536, her armament was listed as comprising 15 bronze guns and 56 wrought-iron guns of various sizes, as well as a complement of handgunners and bowmen.

This inclusion of bronze artillery represented a true departure in naval warfare, and marked the start of a century-long revolution in warship design and employment. Earlier wrought-iron guns were breech-loaders that lacked the power and range of the modern bronze weapons. By the 1540s improvements in casting technology allowed large bronze objects to be manufactured; although reliable cast-iron guns were not available for another 70 years, experimental models were produced earlier.

Bronze guns gave warships formidable firepower for the first time. The problem was, for much of the 16th century, that tactical ability and an understanding of the full potential of naval artillery lagged behind production of the weapons themselves. Most naval engagements of the century were

above: *The Tudor warship Mary Rose, as depicted on the "Anthony Roll" of 1546. From the mid-16th century, warships carried a heavy armament of artillery, but still relied on soldiers to board the enemy vessel. The information produced by the excavation of the warship revolutionized our understanding of how these ships operated.*

1533	1534	1535	c.1540	1545	1569	1571	1577–80
Henry VIII marries Anne Boleyn.	Baghdad, Mesopotamia, and Tunis are captured by Ottoman Turks.	Sir Thomas More refuses Acts of Supremacy oath and is executed.	The Spanish reach California.	Date of the *Mary Rose* wreck, sunk shortly after its launch.	Dutch merchant Gerhard Kremer publishes the first complete map of the world.	The Philippines are conquered by the Spanish.	Francis Drake sails around the world.

above: *The large trading ships of the 16th century were constructed such that artillery could be carried by piercing the hull to make gunports. Many of the ships of the Spanish Armada were converted merchantmen, and would have resembled the vessel depicted here. "A Carrack before the wind." Oil painting in the style of Peter Breughel.*

inconclusive, although one innovation gave the English a marked superiority over their foes during the Spanish Armada campaign of 1588.

By the mid-16th century, English and Dutch naval designers had begun to mount their large artillery pieces on four-wheeled carriages. The Spanish still used the older two-wheeled gun carriage, which was harder to handle in the cramped conditions of a gundeck in action and slower to reload.

This was partly due to the tactical doctrines of the rival fleets. The Spanish saw naval combat as an extension of warfare on land. Their main fighting strength lay in the superbly trained soldiers carried onboard, and artillery was relegated to a minor role. Spanish ships intended to use their artillery in one crashing broadside, then close with the enemy and board them, where their soldiers could be relied upon to win the battle. There was no need to emphasize the speedy reloading of guns, as one shot was enough to decide the battle. This tactic proved successful in actions against the Ottoman Turks in the Mediterranean and the Portuguese, but the English countered it with a novel tactic of their own.

New tactics in the Channel

The superior numbers aboard the Spanish vessels and the superior skill of their soldiers meant that any attempt at mêlée would mean certain defeat for the English. The alternative was to keep out of range, and to harass the Armada from a distance by using naval artillery. An emphasis was placed on the reloading of artillery pieces, a feat made easier by the design of the English gun carriages.

The English had also refined their ships to suit this new tactic. Rather than the more cumbersome carracks and galleons of the enemy, the royal ships that spearheaded the English fleet were less unwieldy, lacking the towering superstructures of their opponent's vessels. This made them faster and more maneuverable, and allowed them to keep the Spanish at a distance. A combination of revolutionary naval tactics and superior ship design gave the English an edge during the hard-fought campaign.

As the Armada sailed up the English Channel, it maintained its cohesion as a fighting unit; another Spanish tactical idea. The English gunnery was unable to stop the fleet, and only a mixture of contrary winds and a bungled rendezvous with their waiting infantry and transports prevented a landing. Fireships rousted the Armada from its anchorage off Gravelines, and in the ensuing scramble the Spanish fleet lost its cohesion. This allowed the English ships to pound the Spanish at close range, and showed that artillery could at last play a decisive role in naval combat.

1588	1592–98	1595	1600	1610	1618	1626	1628
Date of *La Trinidad Valencera* wreck. Spanish Armada is defeated on attempt to invade England.	Korea is devastated by Japanese invasion.	The East Indies are colonized by the Dutch.	The English East India Company is formed.	Galileo is the first to observe the stars through a telescope.	Beginning of the Thirty Years' War.	New Amsterdam founded by Dutch (later becomes New York).	Date of the *Vasa* wreck, a Swedish warship.

The battered Armada missed its rendezvous with its invasion army and, because of the wind direction, had no option but to continue into the North Sea. They faced a dangerous voyage around the British Isles before they could return to Spain. As the fleet limped around the north of Scotland it was struck by bad weather, and many of the ships were wrecked along the western coast of Ireland. The Spanish failure was a spectacular and costly one.

Line of fire

On both sides, royal warships or galleons spearheaded the fighting, supported by armed merchant vessels. These merchant carracks and *naos* were unable to carry heavy armament, and reflected the increasing specialization of warships, a trend brought about by the introduction of artillery. By the early 17th century, ships like the Swedish *Vasa* (*pages 98–99*) or Spanish *Nuestra Señora de la Atocha* (*110–111*) formed the backbone of contemporary navies, while smaller vessels and armed or converted merchantman craft were relegated to a subsidiary role. This trend continued as naval tactics developed.

Although the basics of warship armament during the age of sail were seen on the *Mary Rose*, it would be another century before naval artillery was used to its best advantage. In the naval engagements of the early 17th century, the Spanish theory of mêlée slowly fell into disuse and artillery was the preferred type of combat. The best way to fight a ship using artillery was to sail a fleet in line, pointing as many guns at the enemy as possible. The *Vasa* showed that as early as 1628 ships were technically able to handle the problems and maneuvers required to sail in a line, one behind the other. This was achieved during the mid-17th century, probably during the series of engagements between English and Dutch fleets known as the First Dutch War (1654–56).

Commanders, such as Blake for the English and De Ruyter for the Dutch, experimented with lines of battle, setting the pattern for sea battles for the next two centuries. In a period of a hundred years following the sinking of the *Mary Rose* in 1545, ship-mounted guns had come into their own.

below: By the mid-17th century, warships relied exclusively on naval artillery in battle, and tactical developments led to the introduction of the line of battle. "Before the Battle of the Downs, 21st October 1639, showing Tromp's flagship Amelia." Oil painting by Reinier Nooms.

1645	1646	1652	1653	1654–56	1662	1666	1667
Abel Tasman discovers New Zealand while circumnavigating Australia.	The Bahamas are colonized by the English.	Cape Town, South Africa, founded by the Dutch.	Date of the Duart Point wreck, an English warship.	England and the Netherlands fight the First Dutch War.	Construction begins on King Louis XIV's palace at Versailles.	The Great Fire of London.	England and the Netherlands retreat at the end of their Four Days' War.

THE MARY ROSE

1545

The rediscovery of Henry VIII's warship

England was at war with France in 1545, and King Henry VIII was at Portsmouth, in the south of England, to watch his fleet sail out to do battle. As the king watched from the shore, one of his warships, the venerable *Mary Rose*, suddenly heeled over, caught by a surprise gust of wind. Water poured in through the open gunports and the vessel rapidly filled and sank. Few of the crew escaped, many trapped in the netting rigged over the deck to deter French boarders. It was a tragic end to a ship that had served her country well.

The *Mary Rose* was built in Portsmouth in 1509, and served in the English fleet for the next 35 years. She was refitted in 1536, her hull strengthened and pierced with gunports to take a heavier array of guns. Built during a revolution in warship design prompted by naval artillery, her original design had been too fragile to absorb the recoil of dozens of large weapons. This produced a low freeboard below the gunports, a weakness that would result in her loss.

above: *A 1981 reconstruction of the Mary Rose excavation viewed from the southwest. Water clarity meant that in reality, divers could only see a small section of the wreck at a time.*

Location: Portsmouth Harbor
South coast of
England – The Solent
50° 47' N, 1° 6' W

Depth: Medium (30–100ft)

A number of guns were recovered soon after her sinking, but the wreck was then abandoned. It was briefly rediscovered in 1836 by divers who recovered more guns before it was again forgotten.

From 1956, historian Alexander McKee carried out a search for the wreck, and in 1967 she was relocated through the use of sonar. The *Mary Rose* was completely buried in sand and remained so until 1971, when storms uncovered some of her timbers. Over the next eight years a small-scale excavation and survey revealed the potential cultural value of the surviving hull structure and its contents. By 1979 it was clear that the ship lay on her almost-complete starboard side and, although the port side had rotted away, most of her internal decks were intact.

That year, the Mary Rose Trust was founded to manage work on the wreck, including its excavation and, if possible, recovery. For the next four years an intensive archæological program recovered much of the vessel's contents, carefully recovered her internal decks, and prepared the hull for raising off the seabed. Her oak timbers were strong enough for lifting, so divers slowly surrounded the hull with a frame. Pinned in place, the timbers were further supported by a steel cradle.

The Rose floats into dock

All the engineering and fiscal problems encountered were eventually overcome, and in 1982 the *Mary Rose* finally surfaced once more. The cradle was floated into a dry dock, where it became the support for the ship itself; in 1985 the cradle was rotated so that the now-enclosed hull stood upright, displaying a cutaway view of the ship's starboard side. Slowly the internal decks and fittings were replaced, and the entire waterlogged structure subjected to chemical treatment to ensure the stability of the timbers. A three-stage active conservation program was initiated, which although expected to take 20 years to complete, will fully stabilize the hull of the *Mary Rose*.

Over 22,000 finds were recovered and conserved, including many fragile organic remains, such as cordage, clothing, animal and insect remains, and seeds. These artifacts, together with an analysis of human bones recovered, allowed scientists to accurately reconstruct 16th-century life, including diet, health, hygiene, and even dentistry!

On a larger scale, the massive bronze and wrought-iron guns, carriages, shot, and gunnery tools provide an insight into the transition of warship armament in the 16th century. Of particular interest are the hundreds of arrows, marking the last decades of the fabled English longbowman's dominance of warfare.

Ship's equipment included rigging fittings, navigational instruments, and the everyday tools and equipment needed to keep the ship operational. Together with the personal possessions of the crew and their weaponry, the items recovered from the *Mary Rose* are the finest, most complete assemblage of 16th-century artifacts ever recovered. Many of the finds and the timbers of the ship herself are on display in the Mary Rose Trust Museum in Portsmouth, England.

above: *On October 11, 1982, the hull of the Mary Rose broke the surface of Portsmouth Harbor for the first time in over four centuries. It was raised using a specially constructed steel cradle, then placed on a barge for its journey into Portsmouth dockyard.*

below: *Once in the Ship Hall the hull was rotated so it sat upright. The eventual reward is a well-preserved Tudor warship for future generations to study. A system of water jets keeps the timbers wet, although the water will gradually be replaced by a wood preservative.*

LA TRINIDAD VALENCERA

1586

A Spanish Armada wreck on the Irish coast

above: *The wooden wheel and axle hub of a massive gun carriage bears testimony to the excellent state of organic preservation found on the wreck site. The carriage and attendant gun once formed part of a siege train, designed to support the Spanish army in its invasion of England.*

Location: Kinnagoe Bay
County Donegal
Northwest coast of Ireland –
Atlantic Ocean
55° 22' N, 7° 28' W

Depth: Shallow (0–30ft)

As we have seen, most of the vessels comprising the Spanish Armada were merchant ships converted for the campaign. One such ship was *La Trinidad Valencera*, a Venetian grain-carrier of 1,100 tons (998 tonnes) that was pressed into service in 1586. Organized as part of the Levant squadron, she was rearmed and used as a transport ship for 281 Spanish soldiers. Her new armament consisted of 42 guns of various sizes, from her cargo of siege guns to small swivel guns used for point-blank defense. Her commander was veteran soldier Don Alonso de Luzon.

During the Armada's battles along the English Channel, the *Valencera* played a key role, protecting the lesser-armed ships from English attacks. Although the damage she sustained was slight, it weakened her sufficiently to place her in danger in rough seas. As the Armada rounded the north of Scotland on its long homeward voyage, it was scattered by a storm. Alone and taking on water through her weakened hull, the *Valencera* had no option but to head for the north coast of Ireland and try to run aground. She was beached in Kinnagoe Bay, County Donegal.

Over the next two days, most of the soldiers and crew reached the safety of the shore, aided by local Catholics. On September 16, 1586, the ship broke apart, drowning a number of Spaniards and Irish salvors. English troops arrived and massacred many of the survivors and captured their officers, including Don Alonso. A number were eventually ransomed and returned home to tell of their ordeal.

In 1971, the wreck was discovered by local divers of the Derry Sub-Aqua Club, who found bronze guns, anchors, and gun-carriage wheels lying among the sand of Kinnagoe Bay. The club invited maritime archæologist Dr. Colin Martin to help them investigate the site, and between 1971 and 1984 an excavation was conducted. The objects recovered were conserved by the Ulster Museum in Belfast. Contemporary documents revealed the identity of the wreck, through weight markings on two siege guns that matched entries on the *Valencera*'s lading manifest.

A disposable grain-carrier

Although the wreck was scattered and buried across the bay, excavation revealed a wealth of material, including well-preserved organic remains.

A number of separated hull timbers were identified, and the lack of hull cohesion was explained by the lack of wooden fastenings holding the timbers together, similar to the construction of the Spanish galleon *Nuestra Señora de Atocha* (1622). Martin postulated that using only iron fastenings eased maintenance during an expected short but intensive working life. When they rusted away, the vessel was discarded.

After a preliminary survey it was decided to excavate areas of the wreck that showed signs of organic material. A controlled excavation over several years provided a wealth of material, thanks in part to the preserving qualities of the bay's sand. Artillery proved a major type of find—several guns were recovered, including siege guns, their carriages, and equipment. Ship's guns were also recovered, including parts of a Spanish sea carriage, breech-loading swivel guns, and gunnery tools. These provided a rare insight into the nature of Spanish gunnery during the Armada Campaign.

Artifacts belonging to the soldiers were also recovered, including firearms, edged weapons, armor, and clothing. Incendiary weapons, firepots, and staff-mounted "fireworks" were apparently carried to assist during boarding actions. Military stores included part of a tent, sapling stakes for field fortification, and entrenchment tools. These finds help us understand what made the Spanish army such a potent force in the 16th century.

The fine preservation of material allowed the recovery of a wide range of domestic items, including wooden lanterns, musical instruments, pottery, pewterware, and personal utensils. Ship fittings such as cordage, barrel stave, and rigging fittings were also scattered across the bay. The excavation produced an incomparable collection of late 16th-century Spanish artifacts, and will soon form the centerpiece of a new Spanish Armada museum in Londonderry, Northern Ireland.

above: *The sweep of Kinnagoe Bay on the northern coast of Donegal was the setting for the shipwreck of La Trinidad Valencera, and the subsequent massacre of survivors by English troops. The site is located to the right of the picture.*

THE VASA

1628

A proud warship lost on her maiden voyage

above: *The upper deck of the Vasa, viewed from the forecastle. The ship now forms the centerpiece of the specially constructed ship hall of the Vasa Museum in Stockholm. The incredible preservation of the hull allows students to examine an almost intact early 17th-century warship.*

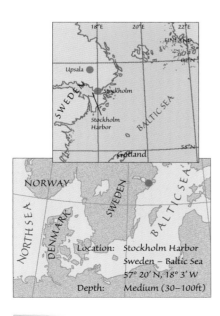

Location: Stockholm Harbor
Sweden – Baltic Sea
57° 20' N, 18° 3' W
Depth: Medium (30–100ft)

This early 17th-century Swedish warship, lost in Stockholm harbor in 1628, occupies a unique place in maritime history. She is the only largely intact sailing warship ever to be recovered from the seabed, a mute reminder of the majesty of these long-lost vessels.

Built in 1626, the *Vasa* was intended to be the pride of the Swedish Navy. At the time, Sweden was a rising European power, with extensive influence in the Baltic region. A powerful navy ensured that this influence would continue, and the 64-gun, 1,200-ton (1,089-tonne) *Vasa* was designed as the floating epitome of that power.

On the afternoon of Sunday, August 10, 1628, Vasa set sail on her maiden voyage across Stockholm harbor, with flags flying and bands playing. A sudden gust of wind caught her and, just like the *Mary Rose*, she heeled over to port and water poured in through the open gunports. The *Vasa* sank within minutes, "with standing sails, flags, and all." It was a devastating loss for Sweden, for not only did the navy lose their showpiece flagship and her 450-strong crew, but also her expensive armament of bronze guns—a loss the small country could ill afford. Attempts were made to salvage the vessel, and in the 1660s a Swedish diver recovered her guns. She then remained all but forgotten in the mud of the harbor.

In the 1950s researcher Anders Franzen discovered that the water in the Baltic Sea was too fresh to support the *Teredo navalis*, or ship's worm. Wooden ships that sank in Scandinavian waters might remain on the seabed in a good state of preservation. In 1956, Franzen searched for and found the remains of the *Vasa* in 100 feet (30m) of water.

A salvage company was consulted, who proposed digging six tunnels under the ship's hull, allowing steel cables to support the hull as she was lifted by salvage pontoons. Because of low visibility, divers had to work blind, blowing the tunnels with water jets through the mud of the seabed beneath the warship. In August 1959 the cables were in place and the *Vasa* was lifted and moved to shallow waters. There she was prepared for her final voyage.

A wealth of finds

Gunports and holes were plugged in the hull and damaged sections were boxed in. Because of her size the *Vasa* had to float into dry dock on her own, so she had to be completely watertight. In the spring of 1961, she was pumped full of air, and on April 24 rose to the surface and was towed into dry dock. Excavation began in 1961, under the supervision of archæologist Per Lundström. An astonishing 25,000 finds were recovered, from hull pieces to personal possessions and ship fittings, including sails. These included perfectly preserved wooden carvings that lay around the wreck site, and from inside the ship the bewildering array of finds included clothes, eating utensils, weapons, storage containers, and even fishing equipment and a backgammon set! It was as if a moment in time had been frozen for posterity.

A temporary museum for the *Vasa* was built in 1961 and opened to the public. Preservation of the remains was the first priority. The waterlogged wood was treated with polyethylene glycol for almost 17 years to stabilize it, while individual pieces were conserved in the museum's laboratory. The hull was rebuilt and new iron fasteners replaced those that had rusted away on the seabed.

Without accurate plans, restoration was a mammoth undertaking. In recent years, modern analysis has revealed new secrets. It appears that the decorative carving surrounding the ship was once elaborately painted and gilded, producing what must have been an imposing and grandiose appearance.

In June 1990 the new Vasa Museum was opened to provide a permanent home for the ship and the artifacts it contained. Designed to fit around the warship itself, the ship hall protects the hull, as well as making it accessible to visitors. The result is a unique opportunity to experience the age of sail at first hand.

below: The main gun deck of the Vasa still contains the four-wheeled truck carriages that carried her main armament on her maiden voyage in 1628. The bronze guns themselves were salvaged soon after the ship sank.

THE DUART POINT WRECK

1653

A lost warship of Cromwell's navy

As head of the newly formed English Commonwealth, Oliver Cromwell launched an invasion of Scotland in 1650. The catalyst was the refusal by the Scots to toe the line and withdraw their tentative support for exiled monarch Charles II. The war ultimately resulted in a Scottish defeat, followed by military occupation.

During this period, resistance continued sporadically, and punitive expeditions were dispatched to deal with them. In September 1653, a small naval force was sent to the west coast of Scotland on one such expedition. The aim was to crush the Macleans of Duart, a highland clan with royalist sympathies. The expedition consisted of six ships under the command of Colonel Ralph Cobbett, an experienced army officer serving in the Commonwealth Navy.

When Cobbett's force arrived off Mull, he found that Duart Castle, the seat of the clan, had been abandoned. While at anchor off Duart Point, a sudden storm scattered the squadron and three of his ships were lost: the *Martha and Margaret* of Ipswich, the *Speedwell* of Kings Lynn, and the *Swan*. The incident resulted in heavy loss of life. A Commonwealth officer reported that it occurred "in the sight of our Men at land, who saw their friends drowning, and heard them crying for helpe, but could not save them."

The *Swan* apparently wrecked close to Duart Castle. The small warship of around 160 tons (145 tonnes) was a pinnace, built in 1641 for the navy of Charles I. The Parliamentarian Navy captured her off Dublin in 1645 and pressed her into service against her former owner.

The wreck was found in 1979, but the diver kept his discovery secret. Worried about the preservation of his find, he reported it to the authorities in 1991. An investigation by the government-funded Archæological Diving Unit showed that serious environmental destabilization threatened the wreck. The site was designated as a

Location: Isle of Mull
West coast of Scotland – Sound of Mull
56° 28′ N, 5° 47′ W

Depth: Medium (30–100ft)

protected historic wreck, and Historic Scotland, the national organization who now controlled the site, issued a license allowing an archæological investigation.

Finds from the stern cabin

The recipient of the license was the Scottish Institute of Maritime Studies at St. Andrew's University, a research body headed by veteran underwater archæologist Dr. Colin Martin. Martin instituted a program of survey, excavation, and protection of the wreck, beginning in 1993 and still underway. This provided the identity of the ship and uncovered a fascinating range of artifacts. Between excavation and survey seasons, the site is covered by sandbags to prevent further erosion; research is being conducted to try to understand why the site is eroding.

Substantial linked pieces of lower hull structure have been found, pinned beneath two separate stone ballast piles, that should provide valuable information about hull construction. Toward the eastern (or seaward) side of the wreck site, an area containing highly decorated carved wooden paneling suggests that this was once the stern of the vessel, where the captain's cabin was located. It appears that, as the ship decayed, the stern structure collapsed in on itself.

Among the artifacts recovered from this stern cabin area were several well-preserved wooden carvings that once formed part of the ship's exterior decoration. Particularly exciting was the discovery of a piece containing a royal crest, the emblem of the Prince of Wales (later Charles II). On a republican ship this find was completely unexpected. Had the captain kept the Swan's former royalist decoration stowed away in his cabin, as security in the event of a restoration of the monarchy? It certainly provides historians with an enigma.

Other finds include the remains of weapons, including part of a pistol lock and the concreted remains of a sword hilt, plus everyday items such as pottery, pewterware, and a range of domestic wooden artifacts. X rayed concretion has revealed the apparently intact workings of a pocket watch, one of the earliest timepieces recovered from a wreck. All these finds are being conserved by the Royal Museum of Scotland, where the entire collection will eventually be housed, a poignant reminder of a troubled era in British history.

opposite: *A conservator is shown attaching a sacrificial zinc anode to one of the concreted cast-iron guns on the wreck site. This form of in situ conservation is being pioneered on the Scottish wreck.*

below: *The wreck site is marked by an interpretative plaque on the shore of Duart Point. Pictured here is Dr. Colin Martin, the project director and a pioneer of underwater archæology in British waters. Also present are Sir Lachlan and Lady Maclean of Duart and Dr. Robert Prescott, Director of the Scottish Institute of Maritime Studies.*

Spain's Treasure Fleets

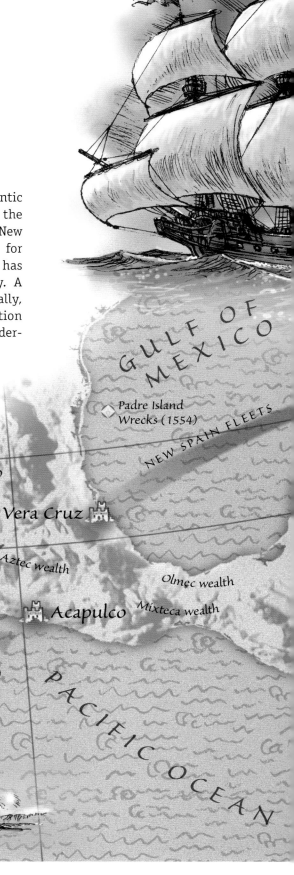

For over two centuries, Spanish galleons sailed the Atlantic Ocean, taking European goods and settlers from Spain to the Spanish Main, and returned laden with the treasures of the New World. These Spanish ships have been a major target for treasure-hunters, and one, the *Nuestra Señora de Atocha* has produced perhaps the largest shipwrecked treasure haul in history. A complex administrative system ensured that these fleets sailed annually, bringing the Spanish crown the wealth it needed to maintain its position as an early modern superpower. The story of this remarkable undertaking, and the galleons that sailed as part of these treasure fleets, holds a unique place in maritime history.

GULF OF MEXICO

Padre Island Wrecks (1554)

NEW SPAIN FLEETS

MEXICO

Vera Cruz

Aztec wealth

Olmec wealth

Acapulco   Mixteca wealth

MANILA GALLEON ROUTE
(from Manila with silk,
(to Manila with silver)

PACIFIC OCEAN

Below: The incalculable wealth of the central and southern Americas, combined with the financial needs of the Spanish king, led to the creation of a great fleet of Spanish treasure ships. Unsurprisingly, the wrecks of some have been among the most valuable salvage operations ever.

ATLANTIC OCEAN

HOMWARD-BOUND ROUTE OF COMBINED FLEETS via Azores

BERMUDA

San Pedro (1596)

FLORIDA

Marvillas Wreck

BAHAMAS

The 1715 Fleet

San Martin (1618)

Nuestra Señora de la Concepción (1641)

LEEWARD ISLANDS

The 1622 Fleet

The 1733 Fleet

Guadalupe & Tolosa (1724)

Tortugas Wreck

Havana

CUBA

HISPANIOLA

PUERTO RICO

WINDWARD ISLANDS

TIERRA FIRME FLEET FROM SEVILLE via Canary Is.

JAMAICA

CARIBBEAN SEA

HONDURAS FLEET

Trujillo

Cartagena

VENEZUELA

San José (1708)

Porto Bello

Panama

COLOMBIA

SOUTH SEAS FLEET

Inca wealth

Spain's Treasure Fleets

I n the 16th century the Spanish Empire covered large parts of Europe and the Americas (the New World). The Spanish king controlled everything from Madrid, aided by the noblemen he appointed as assistants. Lesser nobles often left for the Americas in search of a fortune in the New World. Spanish peasants stayed in Spain, or were conscripted into the army or navy.

The king needed silver from the New World to run his empire. Without the regular arrival of the treasure fleets (*flotas*), Spain would rapidly become bankrupt. Spain was almost always at war in Europe, either fighting the Dutch or fighting religious wars, and warfare cost money. English and Dutch ships raided the Spanish Main, so money was also needed to build armed vessels to protect these *flotas*. By the mid-16th century, it appeared that the Spanish crown was always eagerly awaiting the next fleet, as the king had already borrowed money from European bankers and needed the treasure to pay back his loan.

The headquarters of the Spanish *flota* system operation was in Seville, in the south of Spain. From its administrative building, the Casa de Contratación (or Council of the Indies) supervised every aspect of the ships, men, armament, and cargo involved in the huge operation. This was perhaps the first example of a major civil service department since Roman times, at least one run on such a grand scale and for so long—over two centuries.

below: *As the king's demands for silver to finance wars grew greater, the treasure fleets became more numerous. "Spanish ships approaching a jetty." Painting by Sebastian Castro.*

1520	1530	c.1540	1547	1554	1571	1577–80	1595
Ferdinand Magellan crosses the Pacific Ocean.	The Spanish treasure fleets begin their annual trading voyages.	The Spanish reach California.	Death of King Henry VIII, succeeded by Edward VI.	Date of the Padre Island wrecks, vessels of the New Spain fleet.	The Philippines are conquered by the Spanish.	Francis Drake sails around the world.	The East Indies are colonized by the Dutch.

No passenger was allowed to travel in the ships run by the Casa de Contratación or to carry any cargo without the approval of the council. In effect, they had a monopoly on all transatlantic travel within the Spanish Empire. The whole system of using fleets meant that the ships arrived and departed at set times, and cargoes were loaded under the watchful eyes of royal officials.

The treasure fleet operation

The Spanish monarch was entitled to one fifth of the value of all cargo carried in the fleets, including the gold and silver shipped from the New World to Spain. During the period from 1550 until 1700, huge quantities of treasure were shipped to Spain from the Americas, and only one fleet was lost to enemy attack (in 1628, when the Dutch captured the whole fleet off Cuba). Four major fleet disasters caused by storms upset the delicate operation in 1554, 1622, 1715, and 1733.

This fleet meant that the Spanish king could rely on a steady income from his colonies. Almost every year from 1530 to 1735, with rare exceptions, a fleet sailed from Spain to the Americas. There, it delivered Spanish goods, collected a cargo of treasure and local produce, then returned home to Spain.

When it reached the Caribbean, the annual Spanish convoy split into three units. The Tierra Firme fleet went to Porto Bello to collect silver from Peru, then sailed to Cartagena to pick up gold from Ecuador, emeralds from Columbia, and pearls from Venezuela. The New Spain fleet went to Vera Cruz, where it was loaded with gold and silver from Mexico, and silks, porcelain, and spices from China. The small Honduras fleet called at Trujillo to collect rare indigo dye. All three fleets then met in Havana, Cuba, and sailed home to Spain.

Two other fleets helped bring the goods to Porto Bello and Vera Cruz. The small South Seas fleet ferried Peruvian silver to Panama, where mules carried the silver to Porto Bello. The Manila fleet sailed from the Philippines with a Chinese cargo; once it reached Acapulco in Mexico the goods were transported overland to Vera Cruz. The whole system of Spanish treasure fleets was one of the most complicated and long-lasting maritime trading routes in history.

In its early years, the usual type of ship that formed part of these annual convoys was the carrack (in effect the vessels outlined on *pages 74–79*). Although the annual convoy was controlled by the Casa de Contratación, all but a few of the ships belonged to private Spanish merchants, who paid a tax to trade with the New World. They were protected by armed royal vessels, operated by the Casa on behalf of the King of Spain.

Filling the galleons

These ships became increasingly well armed, and by the mid-to-late 16th century a special type of vessel was developed to perform the role of

above: *Porto Bello was the Caribbean loading port for much of the silver mined in Peru. In 1739, the British fleet bombarded and captured the city, marking the end of the seemingly constant stream of silver flowing from the New World to Spain. "The Capture of Puerto Bello, 21 November 1739." Oil painting by Samuel Scott.*

above: *The intricate links of this exquisite gold chain once belonged to a passenger on a Spanish treasure galleon, which was lost in 1622. As the transport of personal jewelry was not taxed by the king, chains such as these were used as a form of tax avoidance.*

1600	1608	1618–48	1620	1622	1643	1646	1658
Rum is invented by the Spanish in Barbados.	The French found Quebec, Canada.	The Thirty Years' War.	The first ever public library is opened, in Virginia.	Date of the *Nuestra Señora de Atocha* wreck, a treasure fleet galleon.	The city of Santiago, Chile, is completely destroyed in an earthquake.	The Bahamas are colonized by the English.	The Bank of Sweden produces the first ever bank notes.

Spain's Treasure Fleets

above: *The mountain of Potosi in Peru was regarded as the richest silver mine in the world. In the foreground, Spanish engineers and Incan slaves use mercury to extract pure silver from the ore recovered from the mines sunk into the mountain.*

treasure fleet guardian. The galleon was a development of the carrack and the *nao*, but it combined the cargo capacity of a large merchantman with the armament of a powerful warship. The typical galleon was a vessel of around 500 tons (454 tonnes), although they could be as big as 1,200 tons (1,089 tonnes); the latter were mainly used as royal warships.

A particular feature was the height of the superstructure, with pronounced fore- and sterncastles. Their very size made these galleons unwieldy and slow to maneuver. While other nations such as the English also built galleons, theirs were substantially less burdened with superstructure and consequently easier to handle than their Spanish equivalent.

The major advantage of the galleon design was its solidity. It provided a stable platform for artillery, although, as we have seen, Spanish tactical doctrine lagged behind that of its European rivals, and artillery was deemed less important than soldiers capable of boarding an enemy. Galleons also boasted a large cargo capacity, and they were used to transport the government's share of the produce of the New World, mainly silver bullion, gold, and copper.

Galleons also embarked passengers. Being the most prestigious ships engaged in the Indies trade, berths were sold to individuals and their retinues. If you can imagine a ship sailing from Havana to Seville with an overall length of 125 feet (38m), filled with 200 soldiers and sailors, and up to 50 passengers and servants, you will understand the cramped conditions that were endured on these vessels. The ability to defend itself if attacked was seriously impaired by the overcrowded conditions and the decks filled with cargo. Despite these drawbacks, a combination of the convoy system and the royal galleons' imposing appearance usually deterred potential attackers.

End of a golden era

By the early 17th century the Spanish treasure fleet system was in decline, a victim of its own success. The *flota* system had flooded Europe with silver, and the value of the metal plummeted as sailing costs rose. Spain was gripped by crippling inflation, and the economic drain of her involvement in the 30 Years' War (1618–48) took its toll.

The size of the annual *flota* declined steadily, until by the end of the century a typical treasure fleet contained a dozen ships. By this time the galleon had been replaced by regular warships, typical of those used by all major maritime nations. Although the Spanish still called these ships *galeones*, they lacked the grandeur of their predecessors.

A series of economic and maritime disasters befell Spain during the early 18th century and sailings became less frequent. By 1740, the *flota* system was all but abandoned, and individual warships carried the valuable cargoes of the Spanish New World back to Spain. Foreign trade could not be avoided forever and in 1778 Spain officially abandoned the *flota* system, ending an enterprise unique in maritime history.

Although comparatively few flota ships have been discovered, and even less galleons, the system was so well documented that historians know much about its operation. The benefit of shipwreck evidence allows us to see behind the statistics and balances produced by the Casa de Contratación and learn how the ships operated. Few treasure fleet shipwrecks have been fully excavated, although archæological teams working for treasure hunters have provided useful information. These remains of treasure-laden Spanish galleons are perhaps the archetypal image most people have of a historic shipwreck.

While we now know a lot about the cargoes they carried, and archival evidence describes how they were administered, we still know comparatively little about the structure of a Spanish galleon. Perhaps one day archæologists will be allowed to fill this major gap in our maritime knowledge.

below: *The Spanish Main produced more than silver and gold. Native pearl divers are shown working in the pearl beds off the Venezuelan coast. A portion of the riches produced in these areas were loaded onto treasure galleons and sent to Spain to fill the royal coffers.*

1725	1739	1740	1747	1755	1756–1763	1768	1769
Danish sailor Vitus Bering discovers the straits separating Russia and the Americas.	Smuggler and highwayman Dick Turpin is executed.	Decline of the Spanish treasure fleet system; officially ended in 1778.	Afghanistan founded by Ahmad Khan Abdali.	Samuel Johnson publishes the first dictionary.	Prussia and Britain defeat France, Russia, Spain, and Austria in the Seven Years' War.	Captain James Cook explores the Pacific Ocean.	James Watt patents the steam engine.

THE PADRE ISLAND WRECKS

1554 Spain's first treasure fleet disaster

above: *An anchor recovered from the San Esteban, wrecked off Padre Island. During the 16th and 17th centuries, the quality of Spanish ironwork was notoriously poor, and many examples from wrecks have bent or broken stocks.*

Location: Off Padre Island, Texas
USA – Gulf of Mexico
26° 42' N, 97° 12' W
Depth: Shallow (0–30ft)

By the mid-16th century, the Spanish had established themselves as the only European power in the Caribbean, a monopoly that allowed them to freely exploit the resources of the New World. Regular treasure fleets sailed from Seville to the Caribbean basin, then split into smaller flotillas.

One of these was the New Spain fleet, which transported silver from Mexico to Spain, along with the porcelain, silks, and spices brought to Mexico from the Philippines. In April 1554, this fleet of four ships left Vera Cruz in Mexico, bound for Havana, the last stop before the voyage home to Spain. Only one ship, the *San Andres* limped into the Cuban harbor, battered and sinking. The other four vessels—*San Esteban, Espiritu Santo*, and *Santa Maria de Yciar*—were lost in a storm on Padre Island, off the coast of what would become the State of Texas.

Within two months the Spanish launched a salvage expedition that found the ships stranded on the island in less than 20 feet of water. The crews were rescued and almost half of the silver coins and bullion recovered before fresh storms and the approach of the hurricane season prevented further salvage work. By the following year, the hulks had been battered to pieces and lost, taking their remaining treasure with them.

Treasure hunters located the remains of the *Espiritu Santo* in 1967 and salvaged much of its remaining cargo of silver. Texas State archæologists heard about the find and tried to prevent the salvage, prompting a bitter lawsuit that dragged on for 18 years. This legal struggle, known as the Platoro Suit, led to the state gaining jurisdiction over the wreck sites and the recovered objects. The State had to compensate the salvors in full.

The process led to State legislation protecting future historic wreck finds in Texan waters. It also allowed State archæologists to examine wrecks, since the remains of the *San Esteban* were discovered in the intervening period. It appears that the wreck of the *Santa Maria y Yciar* was largely destroyed by dredging operations 20 years before the other craft were discovered.

Treasure beneath the silt

The *San Esteban* was comprehensively excavated between 1972 and 1976. Although few pieces of her hull remained, enough survived to give archæologists a fair idea of the vessel's size. The objects on the site were heavily concreted, with anchors, guns, coins, ship fittings, and other objects fused together in large lumps.

After using a magnetometer to map the site, the archæological team led by J. Barto Arnold III dealt with each concreted lump at a time, recording it, then raising it and preparing it for conservation. The excavation was conducted in poor visibility and, with much of the site covered with silt, the work was extremely arduous. The result of all this hard work was a priceless collection of objects, the most complete and undispersed assemblage ever recovered from a Spanish treasure fleet wreck.

The *San Esteban* was clearly well armed, carrying a powerful array of wrought-iron breech-loading guns (*bombardettas*) and close-range swivel guns (*versos*). It also carried soldiers, as crossbow fragments very similar to those recovered from the St. John's wreck (1564) were found, except environmental conditions meant that their wooden elements were better preserved on this earlier wreck.

The next major group of artifacts related to the cargo. Although only two gold "finger" bars were found, silver bullion and silver coins were recovered in significant numbers. Other remarkable finds included the personal possessions of the passengers and crew: crucifixes, gold jewelry, and valuable pre-Columbian objects, as well as everyday tableware. Ship fittings completed the assemblage, the most impressive being a collection of three navigator's astrolabes, perhaps the earliest known collection in the world.

Together with the objects salvaged from the *Espiritu Santo*, these excavated artifacts provide us with important evidence of Spain's involvement and exploitation of the New World in the 16th century. The collection is now on display in the Corpus Christi Museum in Texas.

above: Hull timbers from the San Esteban retain the marks showing where wooden treenails and iron fasteners were used to bind the hull together. This section of sternpost and lower keel also displays the erosion damage caused by marine life and exposure to the air.

above: During the early 16th century, the most common form of shipborne artillery was the wrought-iron breech-loading gun. Originally, it would have been mounted in a solid wooden bed, and a separate breech chamber would have housed the gun's propellant charge.

THE NUESTRA SEÑORA DE ATOCHA

1622 The world's richest treasure wreck

above: *Priceless artifacts salvaged from the wreck by Mel Fisher. A silver ingot and gold bars are augmented by a conglomerate of silver coins, tableware, gold chains, and a navigator's astrolabe.*

Location: Off the Marquesas Keys
Near Key West, Florida
USA – Gulf of Mexico
24° 40′ N, 82° 6′ W
Depth: Shallow (0–30ft)

A Spanish treasure fleet of 28 ships left Havana in Cuba on September 1622 for its annual voyage from the New World to Spain. It carried the wealth of an empire: gold and emeralds from Colombia, silver from Peru, spices from the Orient, and pearls from Ecuador. While many ships carried passengers and general cargoes, the most wealthy passengers and all of the treasure were concentrated in two ships, the royal galleons *Nuestra Señora de Atocha* and *Santa Margarita*. Both were well-armed vessels of 500 tons (454 tonnes), carrying 20 bronze guns and a crew of around 150 sailors and marines. Each ship carried about two dozen passengers, returning home with their wealth after finding their fortunes in the New World.

During the night the wind grew stronger, and by next morning the fleet was being battered by a hurricane. The ships tried to escape into the relatively safe open waters of the Gulf of Mexico, but eight of them failed to make it past the reefs of the Florida Keys. These included the two treasure-laden galleons.

The *Atocha* struck a reef, which ripped out her bottom. She sank like a stone. The *Margarita* was carried over the reef, only to be battered on a sandbank, two miles beyond. By morning, rescue boats found a handful of survivors from the *Margarita*, but only five survived the sinking of the *Atocha*. After a flurry of salvage work on the *Margarita*, the sands closed over the wreck, while the site of the *Atocha* was never found. The wrecks would remain undisturbed for another 350 years.

Motherlode at the second site

During the 1960s, treasure hunter Mel Fisher successfully salvaged the remains of the Spanish treasure fleet of 1715, lost off Florida's east coast. In 1968 he turned his attention to the *Nuestra Señora de Atocha*. Accounts of the sinking led him to search off the middle of the Florida Keys, but research by Spanish colonial historian Dr. Eugene Lyon prompted Fisher to move his treasure-hunting operation south to Key West. Concentrating on an area near the Marquesas Keys, 40 miles west of Key West, Fisher and his team searched hundreds of square miles of seabed throughout the 1970s, occasionally finding scattered objects from the lost galleons that encouraged them to keep searching.

A group of bronze cannons was found, and within the year, objects were recovered that could be matched to the galleons' cargo manifests, confirming that they were searching in the correct area. The hull of the *Santa Margarita* was found in 1980, but as it had been extensively salvaged soon after it sank, the team kept on looking. In the early 1980s divers picked up a trail of debris: cannons, ship fittings, and coins. They followed the trail, assisted by a team led by archæologist Duncan Matthewson III. Finally, on July 20, 1985, two divers came across a reef standing above the seabed. Instead of rocks, the reef was made of silver bars— Mel Fisher had found the *Atocha*!

The salvors christened the reef the "motherlode"—their haul amounted to 46 tons (41.7 tonnes) of silver, 40,000 coins, hundreds of emeralds and gold bars, plus the priceless possessions of the galleon's passengers. Valued at over $400 million, the *Nuestra Señora de Atocha* is the most financially valuable shipwreck ever found.

Finding the wreck wasn't the end of Fisher's troubles, since he had to fight numerous legal battles before he was allowed to keep his finds. Although much of the treasure was divided between Fisher and his investors, a large portion was donated to a local Maritime Historical Society in Key West, which allowed it to found the Mel Fisher Maritime Museum, an institution named after its largest benefactor. Although it is highly regrettable that the priceless collection was dispersed, enough remains in the museum to enable visitors to experience at first hand the treasures of Spain's New World Empire.

above: Emerald cross, found in a small silver box alongside a matching ring and gold chain.

below: Part of the haul of silver ingots found on the "motherlode" site of the galleon in 1985.

THE 1715 FLEET

1715 Spain's largest maritime disaster

above: Part of the valuable artifacts salvaged from the Spanish wrecks, where treasure hunters found "a carpet of gold coins on the seabed." Unlike on the 1622 wrecks, by 1715, silver was shipped in round cakes cut into wedge-shaped pieces.

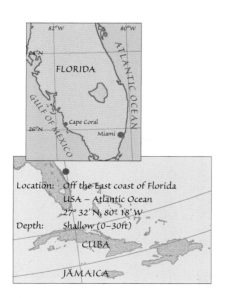

Location: Off the East coast of Florida USA – Atlantic Ocean 27° 32' N, 80° 18' W

Depth: Shallow (0–30ft)

A treasure fleet of 12 ships left Havana in Cuba in late July 1715, bound for Seville, Spain. It formed the combined New Spain and Tierra Firme fleets, a convoy arrangement that was repeated annually. The convoy carried an estimated ten million pesos of treasure and contraband, mostly in the form of silver bullion and coins. As it sailed northward in the confined waters between Florida's east coast and the Bahamas on July 31, six days out from Cuba, the fleet was struck by a hurricane. Despite the best efforts of the fleet commanders, all but one of the ships were wrecked along a 50-mile stretch of Florida's coast, from Sebastian Inlet to Fort Pierce.

Over a thousand Spanish sailors were drowned, almost half of the original complement of the fleet. The only ship to escape was an accompanying French ship, the *Grifon*. Over the next year, the Spanish rescued the survivors and salvaged a good portion of the treasure, despite an attack by pirates on the salvors' camp. As the sands rapidly covered the wrecks, extensive salvage became impossible, and the lost fleet was abandoned.

In 1948, beachcomber Kip Wagner found Spanish coins on the beach near Sebastian. By 1959 he had extended his search from the beach to the sea, and the Real Eight Corporation was formed, an alliance of amateur treasure hunters. The first wreck they found was dubbed "The Cabin Wreck," because of its proximity to Wagner's beach hut. Over the next few years divers recovered substantial quantities of silver coins and wedge-shaped silver ingot segments.

By 1963 the already renowned treasure hunter Mel Fisher and his team of divers from California joined forces with Wagner. Also by this time, the State of Florida was concerned about the amount of treasure recovered from its shores, and it appointed a State archæologist to supervise the salvors' activities. The State issued salvage permits and received 25 percent of anything recovered in its waters. The authorities' share was given to the Florida State Museum Service.

A carpet of gold

The arrival of Fisher galvanized the treasure hunters, and by the end of the year seven of the wrecks had been located and Fisher's winter find of "a carpet of gold coins lying on the seabed" caught the public's imagination. Valued at around $5 million dollars, it was the largest treasure find in American history. It also prompted a rush of would-be treasure hunters and prompted the State to reevaluate its position.

This and other lucrative finds from wrecks with nicknames such as "The Gold Wreck" and "The Wedge Wreck" (after the silver wedges found there) continued to be worked on under State supervision throughout the 1960s and 1970s, but by 1969 the "gold rush" was over. Mel Fisher moved his team south to Key West to look for the *Nuestra Señora de Atocha* and Wagner's group became paralyzed through bitter internal divisions and legal wrangling.

Although salvage companies still operate under State supervision in the area, no more massive treasure finds were made. The presence of State archaeologists ensured that some degree of archaeological recording was maintained and, after careful study, the identity of many of the wrecks was ascertained.

Despite lacking the thoroughness of a professional study, the information that was gathered shed some light on what happened during the terrible maritime disaster. Many of the objects recovered were subsequently sold by the salvors, but they did retain a small portion for display in private museums in Sebastian and Cape Canaveral. The State distributed its share of objects from the 1715 fleet to local museums, as well as retaining a substantial study collection for use by the Florida Museum of History in Tallahassee, the State capital. In 1989, the "Wedge Wreck," believed to be the remains of the *Urca de Lima*, became Florida's first underwater archaeological preserve. The site is open to all divers and the remains are interpreted for them, which creates a unique form of underwater museum.

above: The waters of the Florida Keys and the Bahamas continued to be inaccurately charted until the late 18th century, despite the heavy amount of Spanish maritime traffic. In all, three large Spanish treasure fleet disasters took place in Florida waters.

below: The 1715 fleet wrecked along the desolate eastern coast of Florida, between what are now Sebastian and Fort Pierce. Treasure hunters combing these beaches still recover gold and silver coins washed up on the shore, while salvors still dive for treasure on the remains of the wrecks themselves.

THE GUADALUPE AND TOLOSA

1724 The quicksilver galleons

Quicksilver played a vital part in maintaining Spain's New World Empire. By 1724 Spain had come to rely on a steady stream of silver being excavated from its mines in Peru and Mexico in order to stave off her decline as a world power. Any break in the flow of bullion arriving in the Spanish royal coffers could lead to the bankruptcy of the royal court and the country.

Quicksilver, or mercury as it is known today, was used in the refining of silver ore. Without it, there would be no silver. In 1724, the Spanish ships *Nuestra Señora de Guadalupe* and the *Conde de Tolosa* sailed from Cadiz, bound for Havana in Cuba, and then on to Vera Cruz. Once it arrived in Mexico, the vessels' cargo of 250 tons (226.8 tonnes) of quicksilver would be used in the Mexican silver mines.

After calling for stores and water at Aguadilla in Puerto Rico, the ships reached the northeastern corner of Hispaniola (now the Dominican Republic) when they were struck by a hurricane. They tried to ride out the storm at anchor in Samaná Bay. The anchors failed to hold, and by dawn on August 24, the *Tolosa* was relentlessly dragged onto a reef and wrecked. Less than 40 of the crew managed to survive, seven of whom spent over a month stranded on a mast in shark-infested waters, gathering rainwater and passing store barrels to stay alive.

The *Guadalupe* was slightly more fortunate, running aground on a sandbar that allowed over 500 of her 650-strong crew to reach the relative safety of the shore. The survivors faced a grueling 200-mile trek through the jungle to Santo Domingo, where they told the authorities of their ordeal. Rescue boats were sent to the site and found the masthead survivors of the *Tolosa* and recovered a tiny portion of the *Guadalupe*'s cargo of quicksilver and cannons. The main hull of the *Tolosa* had slid into waters too deep to allow salvage, and the wrecks

above: *A diver demonstrates that mercury is heavier than water by pouring some on the wrecksite. Mercury—used in the extraction of silver from silver ore—was vital to the Spanish economy.*

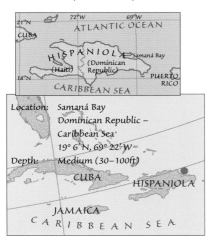

Location: Samaná Bay
Dominican Republic –
Caribbean Sea
19° 6' N, 69° 22' W
Depth: Medium (30–100ft)

were abandoned. The disaster, which had a serious effect on silver production, helped to speed the demise of the Spanish Empire.

Shattered against a reef

In 1976, the Dominican government granted salvage company Caribe Salvage SA a license to excavate the sites. The *Guadalupe* was quickly located and salvaged, although the divers found little mercury. They concluded that either a lot of the cargo had been salvaged by the Spaniards, or else the mercury was stored in the bottom of the hull, where concretion, coral growth, and substantial ship timbers prevented the divers from reaching it.

After a year of largely fruitless excavation, the salvors decided to look for the *Tolosa*. They found her less than eight miles away by using a magnetometer search in the area of the reef described by the original rescue party. There, the pickings were more lucrative. Within weeks the divers had found mercury, pearls, gold jewelry, and, just as important, the well-preserved remains of an early 18th-century Spanish warship.

Over the next year, while Caribe Salvage brought up a steady stream of artifacts under the watchful eyes of Dominican officials, they also recorded what they could find of the ship itself. This enabled them to work out how she was constructed and what happened when she struck the reef. She was a massive vessel, but the force of the hurricane had gashed large holes in the hull, dislodging guns, stores, and masts in what must have been a cataclysmic scene as the ship broke apart on the reef.

Despite the devastation created by the wrecking, the salvors still recovered intact glassware, ceramics, and pewter that formed a fascinating material record of life on a Spanish warship in the early 18th century. The objects were split between the salvors and the Dominican Republic; many of the thousands have been conserved, and are now on display in the Casas Reales Museum in Santo Domingo.

above: *Despite the often cataclysmic destructive processes of a shipwreck, often very delicate objects still managed to survive. This tableware and delicate glassware was recovered from the 1724 wrecks.*

MEL FISHER (1922–99)
Treasure Hunter

Regarded as the world's greatest treasure hunter, Mel Fisher combined personal charm with a tenacity that led him to discover the richest shipwreck ever. His achievements caught the public's imagination and his recent passing marked the end of an era for treasure hunting.

Mel Fisher is perhaps the world's most famous treasure hunter, seen as a hero by some and a looter by others. Throughout his life he was a larger-than-life character who conducted his quest for sunken treasure with a dedication that bordered on obsession, driving his team on despite setbacks. Fisher used the phrase "Today's the day!" as a mantra to maintain his crew's morale during a 16-year search for the Spanish treasure galleon *Nuestra Señora de Atocha*. It came true on July 20, 1985, when he finally found its remains. The dream that had consumed Mel Fisher for over a decade became reality, amid a furor of international publicity.

above: *Treasure hunter Mel Fisher (right) is shown displaying finds from the 1622 treasure wrecks during the early 1980s, along with his sons Kane Fisher (left) and Kim Fisher. In the background is a "mailbox," an excavation tool used on Fisher's salvage boats.*

Mel Fisher was born in Indiana and, after serving in the US Army during the Second World War, moved to California where he opened the State's first diving store. The business prospered and a new shop was opened at nearby Redondo Beach, the first fully-fledged diving center in America. While his wife Deo sold equipment, Mel taught diving and made underwater movies, later broadcast on American television. Fisher organized treasure-hunting expeditions in the Caribbean; although unsuccessful, they allowed him to gather an experienced salvage team.

In 1963, Fisher met Florida treasure hunter Kip Wagner, who invited him to join the hunt for the wrecks of the Spanish treasure fleet of 1715. The next year the salvors found over a thousand gold coins, one of the largest treasure finds of the decade. The partnership recovered over $20 million from the treasure fleet wrecks during the 1960s, but Fisher was growing restless.

By 1969, Fisher had moved to Key West, where he began searching for the *Atocha*. The search would take another 16 years, cost him the lives of his son and daughter-in-law as well as divers, and soak up millions of dollars in legal fees. A trickle of artifacts spurred on the divers, but at times they were almost forced to give up for lack of money.

Treasure hunter/archæologist associates

By 1975 finds of cannons and silver bars indicated that they were looking in the right area, and in a series of legal battles with both the State of

above: *One of the objects recovered from the Nuestra Señora de Atocha was this rare Cinta belt.*

Florida and the Federal Government, Fisher gained the right to keep everything he found. The remains of the *Atocha*'s sister galleon, the *Santa Margarita*, were found in 1980. As well as treasure, hull timbers were discovered, and Mel Fisher hired archæologist Duncan Matthewson III to record them. Archæologists remained with the salvors, working in tandem until 1990.

It is to Fisher's credit that he realized the historical importance of his finds, although it must be stressed that the archæological work was always secondary to treasure salvage. Matthewson and his team did what they could to record what they were allowed, an ethical dilemma that has been discussed earlier in this book.

Then in 1985, after following a trail of finds, the salvage team found the main hull of the *Atocha*—the "motherlode." Valued at $400 million dollars, it is still regarded as the richest find of sunken treasure in history. Although most of the material was dispersed among buyers and investors, a representative sample was kept in Key West, forming a collection in a local maritime museum.

The decade following his find, Fisher fought several more legal battles, and served as a rallying point for the treasure-hunting community against what they saw as the encroachment of legislation designed to put them out of business. Mel Fisher never truly sought wealth through his treasure-hunting; his driving force was the quest itself. Although seen as a mortal enemy by the underwater archæological community, his charisma and enthusiasm made him difficult to dislike as an individual.

Mel Fisher was perhaps the last real treasure hunter, in a climate in which legislation and costs prohibit many from following in his footsteps. His death marked the end of an era. The new generation are large, often anonymous commercial salvage companies, where the motive is profit rather than the fulfillment of a quest.

right: *An elated diver breaks the surface clutching a gold "finger" bar from the site of the Santa Margarita. Together, the two wrecks produced treasure valued at over $400 million.*

ARABIAN SEA

BAY OF BENGAL

below: Improved ship design and sailing skills during the 16th and 17th centuries opened up the lucrative silk and spice routes to the Far East and led to the beginning of the great European trading monopolies.

Ko Chang (16th century)

Vung tau (17th century)

Ravenstein (1725)

Ran Mathu
(late 17th century)

Don Duarte de Guerra (1607)
Admiral Stellingwerf Reef (1643)

Risdam (1726)

Geldermalsen (1752)

INDIAN OCEAN

Trial (1622)

Zuydorp (1712)

Batavia (1629)

Zeewyk
(1727)

Vergulde Draek (1656)

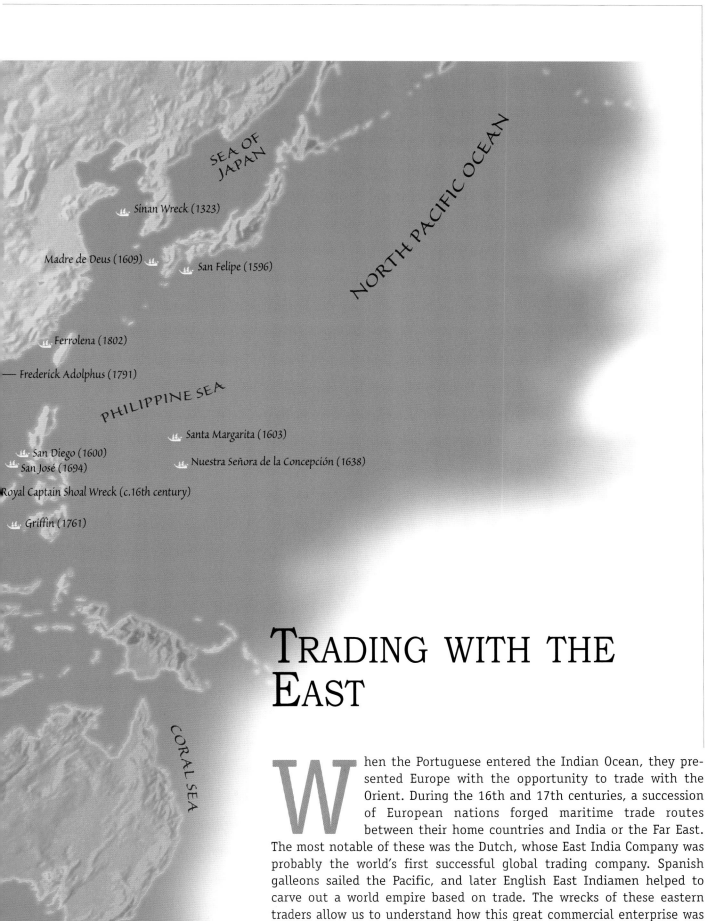

SEA OF JAPAN

NORTH PACIFIC OCEAN

Sinan Wreck (1323)

Madre de Deus (1609)

San Felipe (1596)

Ferrolena (1802)

— Frederick Adolphus (1791)

PHILIPPINE SEA

Santa Margarita (1603)

San Diego (1600)

San José (1694)

Nuestra Señora de la Concepción (1638)

Royal Captain Shoal Wreck (c.16th century)

Griffin (1761)

CORAL SEA

TRADING WITH THE EAST

When the Portuguese entered the Indian Ocean, they presented Europe with the opportunity to trade with the Orient. During the 16th and 17th centuries, a succession of European nations forged maritime trade routes between their home countries and India or the Far East. The most notable of these was the Dutch, whose East India Company was probably the world's first successful global trading company. Spanish galleons sailed the Pacific, and later English East Indiamen helped to carve out a world empire based on trade. The wrecks of these eastern traders allow us to understand how this great commercial enterprise was established.

Trading with the East

When Marco Polo returned to Venice from the Far East in 1295, his tales captivated a continent. The publishing of his memoirs triggered two centuries of obsession, with Europeans dreaming of gaining access to the fabled markets of the Orient. Arab traders in the eastern Mediterranean reinforced Polo's claims by telling European merchants about the wealth of India, and of even greater riches to be had in the Far East.

Developments in European shipbuilding techniques and navigational skills launched the period known as the "Age of Exploration" in the late 15th century. The greatest goal was to find a sea route to the East. Coincidentally, the start of this European bid to explore sea routes came at the same time as the Chinese ceased trading overseas. While Chinese traders had ventured as far west as the Indian Ocean, a more introverted policy was introduced around 1500. The Chinese emperor prohibited overseas trade and the building of ocean-going vessels in a policy known as the Ming Ban. It also created a vacuum in the trading economies of states bordering the Indian Ocean.

In 1498 Portuguese explorer Vasco da Gama reached Calicut in India, after rounding the Cape of Good Hope and sailing across the Indian Ocean. After a hesitant start, Portuguese merchants established a viable maritime trade route between India and Europe, filling the vacuum created by the withdrawal of Chinese traders. The main cargo was spice—although Arab merchant caravans had been bringing spice to Europe for centuries, the Portuguese were able to ship the valuable condiments in bulk and undercut the Arab trade.

above: *The new markets of India and Asia were developed by European traders from the 16th century, and a string of trading ports was established, principally in India, the Philippines, and Indonesia. "Ships trading in the East." Oil painting by Hendrik Cornelisz Vroom.*

Breaking the monopoly

The Treaty of Tordesillas in June 1494 had already divided the known world into Spanish and Portuguese spheres of influence. While the Spanish were allowed to trade to the west (i.e. to the Americas), Portugal retained exclusive control of trade round Africa and into the Indian Ocean. By the mid-16th century, the Portuguese had expanded their trade routes to incorporate commerce with Hormuz in Persia, and even Nagasaki in Japan. The Portuguese monopoly of Indian Ocean

1295	1368	1397	1405	1453	1498	1545	1564–1642
Marco Polo returns from the Far East.	Beginning of China's Ming dynasty.	Norway, Denmark, and Sweden united under the Kalmar Agreement.	The Chinese voyage around the Indian Ocean.	The Byzantine Empire ends as Ottoman Turks take over Constantinople.	Vasco de Gama becomes first person to make a return voyage from Europe to India.	The *Mary Rose* sinks shortly after leaving the dock.	Ivan the Terrible reigns in Russia.

trade would continue until 1581, when Philip II of Spain annexed Portugal, part of his grand strategy of maritime conquest, aimed at the defeat of England and Holland.

Following the defeat of the Spanish Armada in 1588, English and Dutch merchants reevaluated their position. Until the annexation of Portugal, their ships had acted almost like local distributors, buying Portuguese spices and transporting them throughout Europe for a suitable profit. Given the serious blow to Spanish, and therefore Portuguese, sea power, what was to prevent them breaking the Portuguese monopoly and establishing their own trading links with India and the Far East?

Within a decade, these merchants had formed trading companies and were sending ships into the Indian Ocean as rivals to the Portuguese. The Dutch were the first, establishing the Vereenigde Oostindische Compagnie (VOC), or the Dutch East India Company, based in Amsterdam but with offices and docks in most major Dutch ports. In London, the Honourable East India Company (HEIC), created in the early 17th century, fulfilled a similar role.

Each organization was granted a monopoly of trade between their home country and the East, and their financial strengths rapidly made them a dangerous rival to Portugal and Spain. They used specially built ships, designed to carry as much cargo as possible, as quickly as possible, for the smallest outlay of money. The two companies were businesses, some of the first global companies in the world. Their aim was not to conquer territory, but to reap profit.

When Portuguese ships sailed to India they passed the Canary and Cape Verde islands before turning east, then south, following the coast of West Africa. Before they reached St. Helena they curved back into the Atlantic to take advantage of trade winds before running southeast toward the Cape. From there they sailed up the East African coast as far as Mozambique before crossing the Indian Ocean directly toward India.

The rise and fall of British trade

To protect this route the Portuguese built a series of coastal forts, effectively denying the course to their European rivals. The Dutch answer was to avoid the forts and pioneer a new route. From 1613, the preferred VOC voyage sailed into the South Atlantic, avoiding the

below: *The early development of eastern markets was spearheaded by the Portuguese, and Lisbon became one of the busiest and most prosperous ports in Europe. "Portuguese Carracks off a rocky coast." Oil painting in the style of Joachim Patinir.*

1581	1588	1595	1602	1603	1606	1618	1619
Philip II of Spain annexes Portugal.	The English defeat the Spanish Armada.	The East Indies are colonized by the Dutch.	The Dutch East India Company is formed.	Elizabeth I, the last Tudor monarch, dies, replaced by James I.	The Dutch discover Australia.	Beginning of the Thirty Years' War.	Batavia (Jakarta), capital of Indonesia, is founded by the Dutch.

Trading with the East

African coast. Once past the Cape, the ships sailed in a large eastward hook, almost reaching the coast of Australia before heading north toward Indonesia. The voyage took around six months, one way.

The Dutch established a trading base at Batavia on the Indonesian island of Java, enabling them to extend their trading reach into the China Sea. By the late 17th century, the Dutch had extended their reach as far as Japan, while local Dutch traders ranged across the Indian Ocean into the Persian Gulf and the Red Sea.

The English rivals to the Dutch company got off to a bad start through financial mismanagement, and by the mid-17th century the Dutch dominated trade with the East. The HEIC was resurrected in 1690, and its new directors chose to establish their own trading bases in India. During the early 18th century they meddled in Indian politics in an attempt to control internal markets. The Portuguese had all but withdrawn from the field, and by 1700 Portuguese trade was completely overshadowed by the English, who had established trading links from Bombay on India's west coast to Madras and Calcutta on the eastern coast.

below: By the early 18th century, trade between India and Europe was dominated by the British, and the Honou<None>rable East India Company exerted a virtual monopoly. "Fort St George, Madras, c.1731, viewed from the sea."

1626	1629	1638	1641	1646	1652	1654–56	1664
New Amsterdam founded by Dutch (later becomes New York).	Date of the *Batavia* wreck, a Dutch East Indiaman vessel.	Date of the *Concepción* wreck, a Spanish treasure vessel.	The Portugese lose Malacca, Malaysia, to the Dutch.	The Bahamas are colonized by the English.	Cape Town, South Africa, founded by the Dutch.	England and the Netherlands fight the First Dutch War.	Date of the *Kennemerland* wreck, a Dutch East Indiaman vessel.

Throughout the 18th century, the HEIC reinforced its control over the Indian sub-continent, fighting off French attempts at carving out part of the eastern trade. Other European countries that attempted to form trading companies and outposts included Sweden and Denmark. These attempts were short-lived, and the Britain remained the dominant trading nation in the East well into the 19th century.

In part, HEIC's success was due to the Royal Navy. It strangled Dutch trade, and that led directly to the VOC's bankruptcy in 1798. By the late 18th century, the British exerted an almost worldwide control of sea power, a state they maintained until the mid-20th century. Their loss of global naval superiority and the end of the British Empire are far from unrelated.

Victims of a long, treacherous journey

In the mid-16th century the Spanish had explored eastward from Mexico, seeking their own route to the East. In 1571 they established a trading base at Manila, in the Philippines. Unlike their European rivals, the Spanish had abundant stocks of silver, which was a marketable commodity in the Orient. The Manila galleon route shipped silver from Mexico to Manila, where it was exchanged for spices, silks, and porcelain. Unlike the other European nations, the Spanish built many of their ships in the Far East, using local timbers such as teak. After the return journey, the cargo was transported across Mexico to Vera Cruz, where the treasure fleets collected it and sailed for Spain. The collapse of the treasure fleet system early in the 18th century led to the rapid decline of the Manila trade, further hindered by the expansion of Dutch and British trading links in the region.

Given the hundreds of ships that sailed the long journey from Europe to the Orient and back, it's hardly surprising that large numbers of vessels were shipwrecked. Dutch records show that the VOC lost over a hundred ships during the early 17th century, and other trading companies reported similar losses. Three of the four wrecks described in this chapter are Dutch; this is a reflection less on their dominance of the trade than it is that the vessels show an interesting progression of VOC ship development and so allow for interesting comparisons.

The majority of known East India trade wrecks are naturally found in areas prone to storms or that present navigational problems, such as uncharted reefs and congested straits. These areas include the English Channel, the coast of South Africa, the west coast of Australia, the waters of Indonesia and the Philippines, and the mid-Pacific islands of the Marianas. In a handful of cases, these unfortunate mariners left behind a valuable legacy. The information we can gather from their shipwrecks allows us to gain a better understanding of this first great explosion in worldwide trade.

1667	1690	1707	1749	1756	1761	1778	1798
England and the Netherlands retreat at the end of their Four Days' War.	Calcutta is founded by the British.	India's Emperor Aurangzeb dies and the Mogul Empire dissolves.	Date of the *Amsterdam* wreck, a Dutch East Indiaman vessel.	Britain and France begin fighting the Seven Years' War.	The British take France's powerbase in Pondicherry territory, India.	Captain James Cook discovers Hawaii and passes through the Bering Strait.	The Dutch East India Company goes bankrupt.

THE DUTCH EAST INDIAMAN BATAVIA

1629 Mutiny and murder off the Australian coast

above: *Archæologists excavate the lower hull structure of the Dutch vessel Batavia. After 350 years, the solidity of her timbers is in striking contrast to the flimsier construction found in smaller trading vessel shipwrecks of the late 1500s.*

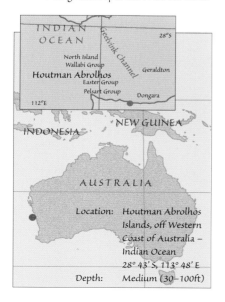

Location: Houtman Abrolhos Islands, off Western Coast of Australia – Indian Ocean
28° 43' S, 113° 48' E
Depth: Medium (30–100ft)

Contrary to popular belief, Captain James Cook was a relative late-comer to Australian waters. The Dutch first discovered the continent in 1606, and their ships regularly sailed along its coast *en route* for the Dutch settlements in Indonesia. Vessels of the Dutch East India Company (VOC) made regular trips between Holland and the Far East, supplying the growing European demand for Asian spices.

By the early 17th century, the Dutch had outstripped the Portuguese as the main importers of spice to Europe. Their favored route was down the African coast to the Cape of Good Hope, due east across the Indian Ocean, then north into Indonesian waters and Batavia, the Dutch capital in the region. On the morning of June 4, 1629, an outward-bound VOC ship called the *Batavia* was following this route when she ran aground on Houtman Abrolhos, a barren pair of islands off the Western Australian coast. Without adequate supplies of water, the survivors would die if they didn't find help quickly.

The ship's captain, Commander Francisco Pelsaert, set out in a launch to reach the nearest Dutch settlement at Batavia (now Jakarta). He was accompanied by his senior officers, many of the passengers, and a handful of sailors, making a total of 48 in the rescue party. This left 268 survivors on the two islands, who had to fend for themselves until help arrived. It took a month to reach the settlement, and a further two for Pelsaert to return with a rescue party. The rescuers found evidence of a grizzly tragedy. In the captain's absence, a group of crewmen had mutinied, killing 125 castaways, including women and children. The mutineers were rounded up, arrested, and taken back to Batavia to face trial and execution. Of the original 316 passengers and crew, only just over a hundred lived to tell the tale of their ordeal.

The wreck was rediscovered in 1963 by a local fisherman and, after a brief salvage attempt, the State Government of Western Australia passed legislation that protected the site. Between 1972 and 1976 the

Department of Maritime Archæology in Western Australia excavated the remains of the *Batavia*, directed by Jeremy Green, a veteran maritime archæologist. The hull fragments and objects recovered from the site are now on display in the Maritime Museum in Fremantle.

A lucrative brick ballast

One of the main finds was a large section of the stern hull structure. This was conserved and reconstructed in the Maritime Museum, and now provides a useful insight into 17th-century shipbuilding techniques. It also shows the Dutch used a strange form of construction, where a shell-first form using a double layer of planking provided the main structure, building up from the keel. Only then was this structure augmented by the addition of conventional ribs and frames for extra support. This runs contrary to the frame-first construction used throughout northern Europe, and remains to be fully explained.

The array of artifacts recovered was equally exciting. The *Batavia* carried a cargo of bricks, trade items, and the luxury goods demanded by the settlers of the Dutch East Indies: silverware, Dutch ceramics, and provisions. A spectacular cargo find was a prefabricated stone portico, the individual blocks designed to fit together perfectly. It was intended to grace the water-port of the Dutch fortress in Batavia. This structure and the numerous building bricks carried by the *Batavia* seem to have replaced the normal ship's ballast; the "paying ballast" would have significantly increased the VOC craft's profits from the voyage, had it reached port.

Enough information was gathered from the shipwreck and archival research to attempt the construction of a full-scale replica. The keel was laid in the Dutch port of Lelystad and fully fitted out. She's now open to the public as a floating museum in Amsterdam harbor. The Dutch shipwrights worked closely with the Australian archæologists; together they have greatly increased our knowledge of early 17th century shipbuilding.

THE NUESTRA SEÑORA DE CONCEPCIÓN

1638

The priceless wreck of a Manila galleon

Location: Off Saipan, Marianas
Islands – Pacific Ocean
17° 2′ N, 145° 0′ E
Depth: Medium (30–100ft)

below: *Fine emeralds and gold chains were recovered in vast quantities from the wreck; a testament to the immense wealth Spain accumulated from her colonies.*

The *Nuestra Señora de Concepción* was an enormous galleon, with a deck length of 150 feet and draft of 1,500 tons (1,361 tonnes). This made her almost three times the size of the *Nuestra Señora de Atocha*, the treasure galleon that sank off the Florida Keys 16 years earlier.

The *Concepción* had one purpose: to safely transport the goods of the Orient from Manila in the Philippines to Acapulco in Mexico on behalf of the Spanish Crown. This was one of the richest shipping routes in history, where every year, silver was transported from the Spanish New World to the Far East, then exchanged for porcelain, gold, silks, spices, and jewels. Established in 1571, the port of Manila was the central Spanish trading center in the East, and its wealth far exceeded that of the rival Dutch, Portuguese, and English trading outposts.

Every year, large Manila galleons such as the *Concepción* would sail the 9,000-mile voyage from Mexico during the spring, taking advantage of the predominantly easterly winds. The return voyage in the late summer could take up to six months, and with the constant threat of typhoons, timing was crucial. They headed on a northeasterly course, almost reaching the latitude of what is now San Francisco, before heading east-southeast toward the Californian coast. After taking on fresh water, the galleons would sail down the coast to Acapulco.

In 1638, the *Concepción* ran into a fierce storm or typhoon when she reached the Marianas Islands, in mid-Pacific. The aristocratic captain and the experienced senior seaman officer disagreed over whether to shelter or run with the storm into the open sea. The poor compromise led to the ship being caught, dismasted, and cast against a reef on the southwesterly corner of Saipan on September 20.

Everyday items and sophisticated trinkets

Only a handful of the 400 passengers and crew survived the wrecking, and many of those who reached the shore were killed by Saipanese natives. Only six Spaniards escaped by boat to Guam; from there they sailed back to Manila to report the tragedy, a journey that took almost a year. The locals pillaged what they could from the wreck, but although the Spanish tried to find the vessel, it took them until 1684. The Spanish salvors raised all but one of the 36 guns on board, but much of the smaller pieces of cargo and personal possessions remained buried among the corals of the reef.

The site of the *Concepción* was discovered in the mid-1980s, and the wreck was salvaged in 1987. Although a commercial salvage operation, an experienced archæological team worked closely with the salvors, ensuring that a high degree of recording was attained. The results have since been published. The collection was dispersed because of its commercial nature, but a useful pool of information remained for further study.

Although little of the vessel's original hull structure remained, it was found that the *Concepción*'s hull was constructed using teak from the Philippines, a suitably hard wood for the rigors of the Manila galleon route.

The artifacts recovered by the expedition showed how far the Spanish trading net extended. Japanese decorative items and weapons and precious stones from India lay next to Chinese porcelain.

The possessions of some of the richer passengers were also recovered, including yards of gold chains, filigree jewelry, and tableware. Everyday items used by the crew were also found, including the usual olive jars, roughly thrown ceramics, and ship fittings. The assemblage is comparable with that recovered from similar Spanish ships such as the *Atocha* (1622), but the Oriental slant to the finds are the unique legacy of Spain's rich trade with the East.

above: *The ship was carrying an eclectic array of finery from the East. Precious stones from India and gold jewelry belonging to the Spanish nobility onboard were just some of the treasures that were recovered from the dive.*

below: *The rocky coast of the southwest corner of Saipan marks the site of the wreck of the galleon.*

THE KENNEMERLAND

1664

A Maunsmas Day windfall for the Shetlanders

The richly laden Dutch East Indiaman *Kennemerland* left Holland on December 14, 1664, on the start of a long voyage to the Dutch East Indies. Like her predecessor, the *Batavia*, she was loaded with goods for the colony. She was sailing around the British Isles rather than through the English Channel because Holland was at war with England.

Although this was her second voyage to the Indies, this was her first through the fierce waters of the North Sea off Scotland. A southerly gale drove her north and, without any warning from the masthead lookouts, the *Kennemerland* smashed against an unseen rock stack. The foremast broke under the impact and fell against the outcrop, allowing the three lookouts to reach safety. They were the only survivors of the 200-member crew. The ship broke in two and the bow settled in deep water beside the stack, while the stern section carried into the bay beyond and was eventually washed onto the beach.

The disaster took place on December 20, 1664, the rock outcrop was Stoura Stack, and the location was the Out Skerries, the most easterly group of the Shetland Islands, 120 miles north of the Scottish mainland. The locals looted the wreck thoroughly, and were reportedly drunk for weeks after finding its cargo of wine and brandy. The event was recorded in a local poem:

The Carmelan [sic] frae Amsterdam cam on a Maunsmas Day,
On Stoura Stack she broke her back, and into the voe she ca.

The Scottish authorities took control of the situation and salvaged what they could. As Holland and the joint kingdoms of England and Scotland were at war, the money recovered was deemed war booty, and when Charles II decided that the local laird (landowner) had kept some of it for himself, he confiscated his estates. In truth the *Kennemerland* carried 120,000 Dutch guilders, and most was turned over to the Crown.

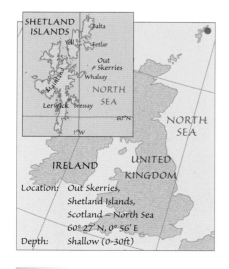

Location: Out Skerries,
        Shetland Islands,
        Scotland – North Sea
        60° 27′ N, 0° 56′ E
Depth: Shallow (0-30ft)

Inhospitable conditions

The wreck was relocated in 1971 by a university diving club. An intermittent excavation was conducted for the following 16 years under the direction of Richard Price. He was assisted by Keith Muckelroy (now deceased), who used the site as a testing ground for research on the environmental influence on wreck formation. Chris Dobbs, an experienced archæologist from the Mary Rose Trust, took over this work in the 1980s.

Much of the excavation was conducted at the mouth of the voe (bay), where the stern section was located and much of the cargo of bricks was found. Underwater vegetation caused problems, with much of the voe covered in a thick forest of kelp. The site's intimidating physical conditions and short diving seasons due to financial difficulties meant that work progressed slowly.

Although no hull structure was recovered, the finds themselves spoke volumes about the cargo and passengers carried on a late 17th-century Dutch East Indiaman. Even more important, the work conducted by Muckelroy then Dobbs gave archæologists a rare understanding of the way the ship was wrecked, the scattering of its objects, and how the hull fell apart over the centuries.

The finds were mainly located beside Stoura Stack and 400 feet further into the voe. All of the anchors found were in the first area, while many of the guns were recovered from the inner region, supporting the theory that the bow and upper hull were dragged past the Stack during the wrecking. Despite the rugged conditions, several well-preserved delicate finds were made, including ornate brass tobacco boxes bearing Dutch designs and five pewter golf club heads, some of the earliest surviving examples.

The majority of the finds from the site are currently on display in Lerwick, capital of the Shetland Islands, although the golf clubs have toured to the Royal and Ancient Clubhouse at St. Andrew's. The excavation of the *Kennemerland* is an example of what can be achieved on an archæological site, where skill, perseverance, and enthusiasm overcome problems created by a limited budget.

opposite: *A diver attempts to examine the wrecksite but is dwarfed by a kelp forest, a form of seaweed that covers much of the area. A study of the distribution of artifacts in this difficult underwater terrain helped to further our understanding of the way ships disintegrate after wrecking.*

below: *These Bellarmine jars of Rheinish stoneware were a popular ceramic form in the 17th century, and are identified by the distinctive face on their neck. A number of these artifacts from the Kennemerland were used to hold mercury.*

THE AMSTERDAM

1749

A well-preserved Indiaman on the beach

Location: Near Hastings, Southern Coast of England – English Channel
50° 57' N, 0° 45' E

Depth: Beached

below: *This drawing shows a diver using an airlift pump to clear silt from the Amsterdam's timbers. The cofferdam can be seen top right.*

The *Amsterdam* was a Dutch East Indiaman built in the Dutch capital in 1748. She left the Texel estuary in January 1749 on the start of her maiden voyage to the Dutch East Indies. An error of judgment led to her grounding on the beach near Hastings, in the south of England. Soon after she was beached, the hull settled in the soft mud and sand of the low tide mark, and the lower hull was consequently extremely well preserved. The wreck was partly salvaged soon after its loss, but the rapid settling of the ship into the mud prevented extensive damage to the hull or recovery of its contents.

The site was rediscovered by local salvors in 1969, and they used mechanical excavation equipment to salvage the wreck. Several objects were removed but the site was damaged by their activities, although the ensuing publicity resulted in the wreck being brought to the attention of archæologists.

Between 1969 and 1970, maritime archæologist Peter Marsden surveyed the site, work which helped identify the wreck and its importance. In 1973, the new Protection of Wrecks Act allowed the site to be protected from further damage. The following year, the VOC

Ship Amsterdam Foundation was created to conduct research and raise funds for an excavation of this important piece of Dutch maritime history.

Everything was in place by the early 1980s, and in 1984–6 three summer excavations were conducted by a joint Anglo-Dutch team, led by Jon Adams. The work involved a partial excavation of the hull. Poor visibility and difficult working conditions necessitated the use of special techniques. A partial cofferdam was built around the wreck, partly to protect the hull from sand pressure as its interior was excavated, but also to provide a fixed datum point when surveying the wreck. A tubular grid supported divers working on the site so they didn't disturb the silt inside the hull, and it too was used as a surveying tool.

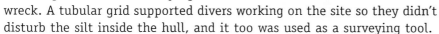

DRAWING OF SHIP'S STERN STRUCTURE REVEALED BY EXCAVATION   AS OF 10.8.84   (NOT TO SCALE)

above: *Underwater archæologist Jon Adams sketched the timber remains in front of him; evidence revealed during the excavation of the Mary Rose. As excavation is essentially destructive, archæologists have to thoroughly record the progress of their work.*

A scarred hybrid

The project was complex due to the size of the hull, the range and quantity of artifacts, and their excellent state of preservation. Impact damage from the mechanical digger used in 1969 and other disturbance damaged the upper layers of the hull, but as the archæologists worked their way down, prime layers of material were uncovered. The archæologists used the *Amsterdam*'s shipbuilding blueprints for reference, but quickly found that the finished product differed from the original design. This was significant, as the VOC (Dutch East India Company) had instituted a standardization policy of shipbuilding in 1742. It would be interesting to discover whether she followed the new standard, or whether conservatism meant that old building features were retained. The findings so far indicate a compromise between the old and new styles.

The *Amsterdam* was over 160 feet long, with a beam of almost 40 feet, and the remaining structure extended 20 feet beneath the surface of the beach, roughly equivalent to the distance from the upper deck to her bilge. As she lay at 20 degrees to port, the starboard side was more eroded than the port. The partial excavation concentrated on the stern section, where the aft section of the lower deck was uncovered. A thick covering of objects lay on her lower deck, including extensive organic remains. The sheer density of finds meant that the excavated area had to be small, mainly due to the conservation demands of the objects.

The original plans allowed the function of certain areas to be identified, such as the sick bay and the captain's cabin. The main cargo area remains to be excavated, but the wide range of personal items such as tableware, silverware, and personal items, plus the plethora of ship fittings, indicate that considerable archæological riches await excavators of the future. Although the finds have not yet found a permanent home, a replica of the *Amsterdam* has been built and can be visited in its namesake city.

PIRATES, SLAVERS AND TRADERS

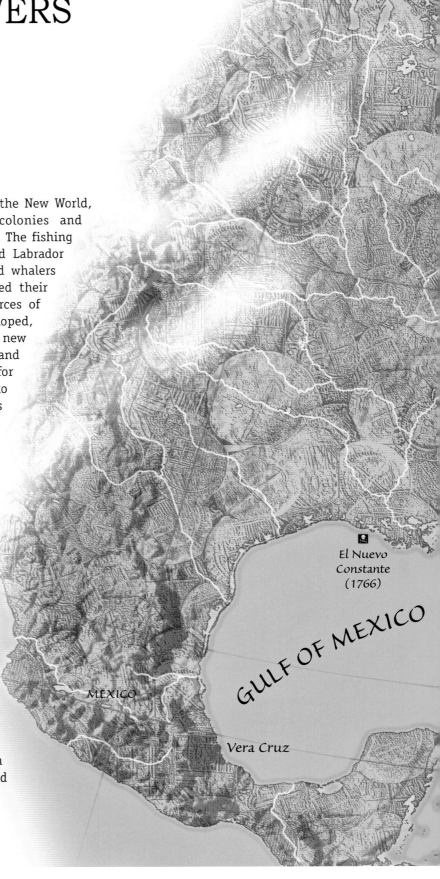

After the initial exploration of the New World, European settlers founded colonies and created a new Atlantic market. The fishing grounds off Newfoundland and Labrador were worked by fishermen and whalers at the same time as the Spanish instituted their treasure fleet system to exploit the resources of their overseas empire. As the colonies developed, particularly those of the English settlers, new industry developed that stimulated growth and further trade. It also created the demand for cheap labor, and the slave trade arose to supply this need. This sorry business reached its peak around 1700, and a unique shipwreck find off Florida allows us to see the tools and restraints of this despicable trade in human suffering at first hand. Around the same time, a century of almost constant hostility between the Spanish and the other European nations came to an end. Privateers who had made a living as a result of this warfare turned to piracy instead. The resulting Golden Age of Piracy lasted for 30 years, but for centuries it has captured the imagination of many who saw romance where only barbaric cruelty could be found. The remains of two pirate vessels discovered in American waters give us the opportunity to travel back to the era of Blackbeard and Bartholomew Roberts. As the American colonies developed, so too did their trading system. By the time of the American Revolution, America held an important place in the world economy and was a bustling center for maritime trade.

El Nuevo
Constante
(1766)

GULF OF MEXICO

MEXICO

Vera Cruz

Marguerite (1707)

NEWFOUNDLAND

FRENCH COLONIES

Quebec

L'Anse aux Bouleaux (1690)

Montreal

NOVA SCOTIA

Halifax

Terence Bay Wreck (c.1750)

Boston

New York

Whydah Galley (1718)

Ronson Ship (c.1750)

Philadelphia

BRITISH COLONIES

James River Bateaux (late 18th century)

Yorktown Wrecks (1781)

Queen Anne's Revenge (1718)

Brown's Ferry (c.1740)

Savannah

below: In the wake of the earliest American colonists came the traders and plantation owners, which in turn led to the slave trade, then the pirates who fed off everyone. The wrecks of these vessels have left a legacy of artifacts that tell us much about the period.

BERMUDA

FLORIDA

St Augustine

ATLANTIC OCEAN

Henrietta Marie (1700)

BAHAMAS

CUBA

Monte Christi Wreck (c.1655)

Wreck of the Ten Sail (1794)

St Anne's Bay Wrecks (c.1750–80)

Port Royal

HISPANIOLA

PUERTO RICO

VIRGIN ISLANDS

Port Royal—submerged city (1692)

Pirates, Slavers and Traders

above: *Fishing vessels operating off the Grand Banks of Newfoundland. The rich fishing grounds of North America attracted fishermen and whalers from the 16th century onward.*

Soon after the discovery of the Americas by Europeans in 1492, following in the wake of the explorers and conquistadors, came settlers and traders. The Spanish, who led the way, settled the islands of the northern Caribbean, and then used them as a base for the colonization of Mexico and South America. Further north, English, Dutch, and French explorers and colonists carved out territory along the Atlantic seaboard of North America, and in the process discovered the natural abundance of the New World.

While the Spanish concentrated on colonization through exploitation, which resulted in the virtual rape of South American culture, further to the north a less hostile approach was adopted. There, the natural resources of the land surrounding the new European colonies were used to produce a growing stream of goods that could be traded. Furs, tobacco, lumber, fish, and sugar all contributed to the economic development of these colonies. As time wore on, subsidiary industries such as cotton-growing and rum-distilling augmented the economic growth of colonies further south and in the Caribbean.

The need for manpower in the new industries led to the use of slaves. Although the slave trade had prospered in the New World since the mid-16th century, its potential was only fully exploited in the late 17th century. While slavery was concentrated in the cotton-, tobacco-, and sugar-producing regions south of the Chesapeake and in the Caribbean, its economic impact left its brutal mark on the development of America. Further to the north, fur-trapping was less manpower-intensive, and French settlements in New France (now Canada) and English ones in New England and New York relied on this trade for the development of their own colonies. Further north still, the superb fishing banks off the coast of Newfoundland and Labrador were discovered by the early 16th century. From Labrador down to Brazil, the Americas were providing the world with new markets, fresh produce, and economic opportunity.

Fishing and whaling vessels

Annual fishing fleets ventured across the North Atlantic to the Grand Banks area off Newfoundland from the early 16th century onward, although it is not known if the English, Dutch, or Basques were the first mariners to discover the region's potential. Certainly, while the English and Dutch concentrated on fishing the Grand Banks, by the mid-16th century the Basques of northern Spain were the most prolific transatlantic whalers.

The Basques were an ancient seafaring people, and Basque ships and captains were at the forefront of Spanish exploration of the New World. Basque whalers had originally operated in the Bay of Biscay, off the northern coast of Spain. As whale stocks dwindled, they moved further afield, and by the time of the loss of the Basque whaling ship in Red Bay, Labrador, the Basques had established over a dozen whaling stations in the area (*see pages 138–139*).

Increasingly during the late 16th and then the 17th century, English, Danish, and Dutch whalers competed amid the whaling grounds off what is now Canada's Atlantic coast. Fishing stations in Nova Scotia turned into permanent settlements and, by the 18th century, the fishing grounds off Labrador, Nova Scotia, and Newfoundland were among the busiest in the world.

Further south, the growth of large plantations and the unhealthy conditions found in the southern colonies and the Caribbean made the use of slaves attractive to many colonists. Although slaves had been brought to the Americas from the very early 16th century, used by the Spanish, it was the English who first turned slavery into a major business and who are largely responsible for the African diaspora.

The earliest English slavers, including the Elizabethan hero Sir John Hawkins, traded slaves to Spanish colonists, mainly in the settlements around the rim of the Caribbean basin. Spanish hostility to interlopers curtailed this activity, but by the mid-17th century England had her own colonies in the region. The capture of Jamaica from the Spanish in 1655, and the settlement of Bermuda and Barbados, created land for English entrepreneurs to exploit.

The triangular trade

After experimenting with other farming methods, the plantation system was adopted in these English colonies, copied from Spanish models. The large sugar plantations created a demand for slaves, and English merchants rapidly provided the human cargoes that the colonists required. The result was a system known as the "Triangular Trade," a highly profitable enterprise for the financial backers and ship captains involved.

In the Triangular Trade, slave ships left London or some smaller English port, loaded with a cargo that could be traded for slaves on the West African coast. This cargo could include pig iron, trade beads or

below: Edward Teach, or "Blackbeard," from Captain Johnson's "A General History of Pirates," published in 1725. Blackbeard was perhaps the most notorious of the hundreds of pirates who plagued the waters of the American colonies and the Caribbean during the early 18th century.

1588	1591	1606	c.1612	1616	1623–1638	1630	1646
The English defeat the Spanish Armada. John Hawkins is knighted.	Spanish and Portuguese mercenaries destroy the Songhay Empire of West Africa.	The Dutch discover Australia.	Approximately 10,000 slaves are taken from Angola, southwest Africa, every year.	Death of William Shakespeare.	The Dutch capture approximately 500 Spanish and Portugese vessels off the Americas.	Brazil is invaded by Dutch colonists.	The Bahamas are colonized by the English.

glass, pewterware or some other commodity required by the local coastal slave traders. Often this varied depending on what the previous slaving ship had brought as cargo, so values constantly fluctuated.

Until around 1700, the Royal African Company regulated trade with the West African coast—"interlopers" could be heavily fined. After this, ships could pay a 10 percent levy to avoid the fine. One such ship was the slave ship *Henrietta Marie*, wrecked off the Florida Keys in 1700 *(pages 140–141)*. Slaves were herded into holding pens, then crammed onto the slave ships for the transatlantic voyage. This section of the

1664	1689–97	1692	1700	c.1700	1701	1703	1704
The Dutch lose New Amsterdam to the English, who rename it New York.	War of the Grand Alliance.	The city of Port Royal, Jamaica, is destroyed in an earthquake.	English slave vessel *Henrietta Marie* wrecked. British pirates make a base of Madagascar.	Beginning of the "Golden Age of Piracy."	Captain Kidd is executed for piracy.	St. Petersburg, Russia, is founded by Peter the Great.	America's first newspaper is published (*Boston News-Letter*).

above: *The development of the Americas created a ready market for slaves, and this trade in human suffering reached a peak during the early 18th century. "The Slave Deck of the Albanez." Watercolor by Francis Meynell.*

Triangular Trade, known as the middle passage, was a period of abject misery for the slaves. Shackled together below decks, in cramped, unsanitary conditions, many of the African human cargo preferred death by jumping overboard to a continuation of this living hell.

Once they arrived in the Americas, the slaves were sold at auction. The ship then loaded up with a cargo of sugar, rum, or other Caribbean commodity, then sailed home to England. Each stage of the voyage produced some kind of financial gain, so slaving trips could be immensely profitable. They also produced untold human misery for the victims of this enterprise.

The golden age of piracy

At the same time as the slave trade was approaching its height, the waters of the American Atlantic seaboard and the Caribbean were plagued by a fresh tide of piracy. Although buccaneers had operated in the Caribbean during the 17th century, using bases at Port Royal in Jamaica and Tortuga, an island off the coast of Hispaniola, they restricted their attacks to Spanish ships and colonies. Some, such as Henry Morgan, even raided major Spanish cities, such as Panama and Cartagena.

Following the cessation of a string of wars involving the Dutch, English, French, and Spanish in 1697, lucrative privateering contracts came to an end. These allowed captains to prey on shipping of an enemy country. While many honest seamen returned to their less lucrative peacetime trading, many did not and created a surge of piracy. This era, sometimes referred to as the Golden Age of Piracy, lasted from around 1700 until 1730. This was the era of many of the most notorious pirates in history, such as Blackbeard, Bartholomew Roberts, Captain Kidd, the women pirates Anne Bonny and Mary Reade, and Henry Every. Many of these operated in American and Caribbean waters, where they preyed on slavers, whalers, sugar carriers, and a host of other ship and cargo types.

Of the two pirate shipwrecks mentioned in this chapter, both vessels were slave ships captured by pirates off the Americas, then pressed into service by their new owners. By the 1730s, stricter law enforcement by colonial authorities and firm action by the world's navies brought the "golden age" to a close. A romantic era in history, it has left a small group of wrecks that allow us to discover more about piracy.

Over a period of more than 250 years, from the early 16th century until the American Revolution, the waters of the American Atlantic coast and the Caribbean abounded with small trading vessels, slave ships, fishing boats, and the craft of those who preyed on them. Understanding the legacy left by these vessels gives ua an insight into the founding years of the American colonies. It also provides us with a chance to learn more about the less noble enterprises that thrived in the colonial system: slavery and piracy.

1709	1715	1717	1718	1721	c.1730	1747	1768
The pianoforte is invented by Bartolomeo Cristofori.	The whale oil industry thrives in Massachusetts.	Date of the *Whydah Galley* wreck, a slave and pirate vessel.	Date of the *Queen Anne's Revenge* wreck, a pirate vessel.	A postal system is in operation between Britain and its American colonies.	End of the "Golden Age of Piracy."	The kingdom of Afghanistan is founded by Ahmad Khan Abdali.	Captain James Cook explores the Pacific Ocean.

THE RED BAY WRECK

1565 A Basque whaler among the frozen waters of Labrador

I n late 1978 a marine archæology team from the Parks Canada organization went to Red Bay, Labrador, to search for a 16th-century whaling ship. Red Bay is a small, remote fishing community on Labrador's southern coast, in the straits facing Newfoundland, over 400 miles north of Halifax, Nova Scotia.

Archival research indicated that in the 16th century, Red Bay had been a bustling whaling station operated by the Basques from northern Spain. In 1565, a Basque whaling vessel, the *San Juan* was lost near the settlement. This was the prize the expedition was after, although the Red Bay project was more than just an underwater archæological expedition. The project would also involve land excavations around the old whaling settlement and a complete study of the area, thereby putting the wreck into its 16th-century context.

The wreck was easily located in 32 feet of water. Test holes revealed well-preserved ship timbers, barrel staves, and even a whale jaw. This was clearly a whaler of the right period, so the excavation and surrounding survey went ahead. Over the next six years, two other whalers and four small boats were found in the bay, all relating to the Basque whaling industry.

Forming the most comprehensive underwater archæological expedition ever undertaken around Canadian waters, the work proved groundbreaking in terms of understanding the Basque presence in 16th-century Canada. The finds recovered from the first wreck helped the archæologists to understand much about the whaling industry. Thousands of barrel staves and hoops were found, many of which still retained a white residue that was identified as whale blubber. Thousands of roofing tiles were present, plus the usual 16th-century finds: an anchor, swivel gun (*verso*), limestone ballast, and rigging fittings.

Well preserved and painstakingly recorded

Of all the finds, the most important was the ship itself. All the timbers were well preserved, and its study greatly helped the understanding of 16th-century ship construction. It was probably a cross between a galleon and a *nao*, with a rounded hull, sharply raked flat stern, and a bluff bow. Loose timbers surrounded the site—exterior planking, beams, knees, and parts of the transom. A large portion of the stern was found, with the rudder partly pinned beneath. A further cohesive piece of

Location: Red Bay
            Southern coast of Labrador,
            Canada – Straits of Belle
            51° 49′ N, 56° 55′ W
Depth: Medium (30–100ft)

structure was found at the bow that revealed details such as mast steps, hawse holes, and the sternpost. Other timbers included a section of an oak mast almost 24 feet long, parts of the bowsprit, and deck planking.

It was decided not to raise the hull, but record it in situ, so that a 1:10 scale model could be produced for further study on land. Following the decision to disassemble the hull structure during excavation, to reach the remains of a small whaleboat pinned beneath it, a six-year timber recording project fleshed out the details required for the model. Each timber was carefully removed, measured, and drawn, then returned to the seabed. Every detail was recorded, including tool marks and constructional details. Surprising features were revealed, such as her semi-shell-first hull construction. In 1984, the timbers were reburied on the site beneath sandbags, tarpaulins, and sand, where they should be preserved from further decay.

Good preservation of organic material meant that recovered items included clothing, shoes, and wooden tools. Combined with finds such as the ship's compass, a compass binnacle, an hourglass, and log reel, the tools showed how the ship was navigated, sailed, and repaired. Items such as the barrels, ship fittings, and whaling tools revealed how the crew worked and lived onboard the vessel.

Now thought to be the *San Juan*, the whaler, together with the other archæological projects in the bay, has given us a much greater understanding of the early whaling industry than was ever thought possible. Parks Canada intend to interpret and display all their recovered finds, as well as their model of the galleon.

opposite: *The underwater archæological team of Parks Canada shown working in the inhospitable waters of Red Bay, with the timbers of the whaler below them.*

below: *Meticulous recording of the whaler's physical remains allowed ship historians to attempt a reconstruction of the ship's lines, combining the wreck information with evidence from contemporary shipbuilding sources.*

THE HENRIETTA MARIE

1700

A poignant reminder of a shameful past

A 1972 treasure-hunting team led by Mel Fisher was looking for the lost Spanish galleon, the *Nuestra Señora de Atocha*, when they came across a shipwreck about 36 miles west of Key West, Florida. For two short periods in 1972 and 1973 the salvors recovered objects from the site, although not in an archæological manner—accurate recording was minimal. The salvors quickly lost interest when they found it contained no treasure. A portion of the artifacts was selected by the State of Florida and removed to Tallahassee, while the rest was stored by the salvage team.

In 1983, archæologists working for Fisher decided to reinvestigate the site. One of the first finds was the ship's bell, embossed with the inscription "Henrietta Marie 1699." Research was conducted to learn more, and the finds suggested an English connection to the vessel, which was possibly a slave ship. These included a tusk from an African elephant and encrusted sets of iron shackles. If it was a slaver, the wreck would prove more valuable than sunken treasure—no slave ship had ever been investigated. For millions of African-Americans, it could provide a direct link to their past.

Archæologist David Moore worked on the project throughout the 1980s, conducting research on both sides of the Atlantic and analyzing the finds. The *Henrietta Marie* was clearly a small vessel, of 120 tons (108 tonnes) burden, yet archival research showed a human cargo of 250 people had once been crammed into her hold. Sufficient hull timbers were examined to allow Moore to gain an insight into her construction, although a proper archæological excavation of the wreck still needs to be undertaken. Archival research filled in the story.

A shameful legacy

She was probably built in France toward the end of the 1690s and captured by the English Navy during The War of the Grand Alliance (1689–97). Sold to private owners and registered in London, by 1697 she was ready to sail on her first slaving voyage. This involved what was known as "the Triangular Trade." Trade goods purchased in London were exchanged for slaves in West Africa, then the slaves were taken to the West Indies and sold. The profits were used to buy rum or sugar, and the ship returned to London, netting a substantial profit from her voyage.

For her second slaver voyage in 1699, she sailed as a "ten-percenter"—10 percent of the profits from the voyage were paid to the Royal African Company, which maintained a monopoly over African trade. She was

above: *One of the first items recovered from the wreck was the ship's bell, launching a historical investigation into the origins of the vessel.*

82°W

FLORIDA
Cape Coral
26°N
Miami
GULF OF MEXICO
Key West

USA
GULF OF MEXICO

Location: New Ground Reef
Near Key West, Florida
USA – Gulf of Mexico
24° 41' N, 82° 5' W
Depth: Medium (30–100ft)

therefore allowed to use the company's facilities in West Africa. Sailing with a cargo of trade goods and pig iron, she headed for New Calabar, where the goods were exchanged for Igbo captives. These were transported across the Atlantic to Jamaica, where they were sold into slavery. The *Henrietta Marie* then loaded an unspecified cargo and began her voyage home to London, rounding the western tip of Cuba. She was never seen again, and it is thought a hurricane drove her onto the desolate New Ground Reef off the Florida Keys. There were no survivors.

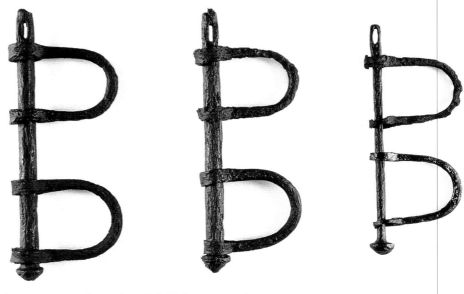

above: *Iron leg shackles (or bilboes) were recovered in a range of sizes, including those on the right, which were designed to fit the legs of a child.*

In 1985, the salvors donated the objects recovered to the Mel Fisher Maritime Museum, in Key West. Research continued over the next ten years, with the aim of creating a nationwide traveling exhibition that would tell the story of the slave trade using the artifacts as a medium. Publicity about this wreck struck a chord with African-Americans. The National Association of Black Scuba Divers (NABS) placed a bronze memorial plaque on the site in 1991 to commemorate the millions of lives lost during the African diaspora. Part of it was inscribed with the legend, "Speak her name and gently touch the souls of our ancestors."

The exhibition attracted major interest, and placed the *Henrietta Marie* in the forefront of a movement by African-Americans to learn about the slave trade, and to try to come to terms with the traumas of the diaspora.

below: *A plaque was placed on the site by members of the National Association of Black Scuba Divers in an emotional ceremony. It honors the millions of lives lost during the African diaspora.*

THE WHYDAH GALLEY

1717

Sam Bellamy's pirate ship

L
ike the *Henrietta Marie*, the *Whydah Galley* was a slave ship, although on her return voyage from the West Indies to London in early 1717 she was captured by the pirate Samuel Bellamy. She was reputedly carrying gold, sugar, ivory, and indigo. Records indicate that she was a ship-rigged galley of 300 tons (272 tonnes) burden and built in London. The term "galley" means she was fitted with oar-ports, allowing her to be rowed when the winds calmed, making her a useful pirate ship. Bellamy was a crewman of Benjamin Hornigold, and when Hornigold refused to attack British shipping, Bellamy was elected captain.

Operating from a base at New Providence (now called Nassau) in the Bahamas, Bellamy preyed on shipping in the Bahamas Channel and the Windward Passage. Once he captured the *Whydah*, Bellamy sailed for Virginia, where he captured more ships off the colony's coast before a storm drove him north into New England waters.

Sometime during the night of May 17, 1717, with Bellamy on board, the *Whydah Galley* struck a sandbar off Cape Cod, Massachusetts. She sank rapidly, taking Bellamy and most of the 146 pirate crew with her. The handful who survived were captured; most were subsequently hanged in Boston. Local salvors may well have picked over the wreckage before the authorities reached the scene, for only two cannons were subsequently recovered by agents of the Governor of Massachusetts.

above: *The recovery of the bronze bell from the pirate ship identified her beyond any reasonable doubt. Here it is shown during the removal of concretion, but the vessel's name is still visible.*

Location: Off Cape Cod, Massachusetts USA – Atlantic Ocean
41° 38' N, 70° 11' W
Depth: Medium (30–100ft)

Another theory is that the violent storm that wrecked the vessel also broke her up, scattering the wreckage for miles along the sandbar, where the remains were quickly covered.

During the 1980s a commercial salvage group led by shipwreck hunter Barry Clifford tried to find the wreck with magnetometers and sonar equipment. In 1984 their work paid off. A bell was recovered, marked "The Whydah Galley 1716." They were looking in the right place.

Modifying a slaver

It was found that debris from the wreck was scattered over a wide area, supporting the theory that the ship broke up soon after it struck the sandbar. Sand had buried the remains, but the salvors employed archæological methods to investigate the *Whydah* wreck.

It was found that the hull was originally over 75 feet long. It was oriented so that it lay roughly parallel to the shore, pointing south. The bell was recovered in the bow section, along with anchors and a cooking stove, and the stern area was marked by personal artifacts. Between them lay a scatter of 28 cannons, making the ship as well armed as a similarly-sized warship. Clearly Bellamy and his crew rearmed the *Whydah* after her capture, converting her from a slaver into a pirate ship. Over 100,000 artifacts were recovered from the wreck, which the salvage team conserved in their own Massachusetts laboratory.

Maritime Underwater Surveys, the organization responsible for the salvage and conservation of the objects, performed their task diligently. The stabilized objects allowed researchers to work out how a pirate ship was armed, equipped, and operated. As a commercial enterprise, there was no requirement to keep the collection together, but the majority of artifacts are now on public display at the Expedition Whydah Sea Lab & Learning Center, a dockside facility in Provincetown, Massachusetts.

The center has been described as "a model for private archæology." Artifacts on display include cannons, navigation tools, small arms, and a fascinating open-view laboratory, where visitors can see objects from the wreck being conserved.

The Whydah Research and Preservation Society was also founded to conduct research into the wreck and to disseminate information about it. While archæological purists have condemned Clifford's activities, the efforts made to interpret and display the finds recovered from the *Whydah* are commendable, and have helped to flesh out the romance of piracy with tangible evidence.

above: Barry Clifford was the driving force behind the project to locate and salvage the Whydah. A conservation facility was created to handle the mass of maritime finds recovered from the wreck site.

below: A conservator holds a freshly cleaned artifact from the pirate ship, in this case the brass decoration from a firearm. As would be expected from a pirate ship, many of the artifacts recovered related to weaponry.

left: The salvage team used sieves to strain recovered seabed scatter for artifacts.

THE QUEEN ANNE'S REVENGE

1718 — The ghost of Blackbeard's flagship

below: *One of the more interesting finds was a syringe, possibly part of a medical chest Blackbeard extorted from the citizens of Charleston.*

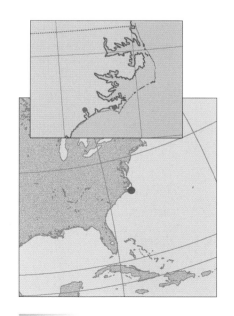

Blackbeard is probably the most notorious pirate of them all. It's believed he was born as Edward Teach in Bristol, England, and began his seafaring life in the employ of Queen Anne, attacking her enemies' ships in the West Indies. When the war ended, he turned to piracy. His mentor, Benjamin Hornigold, retired from piracy in 1717, so Teach took over his ship and crew. The former slave ship was given heavier armament and renamed the *Queen Anne's Revenge*. For the next year he terrorized the Atlantic Seaboard of America and the Caribbean, establishing a base on Ocracoke Island, North Carolina. Teach earned a fearsome reputation, and his nickname stemmed from his appearance. He was a tall man, his face almost covered with hair, and he reportedly decorated his long black beard with plaits and ribbons.

In May 1718 he blockaded Charleston, South Carolina and held hostages for ransom before returning to his lair at Ocracoke. While passing through Carolina's Outer Banks, Blackbeard lost his flagship, *Queen Anne's Revenge*, and another sloop when they ran aground near the modern town of Beaufort, North Carolina. Blackbeard salvaged what cargo he could and sailed on to Ocracoke with the rest of his flotilla. By November 1718, an expedition led by Lieutenant Maynard of the Royal Navy succeeded in finding Blackbeard's base. In a bitterly contested fight, Blackbeard was killed. The surviving pirate crew was taken to Williamsburg to face trial and execution.

A pirate's armory and medicine

In the mid-1990s a commercial salvage organization, Intersal of Boca Raton, Florida, began searching for the wreck, armed with documentary evidence and a search permit granted by North Carolina's Office of State Archæology. Once it was located, Michael Daniel of Intersal formed the Maritime Research Institute (MRI), a non-profit organization intended to undertake the excavation of the site under Daniel's direction. The State of North Carolina retained ownership of the wreck and its artifacts, and steps were undertaken to designate the site a protected State archæological preserve. State archæologists supervised the excavation of the site, assisted by a staff from the North Carolina Maritime Museum, which included archæologist David Moore, who was responsible for much of the analysis of the slave ship *Henrietta Marie*.

The wreck lies in 20 feet of water, and the substantial remains of hull structure have been uncovered. Over the years, these were scattered over an area of approximately 200 by 100 feet, mostly protected by a shallow layer of silt. Analysis of the timbers will show what type was used and when it was cut. Of particular interest to historians will be any evidence of how the ship was converted for use as a pirate ship. State authorities are now almost certain that the wreck is that of the *Queen Anne's Revenge*, and project director Mark Wilde-Ramsing intends to conduct more work on the site on behalf of the North Carolina Department of Archives and History.

Initial finds included 18 cannons, anchors, a ship's bell, and weaponry. The quantity of guns suggests that the ship was a pirate vessel, and three of these weapons have been raised for conservation. Pewter tableware and wine bottles date from the early 18th century, but the most telling find is a syringe. Part of the ransom Blackbeard extorted from Charleston was a chest of medical supplies, reportedly because of rampant syphilis among the pirate crew. It is suggested that the syringe may have formed part of this medical kit.

The *Queen Anne's Revenge* excavation is probably a unique project in the USA—a collaborative effort between a private research and salvage firm and a State-run professional maritime archæological team. While Daniel and his MRI organization have exclusive rights to market replicas of the artifacts and to publish commercial accounts of the story, the State of North Carolina keeps the artifacts themselves. After conservation, it is expected that these objects will be displayed in the North Carolina Maritime Museum in Beaufort.

below: *Despite the poor visibility of the North Carolina coast, archæologists are continuing to survey and investigate the pirate shipwreck. A concreted cast-iron anchor fluke marks the bow area of the vessel.*

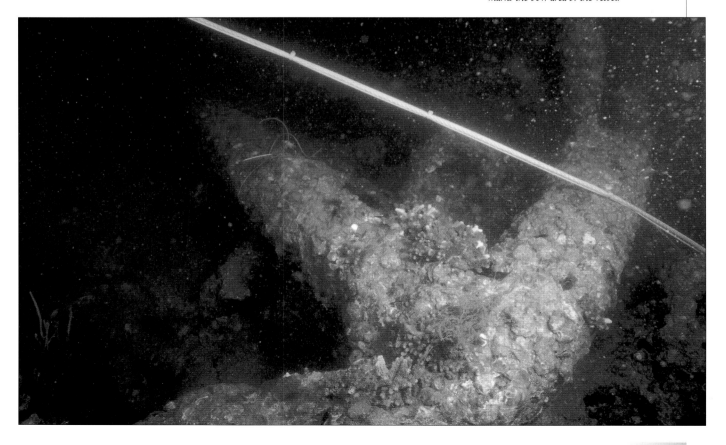

THE AGE OF FIGHTING SAIL

Machault ●

● Hamilton & Scourge

Sapphire ●

Defence ●

● Penobscot Bay

Louisburg Harbor ●

● De Braak

The naval revolution created by the introduction of artillery reached its conclusion in the mid-17th century. From then until the early 19th century there was little change in warship design or armament. Naval actions were decided by the way these ships were employed by their admirals. Early in the 18th century there occurred a period of stagnation in both ship design and naval tactics, when admirals appeared more scared to take risks than they were eager to win battles. This stalemate ended by the later part of the century, when British superiority through skill and better gunnery overcame their deficiencies in ship design. The age of fighting sail lasted for over 150 years, and has left us a large enough legacy of shipwrecks to be able to examine most types and sizes of vessels used during the period. Although evidence from wrecks cannot recreate the beauty and stateliness of these warships, they can provide valuable evidence concerning how they sailed, fought, and acted as a home for their crew.

above: *Prior to the mid-1600s, naval battles were a loose mêlée of individual ships, but increasing armament and better sailing tactics led to the deployment of a fleet in line—a wall of ships to present broadsides that was difficult to break up.*

ATLANTIC OCEAN

Dartmouth
Duart Point

Evstafii

Bonhomme Richard

NORTH
SEA

Vasa

St Nikolai

Catterwater Wreck

Kronan

BALTIC SEA

Colossus

Invincible

Mary Rose

Lutine

Association

Anne

Studland Bay Wreck

Alderney Wreck

BAY OF
BISCAY

Villefranche

Floating batteries

MEDITERRANEAN

Athenienne

Navarino Bay Wrecks

SEA

Columbine

Cambrian

L'Orient

The Age of Fighting Sail

T he naval revolution created by the introduction of artillery reached its conclusion in the mid-17th century. As we have already seen, ships began to carry a substantial armament of heavy bronze guns by the mid-16th century, but it would be another half-century before tactical developments and ship design allowed naval artillery to realize its full potential.

By the start of the Dutch Wars of the mid-17th century, warships armed with artillery had a balanced and powerful broadside capacity, and commanders had the tactical skills to use this tool to its best advantage. The design of the sailing ship required naval artillery to be mounted along the sides of the hull sides, so in order to engage an enemy the ship had to present her side to the target and fire a broadside.

While earlier naval battles resembled a free and loose mêlée of individual ships, naval commanders in the Dutch Wars introduced the deployment of a fleet in line, one behind the other. This created a wall of ships and guns that was difficult to break up, and made the best possible use of the fleet's armament. With the exception of the Dutch Wars between the English and Dutch fleets, these tactics crept into the doctrines of other naval powers, such as the French, Swedes, and Spanish.

At the same time, warship types developed into two groups. The first consisted of ships considered powerful enough to stand in these naval lines of battle. In the mid-17th century, these ships of the line carried 40 or more guns, but the standard size crept up throughout the 18th century. By the Napoleonic Wars (1803–15), ships of the line were expected to carry at least 74 guns, and several vessels carried many more.

The second group initially consisted of warships considered too small to hold their own in a major engagement. One of these group types, the frigate, grew in popularity during the 17th century, fulfilling the roles of scout ship and independent cruiser. Other smaller ships varied widely, but by the 18th century they generally became standardized into craft such as brigs, cutters, and sloops. Another type, the schooner, was widely used as a privateer by the American colonists, and became a warship during the American Revolution. It was loosely based on even earlier Dutch designs.

Arming the ships of the line

Returning to ships of the line, late 17th century warships such as the massive Swedish ship *Kronan* (*see pages 152–153*) acted as national status symbols, and consequently were heavily decorated. Illustrations by marine artists such as Van de Velde the Younger reinforce this statement, backed up by shipwreck evidence. The result was a combination of ostentation and utilitarian power, creating a beautiful instrument of war.

In this period, 70- or 80-gun ships of the line were common, although by the early 18th century, ship designers favored simpler, lighter-armed, and more maneuverable warships. Vessels were also divided into rates, a system that would remain throughout the age of

above: *Naval tactics consisted of engaging in a free-for-all mêlée until the late 17th century. "The Second Battle of Schooneveld, 4th June 1673." Oil painting in the style of Willem Van de Velde the Elder.*

right: *By the end of the 17th century, sailing warships had developed into vessels designed to hold their own in a line of battle. "HMS Resolution in a gale." Oil painting by Willem Van de Velde the Younger*

1654–56	1676	c.1700–1730	1740	1747	1756–1763	1758	1769
England and the Netherlands fight the First Dutch War.	Date of the *Kronan* wreck, a Swedish warship.	The Golden Age of Piracy.	Decline of the Spanish treasure fleet system; officially ended in 1778.	The English and French navies fight the First Battle of Finisterre.	Prussia and Britain defeat France, Russia, Spain, and Austria in the Seven Years' War.	Date of the *HMS Invincible* wreck, a British warship.	James Watt patents the steam engine.

fighting sail. Ships of the line were divided into third rates (50–79 guns), second rates (80–89 guns), and first rates (90 guns and above). Of the ships in this period, the smaller ones are unrated, one was a third-rate, and another a first-rate vessel. The boundaries between the various classes varied slightly throughout the period, but the basic classification remained the same.

National differences in warship building made themselves apparent during the 17th century. French ships tended to be better built and were less prone to be over-gunned, as was common in the English navy. The Swedish *Kronan* (1676) was particularly heavily armed for a ship of her size, and may have been considered top-heavy.

There was no major revolution in warship design during the 18th century, but styles were refined and developed over time. For much of the century, ship design went through a period of stagnation, particularly in Britain, while French and Spanish ship designers produced superior warships.

Updating the Royal Navy

Certain innovations were standard throughout all navies. Early in the century, most navies replaced the spritsail topmast with a longer bowsprit and jib. This eased sailing close to the wind, making warships more maneuverable. Maneuvering was required mainly to stay in line—during the 18th century, naval

1773	1776	1787	1788	1789	1791	1792	1796
The Boston Tea Party.	George Washington reads the Declaration of Independence.	The highest peak of the Alps, Mont Blanc, is reached by French climbers.	English prisoners arrive at Botany Bay for Australia's first penal colony.	George Washington is made the first United States President.	The Constitution Act divides Canada into French- and English-speaking territories.	Revolutionary wars in France; proclamation of the French Republic.	Ceylon is conquered by the British.

The Age of Fighting Sail

commanders were noted for their rigid adherence to the tactical doctrine of maintaining the line of battle at all costs. This tended to reduce risk, but also reduced the potential of gaining a decisive victory. Admirals who flaunted the rules could face disaster, but some, such as Howe or Nelson, saw it as the only way to defeat the enemy.

In 1740, the British captured the 70-gun Spanish *Princessa*. The officers who examined it were startled at its superior design, compared with contemporary British warships. The result was a major upheaval of naval design that resulted in improved vessels. Similarly, another milestone was the British capture of the 74-gun French

1798	1803–15	1804	1805	1812–15	1813	1815	1820
Date of the *HMS De Braak* wreck, a British warship.	The Napoleonic Wars.	Napoleon makes himself Emperor of the French.	The French-Spanish navy is defeated in the Battle of Trafalgar.	The War of 1812.	Date of the *Hamilton* and *Scourge* wrecks, converted merchant schooners.	Wellington defeats Napoleon at the Battle of Waterloo.	American missionaries begin working on the Hawaiian Islands.

left: *The loss of large sailing warships through explosion or sinking was a rarity but, as the largest man-made vessels of their day, they provide a fascinating resource for archæologists. "Loss of HMS Ramillies, September 1782: Blowing up the wreck." Oil painting by Robert Dodd.*

below: *In addition to ships of the line, smaller warships such as frigates and brigs formed a vital function in the navies of the 18th century. "A frigate off Liverpool." Oil painting by Robert Dodd.*

warship *L'Invincible* in 1747 (*pages 154–155*). *The Invincible*, as it was renamed by the British Royal Navy, provided the basis of a new group of ships, the 74-gun ships of the line that would form the backbone of the British fleet until the end of the Napoleonic Wars.

A combination of battle experience during the Seven Years' War (1756–63) and this new-found wealth of design information created a naval phenomenon. By the end of the war, the British Royal Navy was widely seen as the finest in the world, its ships and seamen capable of defeating rival navies with ease. This reputation would falter during a poor performance during the American Revolution, and again following losses in single-ship actions at the hands of the American navy during the War of 1812. Despite these setbacks, it remained the foremost naval power in the world, consistently defeating forces set against it.

The versatile frigates and brigs

Naval supremacy was not gained by large ships alone. During almost a century of warfare between Britain and France, and occasionally involving the fleets of other nations, small ships such as brigs, cutters, and schooners were called upon to fight, often in places where larger fleets were unable to go. Frigates were the prime example of these smaller ships, although some, such as the American 54-gun super-frigates like the *USS Constitution*, were as powerful as some smaller ships of the line. The introduction of carronades—short guns with great close-range firepower— gave many smaller ships a powerful punch, compared to their size.

Frigates and brigs were small, swift warships that had numerous uses. They escorted convoys, scouted for the enemy, and cruised in enemy shipping lanes. A typical frigate was a vessel with guns mounted on a single deck, compared with the two decks of a third-rate ship of the line. Small brigs such as the *De Braak* (*pages 156–157*) were also extremely valuable in maintaining naval lines of communication. During the Revolutionary War and the War of 1812, both the Americans and the British pressed local craft into naval service on the Great Lakes, or built new warships from scratch (*pages 158–159*).

After the Napoleonic Wars, warships slowly developed during the first half of the 19th century. First, metal was introduced into warship construction to reinforce the wooden hulls. While the size of armament increased, ships became increasingly vulnerable to gunfire, but nothing was done to improve protection. Although as early as the 1830s designers suggested building warships using steel, the concept was rejected.

One major innovation was the adoption of steam power. From the 1840s onward, the world's navies reluctantly agreed to the use of steam for propulsion, but sails were still retained for reasons of liability and economy. These warships created a transitory type, between the age of fighting sail and the introduction of the ironclad. The introduction of iron warships in the 1860s made them obsolete, and the days of the wooden warship were over.

1823	1833	1834					
President Monroe forbids European interference in the western hemisphere.	The British Empire abolishes slavery.	The analytical engine, a mechanical computer, is invented by Charles Babbage.	Mexicans beat the Texan army at the Alamo.	Queen Victoria is crowned.	Navies use steam-propelled vessels.	Ironclad warships are introduced, replacing wooden vessels.	Passports are used in the United States.
		1836	**1837**	**c.1840**	**c.1860**	**1861**	

THE KRONAN

1676 The pride of Sweden

above: *A skull and a partially buried bronze gun form part of the scatter of artifacts that mark the well-preserved remains of the Swedish warship Kronan.*

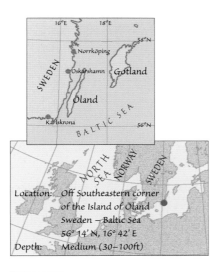

Location: *Off Southeastern corner of the Island of Öland Sweden – Baltic Sea 56° 14' N, 16° 42' E*
Depth: *Medium (30–100ft)*

When she was launched on July 31, 1668, the *Kronan* (Crown) was one of the most impressive and powerful ships in the Swedish navy. She was designed by the English shipbuilder Francis Sheldon and built at the Royal Shipyard in Stockholm. Although work began in 1665 and she was launched three years later, the *Kronan* was not commissioned until 1672, due to defense cuts.

Sweden allied herself with France in 1672, a move that brought war between Sweden and the nations of Holland and Denmark. The *Kronan* was rushed into commission to reinforce the Swedish fleet. She was an impressive warship—a three-decked vessel of 197 feet, with a 43-foot beam and a displacement of 2,140 tons (1,941 tonnes). She was armed with an impressive 124 bronze guns and served by a crew of 500 sailors and 300 marines.

In May 1676, the Swedish fleet sortied to engage the joint Danish-Dutch fleet, meeting off the eastern coast of the Swedish Baltic island of Öland on June 1. At noon, just as what would become "The Battle of Southern Öland" was about to begin, the *Kronan* inexplicably blew up, then capsized and sank, all but 50 of the crew with her.

The wreck was discovered in August 1980 by Anders Franzén, the renowned Swedish maritime archæologist and historian who discovered the *Vasa*. The remains of the *Kronan* were in 85 feet of water, lying on a flat, sandy seabed, some four miles from the southeastern coast of the island. Soon afterward, a survey of the site was conducted and plans were made to excavate the wreck.

Scattered and burnt timbers

The preservative qualities of the water in the Baltic meant that the wooden remains of the warship were in excellent condition. The surviving timbers of the *Kronan* were scattered over a 120 foot by 60 foot area, the main section being the aft two-thirds of her port side, a continuous structure lying flat on the seabed with the inner face uppermost. Scattered and burnt timbers were strewn over the remainder of the site, evidence of the catastrophic explosion that sank the vessel. The wreck still lies with her bow facing south, the direction she was heading as she prepared for battle in 1676.

From 1981 onward, the site was excavated by an archæological team under the supervision of the Kalmar Läns Museum, located in southeastern Sweden, close to Öland. Test trenches were opened to determine the extent of the remains. In early 1983 a survey grid was laid over the wreck that permitted an accurate survey of the site. It was also used to provide a frame of reference for a photographic survey, so a photo-mosaic map of the site could be assembled. This work revealed that most of the *Kronan*'s starboard side had been torn apart by the explosion, and there was extensive damage to the forward part of the ship.

The excavation produced a wealth of finds, many in superb condition. Over 22,000 artifacts have been recovered, ranging from 44 of her large bronze guns and their associated carriages, equipment, and shot, to human remains—the scattered remnants of her crew. Other strikingly well-preserved finds include clothing, musical and navigational instruments, tableware, and chests containing personal possessions, as well as a hoard of gold coins, presumably the remains of the *Kronan*'s pay chest. Elaborate carvings that once decorated the hull have been recovered with the chisel marks of the sculptor still visible. As work continues, a further thousand objects are recovered each year, making this project one of the largest underwater archæological projects in Europe.

It is expected that excavation work will continue until at least 2003; so far, two-thirds of the hull and scattered remains have been surveyed and excavated. One future objective is the raising of the cohesive port side of the wreck, but even without the hull itself, the objects are a fascinating legacy of Sweden's golden age. The conserved finds from the Kronan are displayed in the Kalmar Läns Museum, near Öland.

below: *The Kronan was ripped apart in a catastrophic explosion that claimed the lives of 750 of her crew. "The Battle of Southern Oland, June 1st, 1676." Oil painting by Claus Moinichen.*

HMS Invincible (L'Invincible)

1758

The remains of a Royal Naval ship-of-the-line

above: *A diver working in the magazine amid numerous gunpowder barrels. Diving in the murky depths of British waters always makes for difficult excavating, no more so than with this expedition.*

Location: Portsmouth Harbor
South coast of England –
The Solent
50° 46' N, 1° 6' W
Depth: Medium (30–100ft)

Fisherman Arthur Mack was working off Portsmouth, in the south of England, in May 1979. His nets were caught in an underwater obstruction, so he returned to the area with local diver John Broomhead, who reported finding the remains of a large wooden shipwreck. Artifacts raised were dated to the mid-18th century. Mack sought assistance from a Royal Naval diving club, who investigated the wreck under the direction of John Bingeman, a naval officer and amateur archæologist. Further finds pointed to the wreck being the remains of *HMS Invincible*, a warship that was stranded off Portsmouth in 1758, and the wrecksite was subsequently protected by law. In 1981, a wooden tally stick used to tag folded sails was recovered. It bore the words "Invincible Flying Jib," identifying the wreck beyond doubt.

HMS Invincible was originally a French ship, built at Rochefort and launched in 1744. Commissioned as *L'Invincible*, she was a considerably better-designed vessel than British ships of the same period. The new warship saw service in the West Indies before forming part of an escort to a large French convey that was overtaken by the Royal Navy at the First Battle of Finisterre in May 1747. The battle was a disaster for the French, who lost eight warships, including *L'Invincible*.

Her name was Anglicized and she was commissioned into the Royal Navy, serving with distinction. During the Seven Years' War (1756–63), *HMS Invincible* sailed from Portsmouth as part of a fleet bound for Canada in February 1758. She ran aground on a shoal off her home port, and before she was refloated, fell over on her beam ends under punishment from heavy seas, and subsequently became a total loss. The *Invincible* was partly salvaged in 1758—the guns and other valuable items were removed before the wreck was abandoned.

Between 1981 and 1990, the site was partially excavated by John Bingeman and a team of volunteers, including professional archæologists from the Mary Rose Trust. In the early years, test trenches were dug across the site to determine the coherence of the hull structure.

Auctioning history

In 1981, the Invincible (1758) Committee was formed to orchestrate work on the wreck, with Bingeman as its chairperson. The naval divers were involved in the Falklands War in 1982, and the Mary Rose volunteers were busy raising their own vessel, but excavation work was renewed in 1983–4, revealing enough of the hull structure for the timbers to be compared with the ship's original plans.

An area identified as the store rooms for the gunner and the boatswain was excavated, and it was found that the anærobic mud of Portsmouth harbor had helped to preserve the contents. These rooms, located in the bow of the ship, yielded an array of artifacts relating to seamanship and gunnery, and have helped our understanding of how an 18th-century warship operated.

A trench dug at the stern of the vessel uncovered officers' cabins and store rooms, where shoes and personal items were recovered, the former probably belonging to the ship's cobbler. In subsequent years a detailed survey of the site revealed that the warship had split down her center line, and further excavation determined that this was a result of the wrecking process rather than salvage operations. Excavation work was discontinued in 1990.

The growing number of finds forced the group to establish their own conservation facilities. While a number of the items were eventually displayed in the Chatham Historic Dockyard in southeast England, controversy surrounded the rest of the collection. The Invincible (1758) Committee decided to auction off many of its finds at Christie's in London, a move that brought the wrath of the archæological community upon it. The auction was forced on the volunteer group by financial circumstances, but the consequent dispersal of a valuable historic collection can only be regretted.

Despite this, the project caused extensive research to be undertaken into *HMS Invincible*, and the combination of this research and excavation work has furthered our understanding of the ships that formed part of the line of battle during the age of sail.

above: *A 30-minutes-and-28-seconds sandglass. Thirty-minute sandglasses were rung during watches as a "clock," i.e. the ship's bell was rung once at 08:30, twice at 09:00, etc.*

below: *HMS Invincible of 74 guns, after her capture from the French, in 1747. Engraving.*

HMS DE BRAAK

1798

The commercial destruction of Delaware's treasure ship

I n the afternoon of May 28, 1798, the Royal Naval brig *HMS De Braak*, of 16 guns, approached the Delaware River, escorting a captured Spanish prize, the *Don Francisco Xavier*. As she prepared to drop her anchor off Cape Henlopen, near Rehobeth Beach, a freak squall hit the vessel, heeling her over so much that she took on water, capsized, and sank within minutes. Captain James Drew, 34 crewmen, and 12 Spanish prisoners were drowned. The survivors boarded the *Xavier* and made their way to Philadelphia, where they informed the British consul of the tragedy.

In late July 1798, *HMS Assistance* was sent from Nova Scotia to the Delaware to see if *HMS De Braak* could be salvaged. The operation was declared feasible, and British salvage boats arrived. During that summer they tried in vain to raise the brig.

above: *The British brig De Braak was captured from the Dutch, and was typical of the small vessels that acted as scouts and message-carriers for the sailing fleets of the Napoleonic era.*

Stories that *HMS De Braak* carried treasure captured from the Spanish spread throughout the region, and attempts to find the wreck were made throughout the 19th century, aided by a location supplied by a Delaware River pilot, Gilbert McCracken. As the treasure legend grew with time, greater efforts were put into the search for the ship, but all without result. Maritime history books even recorded the existence of treasure as fact, stating "she carried 70 tons of copper ingots and a large amount of gold and silver bullion and specie," despite scholarly proof that no treasure was ever carried. The effect was to cause a cultural disaster.

Irresponsible salvors

In April 1984, commercial salvage company Sub-Sal located the wreck using a side-scan sonar array. Objects recovered from the site identified the wreck, and the company applied for and was granted legal custody of it. Sub-Sal began salvage operations in earnest in 1985, raising the hull to see if precious goods lay beneath its timbers and dredging the site for treasure. Both of these actions caused irreparable damage to the wreck assembly and brought intensely negative publicity to bear on the salvage operation. State archæologists who inspected the operation were horrified at the seemingly wanton destruction of an historic shipwreck.

The raised hull was moved into a temporary concrete cofferdam at the nearby town of Lewes, Delaware. In 1990 it was moved to a wet-storage building nearby. Flagrant violations of State and Federal laws, including the disposal of human remains and the illegal disposal of

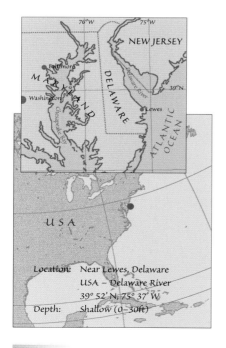

Location: Near Lewes, Delaware
USA – Delaware River
39° 52' N, 75° 37' W
Depth: Shallow (0–30ft)

artifacts, led to the salvors' loss of custody. Harvey Harrington, the salvor who first rediscovered the wreck, was accused of raising artifacts without a State permit and using them as fund-raising collateral. In 1992 the courts awarded the wreck to the State of Delaware, who attempted to salvage what information they could from the remains left by Sub-Sal.

The State of Florida took steps to save the hull from decay and accepted the responsibility to conserve the artifacts recovered by the salvage team. Over 26,000 objects were recovered, the entire collection being appraised by Christie's at under $300,000. It is estimated that Sub-Sal spent ten times that amount in its recovery operation, looking for lost treasure that never existed. A large group of the conserved artifacts were placed on display in the Zwaanendael Museum in Dover, Delaware, part of Delaware State Museums, themselves part of the State's Division of Historical and Cultural Affairs.

Many historians and underwater archæologists consider the salvage of *HMS De Braak* one of the worst maritime archæological disasters in recent history. If one good thing arose from the incident, it was that the controversy surrounding the wreck helped the archæological community to lobby Congress for a change in the law. In 1988, the Abandoned Shipwreck Act came into effect, preventing such destruction in the future.

below: *The remains of the hull of the De Braak were protected by a cofferdam soon after she was raised from the Delaware River. Intervention by the State helped preserve the remains from further decay.*

THE HAMILTON AND SCOURGE

1812

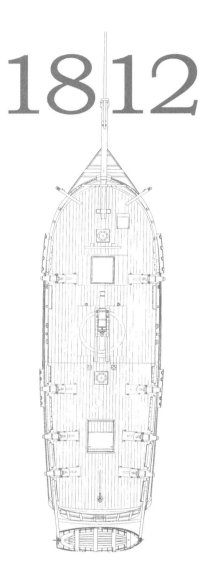

above: *The plan of the schooner Hamilton shows how perfectly these vessels were preserved.*

Location: Near Niagra, Ontario
Canada – Lake Ontario
45° 46' N, 78° 58' W
Depth: Deep (100–175ft)

The ghost schooners of the Great Lakes

During the War of 1812 (actually 1812–15) between Britain and the United States, the Great Lakes between Canada and the USA became a battleground. While small armies invaded and counter-invaded each other's territory, a bitter naval war for supremacy was fought on the lakes. Both sides converted merchant ships into warships, and started naval shipbuilding programs in a form of backwoods arms race.

The *Hamilton* was originally an American merchant schooner called the *Diana*, purchased by the US Navy in 1812; the *Scourge* was an impounded Canadian merchant schooner originally named the *Lord Nelson*. Both were topsail schooners designed to operate in Lake Ontario, the *Hamilton* being 73 feet long and the *Scourge* 57 feet in length. During the winter of 1812–13 they were refitted to carry between eight and ten carronades each. A carronade is a form of short-range gun with considerable destructive power.

In August 1813, the British and American fleets on Lake Ontario made contact with each other near Niagara, and after some maneuvering the fleets retreated and prepared for a battle on the following day. Early in the morning of August 8, a sudden squall caught the fleet, and the two schooners heeled over and capsized, sinking within minutes. It was concluded that the armament fitted to the ships made them top-heavy and vulnerable to capsizing. Of the joint complement of 61 officers and men on the two ships, 53 crewmen were lost.

In 1973, Dr Daniel Nelson was working on behalf of the Royal Ontario Museum and located the two wrecks using a magnetometer, a finding confirmed by a side-scan sonar survey two years later. The sonar images were dramatic, showing the *Hamilton* lying undisturbed and upright in 300 feet of water, her masts still intact. The *Scourge* was located a quarter of a mile away, also in near-perfect condition. Subsequent exploration of the wrecks by an unmanned submersible, or remotely operated vehicle (ROV), confirmed the identity of ships and their amazing state of preservation.

Computer-generated merchant schooners

Ownership of the vessels was transferred to the City of Hamilton, Ontario, by the US Navy, and in May 1982, the Hamilton-Scourge Foundation was established to oversee investigative work. Together with the National Geographic Society, the foundation undertook a full photographic and video survey of the two wrecks. Archæologists Ken Cassavoy and Kevin Crisman interpreted the results, producing plans that showed that, apart from the loss of cordage, the ships looked much the way they would have when they sank, preserved by the cold waters of the lake. Both lay upright, with a 16–18 percent list to port.

The *Hamilton*'s armament was still in place, and the ship's boat remained attached to the davits on her stern. Her figurehead, the goddess Diana, was well preserved on her bow, and small arms and cutlasses littered her deck. The distribution of artifacts on the deck of the *Scourge* also indicated her heeling to port as she sank. Of special interest are the cutlasses and boarding weapons, stowed ready for use toward the stern and in racks beside the guns.

In 1990 a highly publicized survey was conducted by Dr. Robert Ballard, of the Woods Hole Oceanographic Institute. He was assisted by Dr. Margaret Rule, Director of the Mary Rose Trust. The groundbreaking three-dimensional mapping project used an electronic still camera (ESC) linked to a computer to produce a high-resolution photo-mosaic of the site and a computer-generated model.

Although no human has set foot on the decks of the *Hamilton* and *Scourge* since 1813, archæologists now have detailed information about them. Their excellent condition makes the evidence produced by the video and photographic surveys of immense value to students of early 19th-century vessels. Advances in mixed-gas diving technology means that there may be a growing danger to the wrecks from attention by clandestine salvors. Further preservation measures or even archæological recovery may have to be contemplated in the near future if this unique maritime resource is to be protected.

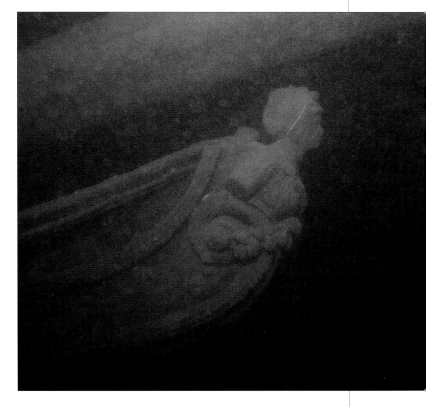

above: *The figurehead of the Hamilton is a bust of the Greek goddess Diana, reflecting the vessel's name before she saw service with the US Navy.*

below: *A carronade protrudes through the open gunport of the Hamilton as if the ship was still prepared to sail into action against the British fleet.*

Breadalbane (1853) ■

Maud (1930) ■

Titanic (1912) ■

Marco Polo (1883) ■

■ Humbolt (1853)

Lord Western (1853) ■

■ Beaver (1888)

Ericsson (1892) ■ ■ Isabella (1830)

Lucerne (1886) ■ ■ Indiana (1858)

■ Phoenix (1819)

Columbus (1850) ■

■ Andrea Doria (195

Lydia (1908) ■ ■ Sterling (1855)

King Philip (1878) ■

Modern Greece (1862) ■

■ Central America (1857

Winfield Scott (1852) ■

■ Spring of Whitby (1822)

Maria Louise (1917) ■

NORTH PACIFIC OCEAN

SOUTH PACIFIC OCEAN

SOUTH PACIFIC OCE

THE SPIRIT OF COMMERCE

While warships were extensively painted and described, merchant ships were the unsung heroes of maritime history. The small sailing ships that traversed the oceans of the world in the last century of the age of sail were soon replaced by faster steamships, but not before they had one last hurrah. The mid-19th century was the age of the clipper, perhaps the ultimate—certainly the most sublime—expression of the sailing ship that has been devised. By the late 19th century, steam had become the dominant means of propulsion and, as reliability increased, passengers used increasingly impressive steamships to cross the Atlantic. This led to the age of the transatlantic liner, typified by the beautiful lines of the *Titanic* and the *Mauritania*. Following two World Wars, the boom in commercial maritime traffic has been dramatic, and the supertankers of today are far removed from the small sailing ships of 200 years before. Even today, ships wreck, and today's maritime loss might provide tomorrow's maritime archæological information.

NORTH ATLANTIC OCEAN

NORTH ATLANTIC OCEAN

■ Titanic (1912)

Royal Charter (1857) ■

Lusitania (1915) ■

Earl of Abergavenny (1805) ■

■ Eric Nordevall (1856)

■ Hindostan (1803)

SOUTH ATLANTIC OCEAN

above: By the 1870s, commerce required reliability, and that meant adopting steam power, although for a while sails were retained as insurance against frequent mechanical failure.

Leonora (1874) ■

Falkland Island Wrecks (1853–72) ■

INDIAN OCEAN

Rapid (1811) ■

SOUTH PACIFIC OCEAN

Day Dawn (1886) ■ ■ James Matthews (1841)

William Salthouse (1841) ■ ■ Monumental City (1853)

The Spirit of Commerce

above: *The advent of fast clipper ships in the 1840s provided a chance for sail to rival the spread of steam for a brief period, and produced some of the most beautiful sailing vessels ever created. "The clipper Flying Cloud." Oil painting by an unknown painter of the American school.*

An earlier chapter traces the development of Atlantic maritime trade during the 18th century; this section of the book takes up the story on the eve of the American Revolution. It has been said that, unlike warships or the more glamorous East Indiamen, merchant ships often spent their entire working lives without attracting the interest of maritime painters or chroniclers. It is for exactly this reason that underwater archæology is able to perform an invaluable function by filling gaps in contemporary records. Although the development of merchant ships over the past 200 years is a vast subject, certain general phases can be traced.

During the late 18th century, large merchant vessels were usually ship rigged, with three masts and square-rigged sails. If we ignore the well-armed merchant ships of the various East India companies, merchant vessels carried a small armament or none at all, even in times of war. Certain maritime nations such as Britain instituted a convoy system during hostilities, probably the first example since the days of the Spanish treasure fleets. Warship escorts were even provided for whaling and fishing fleets, if they were considered at risk.

Smaller ships rarely carried guns, and while larger vessels were generally similar to one another, small vessels could be divided into numerous types. They were classified by their style of rigging, and if this changed, so would the designation of the vessel. These smaller ship types included snows, brigantines, schooners, fluyts, hoys, brigs, and barques; more varieties than can easily be listed. For example, a brigantine was a small, two-masted vessel with square sails. If she changed her sailing rig slightly, she became a snow. An example of one of these is the British vessel *Betsy*, which operated as a collier before being pressed into service as a small transport ship during the American Revolution (*see pages 166–167*). These slow, often coastal craft remained in use until the mid-19th century, when they were replaced by coastal steamships.

below: *The advent of steam meant that maritime commerce was no longer limited by the vagaries of wind and current. "Great Western riding a tidal wave, 11th December 1844." Oil painting by Joseph Walter.*

Descendants of the schooner

The schooner was a uniquely American design, although its ancestry can be traced to Dutch ships of the 17th century. The first schooners of the early 18th century had a single mast, carrying a gaff-rigged mainsail and at least one jib, identical to later cutters. By the mid-18th century, "schooner" was used to describe small, two-masted vessels, usually carrying fore-and-aft- or gaff-rigged sails and jibs. Massachusetts has been credited with the first development of the true schooner, although typical designs varied slightly in style and sail plan.

In the early 19th century, schooners and variants of them formed a major portion of the

1769	1775						
James Watt patents the steam engine.	Beginning of the American Revolution.	Date of the *Betsy* wreck, a British merchant vessel.	George Washington is made the first United States President.	The Napoleonic Wars.	Michael Faraday invents the electric generator and electric motor.	The first ever passenger railway in use, in England.	Queen Victoria is crowned.
	1781	1789	1803–15	1821	1825	1837	c.1840

above: *This mid-18th century harbor scene shows the small craft that formed the basis of the maritime trading fleets of the world. "A Danish Timber Barque." Oil painting by Samuel Scott.*

small mercantile craft operating on both sides of the Atlantic, although they remained a predominantly American design. In European waters, identical ships tended to use square sails on their mainmasts that resulted in them being classified as brigantines! The whole system of nomenclature used throughout the 18th and early 19th century was confusing and changed frequently, with several ship types overlapping.

During the 1840s, a derivative of the schooner rose to prominence. This was the clipper ship. It made a gradual appearance, its roots tracing back to the classic American schooner designs of the late 18th century. For a time, a clipper referred to any fast ship, but its use gradually became standardized. A more extensive overview of clipper development is included with the description of the remains of the American clipper *Snow Squall*, lost in 1864 (*pages 168–169*).

An early derivative was the Baltimore clipper, a schooner-type of vessel with a sharp bow and narrow hull. The great American clipper ships of the 1840s and 50s tended to be three-masted, with square-rigged sails and similar racy lines to the earlier Baltimore clippers. In Britain, tea clippers were usually larger, and the *Cutty Sark* (1869), a surviving example of a late tea clipper, used iron frames in her construction to allow increased hull space. With up to 18 square sails and eight jibs, it resembles the ultimate development of the sailing ship, although she was dwarfed by the five-masted iron sailing ship, *Preussen* (1902), of Germany. While smaller sailing craft remained in use well into the 20th century, commerce required speed and reliability, and by the 1870s this meant the adoption of steam power.

Paddle versus propeller drive

While the first steamships were developed in the late 18th century, they were used in working ships by 1807, when Robert Fulton designed steam

Navies use steam-propelled vessels.	*SS Great Britain* is the first propeller-driven craft to cross the Atlantic Ocean.	Famine in Ireland due to potato blight causes emigration to the United States.	The United States defeats New Mexico in the Mexican War.	Karl Marx issues the Communist Manifesto.	The Crimean War.	Charles Darwin publishes *The Origin of the Species*.	Ironclad warships are introduced, replacing wooden vessels.
1843	1845	1846	1848	1854–56	1859	c.1860	1861–65

vessels to carry passengers on the Hudson River. Steam ships capable of engaging in commercial trade were gradually adopted in the early 19th century, often using paddle-wheel designs. The first true propeller was only invented in 1839. By 1845, the propeller was deemed superior to the paddle wheel, although paddle wheels remained in use at sea until the late 19th century.

The first propeller-driven ship to cross the Atlantic was the *SS Great Britain* in 1843, maintaining a steady speed of 9 knots. She retained masts and sails in case of mechanical breakdown. This small craft was dwarfed 15 years later when the *SS Great Eastern* was launched, a massive iron paddle-wheel vessel of 27,000 tons (24,494 tonnes). Although capable of carrying 4,000 passengers, making her the first true liner, she was plagued by poor performance, and was used as a transatlantic cable-layer instead. Despite this costly failure, other designers attempted to create reliable passenger and cargo ships on less ambitious scales.

As late as the 1880s, masts and sails were retained on steam ships, such as the passenger ship *Oceanic*, completed in 1871, and the *City of New York*, of 1888. Cargo ships also developed steadily, although surprisingly, many retained features found on older sailing ships until the 1890s. These included a steering position far aft, raised quarter-deck, and the retention of masts and sails. Until the early 20th century, most smaller craft, such as coastal trading vessels and fishing boats, remained driven by sail rather than steam.

below: *The enormous size of the steam passenger liners of the Edwardian era offered passengers the opportunity to cross the Atlantic in unparalleled luxury. Here the Cunard liner* Mauritania *is shown berthed at the dockside.*

The American Civil War.	Date of the *Snow Squall* wreck, an American clipper.	Assassination of Abraham Lincoln.	Russia sells Alaska to the United States for $7.2 million.	The Suez Canal is completed.	Queen Victoria becomes Empress of India at the suggestion of Prime Minister Disraeli.	The Statue of Liberty arrives in New York.	The modern Olympics begin in Athens, Greece.
1864	1865	1867	1869	1877	1885	1896	1903

The age of ocean liners

The largest development in steam passenger liners came in 1899. A second *Oceanic* was launched, 704 feet long and with a displacement of 28,500 tons (25,855 tonnes), when fully loaded, making her even larger of the *Great Eastern* of 40 years earlier. She was built as a pure steamship, with no sails to provide auxiliary power. Unlike the earlier huge passenger vessel, travelers were not intimidated by her, and her elegance and style acted as a magnet. Within six years, two sister ships were produced: the *Lusitania* and *Mauritania*. The luxury liner had arrived. The

below: *The Mauritania's sister ship, the Lusitania, likewise epitomized the grace of these luxury vessels as they vied for the coveted Blue Ribbon award for the fastest Atlantic crossing.*

Mauritania was, perhaps, the most successful transatlantic liner ever and held the Blue Ribbon award for the fastest crossing by a passenger vessel for 22 years. Her fame, however, was overshadowed by the most famous liner of them all, the doomed White Star Line vessel, the *RMS Titanic* (*pages 170–171*).

Although other transatlantic liners would be built after her loss in 1912, the sinking of the *Titanic* marked the end of the era of Edwardian confidence in maritime engineering. Following the First World War, liners such as the *Normandie*, *Queen Mary*, and *Queen Elizabeth* maintained the tradition of transatlantic liners, but they never regained the glamour that had surrounded Edwardian liners. During the Second World War, British liners were used as fast troopships, and an increase in war-built shipping led to a vast increase in mostly American commercial cargo capacity.

By the 1950s, air travel was making liners obsolete, although at least until the early 1960s many preferred the lazy luxury that ships offered. Transatlantic liners like the *Rotterdam* and the *Andrea Doria* were still popular, although the sinking of the latter created a lack of confidence in sea travel (*pages 172–173*). From the 1960s onward, cargo liners, large specialist freezer ships, massive oil tankers, and container ships were crossing the oceans of the world in their thousands, making commercial maritime activity more prevalent than at any time in history. With increasing automation, accurate radar, and satellite navigation, it is little wonder that many mariners look back with nostalgia to the days of sail.

The Wright brothers make their first flight.	Date of the *RMS Titanic* wreck, a transatlantic liner.	The First World War.	Death of Vladimir Lenin.	Ibn Saud forms the kingdom of Saudi Arabia.	The first regular television broadcasts.	Second World War; English liners brought into service as supply ships.	Date of the *Andrea Dorea* wreck, a transatlantic liner.
1912	1914–18	1924	1932	1936	1939–45	1956	

THE BETSY

1781

Earl Cornwallis' supply ship

above: *"The Siege of Yorktown 1781."*
The American commander George Washington and his staff view the York river prior to the defenses being taken. The masts of the scuttled British fleet—one of which would have been the Betsy—are clearly seen in the background.

Location: Off Yorktown, Virginia
USA – York River
37° 18′ N, 76° 42′ W
Depth: Shallow (0–30ft)

By 1781, Britain's struggle to contain the rebels in her American colonies had reached an impasse. After a spectacular but indecisive campaign in the Carolinas, Charles, Earl Cornwallis, moved his small British army into Virginia to link up with reinforcements. Instead, he found himself besieged at Yorktown, penned in by a larger French and American army under George Washington. By mid-September, Cornwallis concluded that further resistance was futile, and he surrendered on October 17, 1781. The disaster helped to force the British government to end the war, and peace was signed less than two years later.

During the siege a number of small British merchant ships and transports were trapped in the York river. These vessels were scuttled just before the surrender but their location was never recorded. In 1978, an underwater survey of the river near Yorktown revealed the resting place of six wrecks, one being the small warship *HMS Fowey*, the remainder small merchant vessels, all dating to the siege. A trial excavation was conducted at each of the six sites to determine preservation and suitability for a larger investigation. One of these, a merchant brig tagged "YO88" by the archæologists, was earmarked to be the subject of a full-scale excavation

The wreck was situated about 500 feet off the shore, in an area swept by strong currents. Underwater visibility was less than two feet), so a method was sought to improve conditions and protect the site during excavation. The solution was to construct a metal cofferdam around the

wreck, joined to the shore by a pier. Unlike the cofferdam used in the excavation of the Skudelev ships (*pages 70–71*), this one contained water, filtered through sand to improve visibility. Soon after its completion in the summer of 1982, underwater visibility improved until the archæologists could see 25 feet or more. As with the excavation of the *Amsterdam* (*pages 130–131*), the cofferdam was also used as a plotting tool, providing fixed datum points for measurements.

Collier serves a Foot regiment

The operation, known as The Yorktown Shipwreck Archæological Project, was funded by the Virginia Department of Historic Resources. The excavation was conducted between 1982 and 1986 under the direction of maritime archæologist John D. Broadwater, who overcame myriad technical and logistical problems with apparent ease. The result was a thorough survey of the small vessel and a better understanding of the use of shipping during the final days of the siege.

The preserved remains of the brig were 72 feet long, which gave her an estimated displacement of just over 176 tons (160 tonnes). She had a squat appearance with a broad, flat bottom and a bluff bow. Her timbers were white oak, and her construction was extremely simple and workmanlike, although solid, with a heavily reinforced bow. Her hull was designed for maximum cargo capacity; it was concluded that she was once a collier.

Archival research revealed that she was the *Betsy*, a collier built in Whitehaven, northern England, in 1772. She sailed between England and Ireland carrying coal until leased to the Navy in 1780 as a victualing (supply) boat. She was sent to America, only to be trapped with Cornwallis at Yorktown. Documentary evidence records that all the British merchant vessels at Yorktown were scuttled immediately before the surrender.

The wreck of the *Betsy* showed that a hole was cut into her starboard side below the waterline. As she had been scuttled, the archæologists did not expect to find any artifacts, but a handful of British uniform buttons from the 43rd Regiment of Foot were present. This regiment had been transported to America in three ships, one of which was the *Betsy*. The remains of furniture found in the stern cabin area included fragments of chairs, tables, and dressers.

The excavation of the *Betsy* has given us a better understanding of the thousands of small, unsung, and unremarkable craft that plied the waters of the world in the late 18th century, and whose passing went unrecorded in history books.

above: *Yorktown 1781. One of Virginia's busiest ports during the first half of the 18th century, Yorktown began to decline in commercial importance after 1750. The siege hastened the town's decline.*

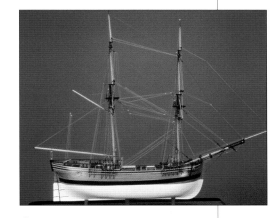

above: *This model of the Betsy is from a collection belonging to John Broadwater, head of the expedition that excavated the ship from its watery grave.*

below: *The British forces needed to block the French fleet from sailing up the York river to attack the town. Supply vessels such as the Betsy were holed below the waterline and set in position to prevent this crisis arising.*

SNOW SQUALL

1864 The last American clipper ship

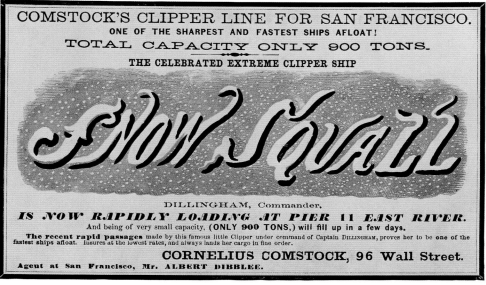

COMSTOCK'S CLIPPER LINE FOR SAN FRANCISCO.
ONE OF THE SHARPEST AND FASTEST SHIPS AFLOAT!
TOTAL CAPACITY ONLY 900 TONS.
THE CELEBRATED EXTREME CLIPPER SHIP

SNOW SQUALL

DILLINGHAM, Commander,
IS NOW RAPIDLY LOADING AT PIER 11 EAST RIVER.
And being of very small capacity, (ONLY 900 TONS,) will fill up in a few days.
The recent rapid passages made by this famous little Clipper under command of Captain DILLINGHAM, proves her to be one of the fastest ships afloat. Insures at the lowest rates, and always lands her cargo in fine order.
CORNELIUS COMSTOCK, 96 Wall Street.
Agent at San Francisco, Mr. ALBERT DIBBLEE.

above: *A Clipper Card announces the departure of the Snow Squall from New York on one of her voyages in the 1850s. Clippers provided the fastest means of transportation from one side of the United States to the other.*

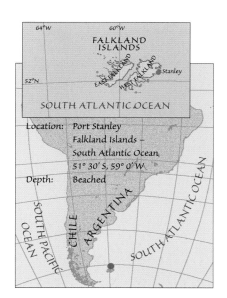

FALKLAND ISLANDS
Stanley
SOUTH ATLANTIC OCEAN

Location: Port Stanley
Falkland Islands –
South Atlantic Ocean
51° 30' S, 59° 0' W
Depth: Beached

The clipper was seen as the ultimate development of the sailing ship—many believe it to be the most beautiful type of ship ever constructed. The name was often applied to any fast ship, but by the mid-19th century "clipper" normally referred to a specific group of craft, with a specific appearance. Clippers had slender hulls in proportion to their length, with slim, heavily raked bows. They were designed to carry the maximum possible amount of sail for their size, and the name became synonymous with speed.

Common styles of these vessels included the tea (or China) clipper, the American (or Californian) clipper, and even the coffee or opium clipper. Of these, the first two types were the most common, being ship-rigged craft with an emphasis on speed rather than cargo capacity. "Extreme clippers" were the ultimate development of fast, low-capacity ships. American clippers became famous during the Californian Gold Rush, where a good clipper could make the journey from New York to San Francisco in under three months. The American clipper era only extended from around 1845 to 1859; few were launched before 1850 and few were built after 1857.

Britain is fortunate enough to have a surviving example of a tea clipper, the *Cutty Sark*. Unfortunately, the American clipper was not preserved, and precise details of its construction, or even the materials used to build it, were believed unavailable. While there were many of these ships that regularly sped between America and China or Australia, it was thought that there was no surviving example. Then, in the 1970s, maritime historians discovered the remains of an American clipper called the *Snow Squall* near the Falkland Islands, in the South Atlantic.

Extreme career

Research revealed that this last American clipper had a remarkable career. The *Snow Squall* was an extreme clipper built in 1851 by shipbuilder

Alfred Butler, at Cape Elizabeth, Maine. She was 157 feet long, with a beam of 32 feet and a displacement of 742 tons (673 tonnes). Her owner, Charles Green of New York, used her to make regular sailings between San Francisco, Shanghai, and New York, with occasional detours to London or Sydney. She was badly damaged by a collision in 1857, but was repaired.

When the American Civil War broke out in 1861, the *Snow Squall* continued her runs between New York and the Far East—in 1862 she was even chased by a Confederate raider. In January 1864 she left New York, bound for San Francisco, but she ran aground in the Straits of La Marie, near Cape Horn. She freed herself and limped back to the Falkland Islands, leaking badly. Her cargo was landed in Port Stanley, but her hull was beyond repair, and she was condemned.

The cold air of the South Atlantic preserved the *Snow Squall* from decay. She was identified in the 1970s, but it was only after the Falklands War (1982) that she was examined. Five expeditions between 1982 and 1987 resulted in the forward 35 feet of her bow being surveyed and excavated by the Peabody Museum, of Massachusetts. Her stern was incorporated into the stonework of a jetty, and was deemed beyond recovery.

Divers attached lifting chains around her hull in 1987 and then removed the rotten midships section and floated the bow into a cradle. The remains of the *Snow Squall* were transported back to Maine, where the Spring Point Museum took responsibility for its continued preservation and display. By 1995 the museum found the conservation costs were too much, and the *Snow Squall* was moved to the Maine Maritime Museum in Bath.

A study of the vessel's construction revealed that ten species of wood were used in her construction, and a copper/zinc alloy was used to protect her lower hull. The remains of the *Snow Squall* have acted as a catalyst for research into the American clipper, and provide a tangible reminder of the romance of the last days of sail.

below: *The remains of the Snow Squall rotted on a beach at the Falkland Islands until maritime preservationists rescued her from further decay.*

RMS Titanic

1912

The rediscovery of the world's most famous shipwreck

above: *The Titanic left Southampton on her maiden voyage in April 1912, bound for New York, via Cherbourg in France and Queenstown in Ireland.*

below right: *The ghostly bow of the Titanic looms out of the darkness 13,000 feet below the surface of the Atlantic Ocean.*

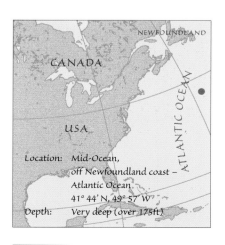

Location: Mid-Ocean,
  off Newfoundland coast –
  Atlantic Ocean
  41° 44' N, 49° 57' W
Depth: Very deep (over 175ft)

The story of the loss of the "unsinkable" liner and the human tragedy surrounding it has been told and retold. However, details of her rediscovery and subsequent salvage, although widely publicized at the time, have received only transitory fame.

The *Titanic* was built by Harland and Wolf for the White Star Line. On April 10, 1912, she left Liverpool on her maiden voyage, bound for New York. Four days later, she was within a day's sail of her destination when she received warning of icebergs ahead. Just before midnight on April 14, she struck an iceberg that ripped a large gash in her starboard hull. Almost two hours later, she sank, taking 1,490 passengers and crew with her.

The loss of the *Titanic* came to symbolize the end of the confident Victorian and Edwardian eras; almost a prelude to the catastrophic trauma created by the First World War. For almost 70 years, the wreck was too deep to find, lying 13,000 feet, or almost 2½ miles, beneath the surface of the Atlantic.

With technological developments in deep-diving, remotely operated vehicles (ROVs) and sonar equipment, it was inevitable that the *Titanic* would become the focus of a deep-sea search. In 1985, Dr. Robert Ballard of the Woods Hole Oceanographic Institution led an expedition to relocate the ship, in association with Jean-Louis Michel of the Institut Français de Recherches pour l'Exploration des Mers (IFREMER). The team found the *Titanic* on September 1 using a towed side-scan sonar array, and the discovery was revealed amid worldwide media attention.

Video images supplied by the ROV *Jason Jr.* provided evidence of how the liner broke up, and of her surprisingly good state of preservation. Eyewitness accounts report that the *Titanic* broke in half just before she sank, and when the wreck was located, it was in two sections. Video cameras also revealed a narrow, intermittent gash in her side, presumably the damage created by the iceberg.

Salvors' legal battle

Robert Ballard returned to the site in 1986 to conduct a more thorough survey of the wreck and the debris field surrounding it. Ballard vowed to keep the location of the *Titanic* a secret and was totally opposed to her disturbance. He wrote of the wreck, "It is quiet and peaceful, and a fitting place for the remains of this greatest of sea tragedies to rest. May it forever remain this way, and may God bless these new-found souls." He was not to have his way.

In a highly controversial move, a commercial salvage organization located the wreck and recovered over 300 artifacts from the debris field surrounding the *Titanic*'s last resting place. They were assisted by IFREMER, the French research group who had helped Ballard to find the wreck. Two salvage companies, Marex Titanic, Inc. and Titanic Ventures, Inc., became involved in litigation over ownership of the site. RMS Titanic Ltd., an offshoot of the latter company who were involved in the recovery of the objects, were deemed "Salvor in Possession." This gave them the exclusive legal right to recover what they wanted from the wreck.

As the *Titanic* lay in international waters, there was little that Ballard, national governments, or public opinion could do about it. It is ironic that Ballard, as the original finder of the site, was legally able to apply for its ownership. He chose not to do so, believing that salvors would honor the sanctity of the wreck.

RMS Titanic Ltd. organized several more expeditions to the site, in 1993, 1994, and 1996. Each expedition resulted in the raising of more artifacts, and these were conserved and researched, and then the company displayed them. First shown in the National Maritime Museum in London, this collection now forms the centerpiece of a traveling *Titanic* exhibition.

A recent expedition to recover a portion of the hull failed, but whatever the future holds for the wreck of the *Titanic*, it seems unlikely that the publicity surrounding her will go away, or that her remains will be left in peace.

above: *A story of hubris—the "unsinkable" Titanic foundered in under two hours and due to the lack of sufficient lifeboats almost 1,500 souls lost their lives in the icy Atlantic wastes.*

below: *Since 1985 repeated visits by remotely operated submersibles to the wreck have resulted in some decay to the surviving structure of the liner.*

left: *Many areas of the upper superstructure and weather decks of the Titanic were undamaged during her sinking.*

ANDREA DORIA

1956

The sinking of one of the last passenger liners

The *Andrea Doria* was one of the last great transatlantic passenger liners. By 1956, the increasing speed and convenience of air travel was putting such ships out of business. Despite this, many preferred the more sedate transit offered by liners, and over 1,700 people were aboard the *Andrea Doria* when she sailed for New York.

She was built in the Ansaldo shipyard in Genoa, northern Italy, and named after a famous Genoan naval commander of the mid-16th century. The vessel was owned by the Italia Line, whose green, white, and red colors were painted on the ship's funnel. The company fitted out the 656-foot long liner with all the luxuries required on a transatlantic voyage: dining rooms, lounges, ballrooms, cinemas, and swimming pools.

The *Andrea Doria* was only four years old in 1956, and was then regarded as the last word in modern ship design. Like the *Titanic* of over 40 years earlier, she was divided into three classes; on her last voyage she carried 190 first-class passengers, along with 267 cabin class, and 677 tourist class travelers. The rich preferred the luxury of a liner to air travel, and to the poor immigrants in the lower decks, sea travel was the cheapest way to reach America.

She left Genoa on April 17, 1956, bound for New York, and after stops in Cannes and Gibraltar, she headed out into the Atlantic. The passengers and crew quickly settled into a shipboard routine. On the night of July 25, the *Andrea Doria* was a day away from New York. She ran into a fog bank off the coast of Nantucket and Captain Calamai reduced her speed by a fraction. Fog is a common feature of the Nantucket coast, where the warm Gulf Stream meets colder waters moving south from Labrador. The liner was equipped with the latest radar device, and there seemed little cause for concern.

An inexplicable, fatal error

At 10:45pm, another vessel was picked up on the radar, heading on a reciprocal course. At 10:55, the two ships were only seven miles apart, and closing at the rate of almost a mile a minute. Shortly after 11:03, the ships sighted each other. The other vessel was the *Stockholm*, a liner of the Swedish-American Line, and, sensing the danger, it altered course to starboard to avoid a collision. The maritime rules of the road say that in these situations, both ships should turn to starboard. Inexplicably, Captain Calamai turned his liner to port, directly into the path of the oncoming *Stockholm*.

above: *The ship's bell of the Andrea Doria was recovered by salvors in 1985.*

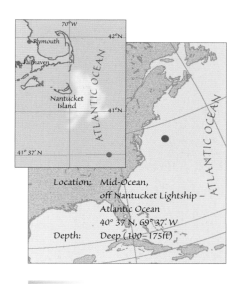

Location: Mid-Ocean,
off Nantucket Lightship –
Atlantic Ocean
40° 37 N, 69° 37' W
Depth: Deep (100–175ft)

At 11:10pm, the bow of the *Stockholm* smashed through the side of the *Andrea Doria*, killing over 50 passengers and crew. The damage proved fatal, and the surviving passengers and crew took to the lifeboats. As other ships arrived on the scene, including the French liner *Île de France*, the *Stockholm* limped back to port. Early in the morning of July 26, the Italian liner rolled over and sank in 240 feet of water. Apart from those killed in the collision, all her passengers and crew were rescued.

Her designers claimed that the *Andrea Doria* was unsinkable. Although only one of her 11 watertight bulkheads was breached in the collision, they only extended a little above her waterline. The liner's ballast tanks were only partly full, and once breached they allowed seawater to enter. The *Andrea Doria* listed heavily to starboard, which allowed water to creep above the bulkheads, and she filled one compartment at a time.

In 1956 the upper superstructure lay just within reach of divers, and immediately after the sinking they photographed her for the newspapers. One of these divers, Peter Gimbel, became convinced that there was a fortune to be had in jewels and gold, secured in the liner's safe. He organized an expedition in 1985 to locate and recover the safe. Under the gaze of millions of live television viewers, it was retrieved and opened. All it contained was exceedingly damp paper money.

below: *A diver pushes the limits of safe diving as he examines the bell of the liner, partly hidden by marine growth.*

ROBERT BALLARD
Undersea Explorer

Dr. Robert Ballard harnessed the deep diving potential of the US Navy to study the scientific and archæological mysteries of the deep waters beyond the reach of divers. His discovery of the Titanic in 1985 caught the attention of the world and demonstrated the potential of deep-water wrecks.

Robert Ballard was always fascinated by the sea. As a boy in southern California, he scrutinized sea creatures on the beaches of the Pacific coast, and as a teenager he learned scuba diving to see more. He attended the University of California, where he studied geology and chemistry, then the University of Hawaii, where he performed postgraduate work in marine geology. In 1967 he joined the US Navy as a scientist and was assigned to the Deep Submergence Laboratory at Woods Hole Oceanographic Institution, Massachusetts.

Over the following 30 years, Ballard participated in and then led over 65 underwater expeditions, many of them involving the use of deep-water equipment, including manned submersibles, remote-operated vehicles, underwater laboratories, and even the US Navy's research submarine. In 1973–4 he explored the Mid-Atlantic Ridge, a mountain range in the middle of the Atlantic Ocean. Ballard then earned a doctorate in marine geophysics from the University of Rhode Island; his field of research was plate tectonics.

Research over the following decade confirmed his theories through several unique discoveries. In 1977, near the Galapagos Islands off the Pacific coast of South America, Dr. Ballard and his research team discovered giant worms clustered around hot underwater geysers. Two years later, he found "smokers" off the coast of California—underwater volcanoes that spewed hot liquid.

Dr. Ballard and a Woods Hole team worked in conjunction with a French group in 1985 to search for the wreck of the *Titanic*. It was located and explored by submersibles, and the photographs from the project captured the imagination of the whole world. Ballard even designed a robot, the Jason Jr., to enter the *Titanic* and photograph its interior, and he returned the following year to conduct a more extensive survey. Ballard was opposed to commercial exploitation of the wreck and he was deeply upset when objects were recovered by a salvage company soon afterward.

The *Titanic* expedition peaked Ballard's interest in the deep water exploration of shipwrecks, and further expeditions were mounted to discover and survey the last resting places of the German battleship *Bismark* (1941), the *Lusitania* liner (1917), and the Japanese and American warships

above: *Dr. Robert Ballard has undertaken many deep sea expeditions, pushing modern technology to its limits in the quest for knowledge of what lies at the bottom of the deepest oceans.*

below: *A remotely operated vehicle (ROV) examines the forecastle of the Titanic, revealing that her anchor cables and winches are still in place.*

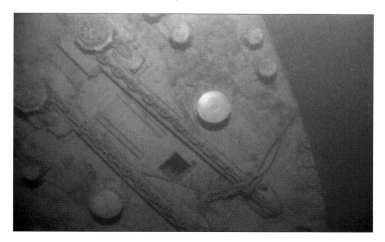

above: *From the depths of the Atlantic, Ballard's crew take a picture of the Titanic where she lies on the Atlantic sea bed. Here, the deck of the bow is clearly visible, complete with anchor moorings.*

top right: *Ballard (seated) helps the "pilot" Dudley Foster to operate a small manned submersible during the investigation of the Titanic in 1986.*

sunk in the battle off Guadalcanal (1942) that gave the "Ironbottom Sound" waters their nickname.

JASON's legion of projects

The potential of submersibles was still to be tested in archæological work, so he organized the JASON Project, a scheme to allow thousands of students to link up with the survey team by satellite, and share in the excitement of the work. *Jason* was also the name of the manned submersible used in the operation. In 1989, Dr. Ballard initiated the project by following ancient trade routes in the Mediterranean Sea, where he discovered and surveyed the remains of a Roman merchant vessel in the process. In the following year, the JASON II Project moved to the waters of the Great Lakes. Ballard and his crew used the submersible to investigate the wrecks of the *Hamilton* and *Scourge*, naval schooners that sank during the War of 1812.

In 1991, Ballard's team and a scientific crew returned to the Galapagos Islands for the JASON III Project, exploring them above and below water. The JASON IV led the research team to study hydrothermal vents the next year, while JASON V explored the waters off Belize. JASONs VI and VII focused on the waters of Hawaii and the Florida Keys respectively. The latter involved work on shipwrecks and the latest expedition is studying geysers in America and Iceland. Each of these involved linking the research team with schoolchildren via satellite. The project is expected to continue into the new millennium.

Dr. Robert Ballard is the author of many books that describe his explorations, he has received numerous awards, and he frequently appears on television. His lasting contribution to the study of historic shipwrecks is proof that deep-water technology can be used effectively to conduct archæological investigation. He has also imbued millions of adults and children with a respect for the past, for the sanctity of shipwrecks, and the value of the information they contain.

below: The story of naval warfare in the 20th century was the building of ever-more powerful ships in artillery, armor, and speed, culminating in the super-dreadnoughts, which were designed to rule the seas.

NORTH PACIFIC OCEAN

NORTH ATLANTIC OCEAN

USS Monitor (1862)
HL Hunley (1864)
CSS Georgia (1864)
HMS Vixen (1896)
USS Techumseh (1864)
USS Massachusetts (1921)

Midway Wrecks (1942)

The Santiago Wrecks (1898)

I-52 (1944)

Pearl Harbor Wrecks (1941)
USS Arizona & USS Utah

A WORLD AT WAR

SOUTH PACIFIC OCEAN

SOUTH ATLANTIC OCEAN

Graf Spee (1939)

Coronel Wrecks (1914)

Falkland Wrecks (1914)

While the sailing warships of the age of fighting sail changed very little in 150 years, in the 80 years following 1862 warships underwent a revolution. During that time, warships doubled in size, then doubled again. At the start of the 20th century, a new type of capital ship was designed, faster and more powerful than anything else afloat. By the start of the First World War, these vessels had developed into the battleships that would remain in service throughout the Second World War. The supremacy of the battleship was challenged by the torpedo, an equalizer that allowed small ships to challenge large ones. It also provided a weapon for the newly invented submarine, which was to change naval warfare significantly. Although not everyone admitted it, by the start of the Second World War, aircraft and submarines were to decide the outcome of the naval conflict. In a mere 80 years, the developments in naval warfare were staggering, from ironclad to aircraft carrier and beyond. Here this development is traced by looking at a group of shipwrecks, all with their own unique place in this naval revolution.

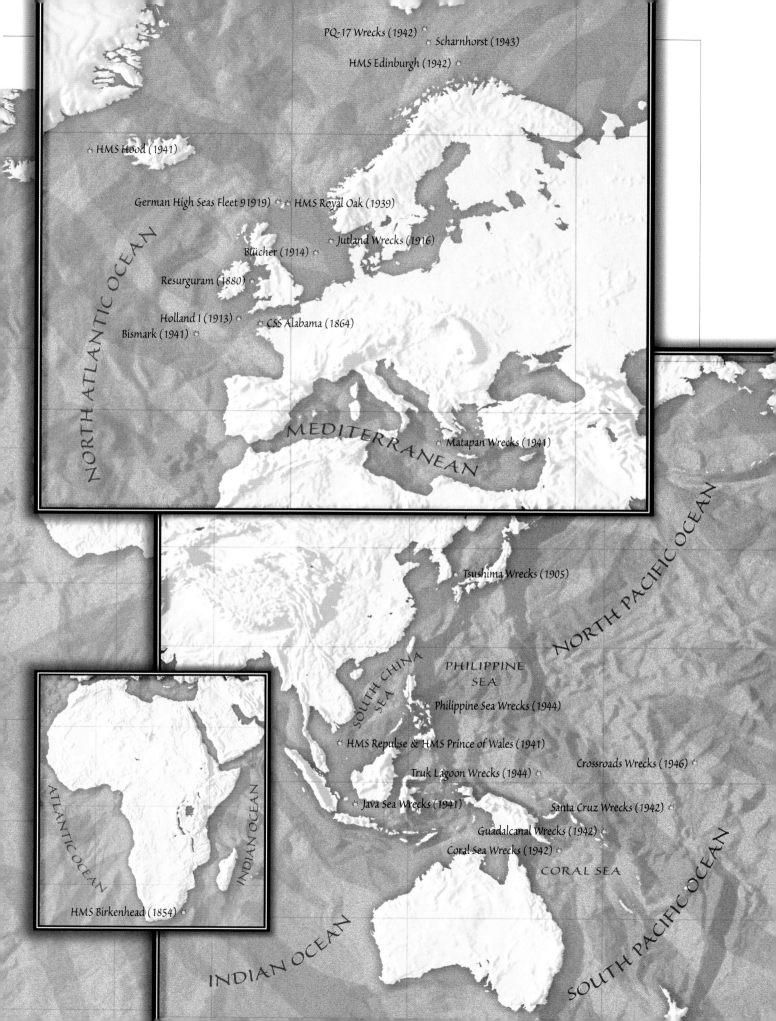

PQ-17 Wrecks (1942)
Scharnhorst (1943)
HMS Edinburgh (1942)

HMS Hood (1941)

German High Seas Fleet 91919)   HMS Royal Oak (1939)

Jutland Wrecks (1916)
Blücher (1914)
Resurguram (1880)
Holland 1 (1913)   CSS Alabama (1864)
Bismark (1941)

NORTH ATLANTIC OCEAN

MEDITERRANEAN
Matapan Wrecks (1941)

NORTH PACIFIC OCEAN

Tsushima Wrecks (1905)

SOUTH CHINA SEA   PHILIPPINE SEA

Philippine Sea Wrecks (1944)

HMS Repulse & HMS Prince of Wales (1941)
Truk Lagoon Wrecks (1944)   Crossroads Wrecks (1946)
Java Sea Wrecks (1941)   Santa Cruz Wrecks (1942)
Guadalcanal Wrecks (1942)
Coral Sea Wrecks (1942)
CORAL SEA

SOUTH PACIFIC OCEAN

ATLANTIC OCEAN   INDIAN OCEAN

HMS Birkenhead (1854)

INDIAN OCEAN

A World at War

above: *Officers of the USS Monitor pose for a photograph after her battle with the CSS Virginia in March 1862. The engagement revolutionized naval warfare.*

By March 1862, the United States of America had been locked in her bitterly fought Civil War for almost a year. A Union naval blockade of Confederate ports caused extreme hardship for the South, and naval designers were asked to find a way to break through. The solution was the ironclad, personified by the *CSS Virginia*.

On March 8, she sortied from Norfolk, Virginia, and caused severe damage to the waiting steam-powered wooden warships of the Union Navy. Her iron sides were impervious to the shots of the Northern ships, and she returned the following day to continue the destruction. Instead, the *Virginia* met another ironclad, the turret ship *USS Monitor* (*see pages 182–183*). Although inconclusive, the battle revolutionized naval warfare. From then on, iron- or steel-clad vessels would be the standard type of warship—wooden-hulled ships instantly became obsolete.

Ironclad warships formed the backbone of the world's major navies by the 1870s; the naval battle of Lissa (1866), fought between the fleets of Italy and Austro-Hungarian Empire, had showed the power of these new vessels. Over the next 20 years, ironclad warships grew in size and performance, although gun technology was slower to develop than the application of armored protection.

New steel production processes meant that armor was increasingly efficient at stopping shells, but the extra protection increased the weight of ships, and engine improvements could barely keep up. Armor tended to be concentrated where it would be most useful, to protect the gun turrets, engine rooms, and ammunition magazines, while less important areas were often left unprotected. This armor was often concentrated in a belt that protected the vital areas. Decks were usually left unprotected, as was the superstructure of an armored warship.

The Dreadnought blueprint of naval supremacy

Offensively, warships were only as effective as their guns. As late as the 1880s, most navies still used muzzle-loading guns, some as large as 80 or 100 tons, capable of firing massive shells. Reloading was a problem, so breech-loading guns were introduced to most new warships by 1890.

At first, ironclad warships carried their guns in a variety of ways. While the *Monitor* was a turreted vessel, the *Virginia* carried her guns in a casemated hull. Turrets were not universally adopted, and casemate mountings were replaced by central batteries that incorporated an armored "citadel" and guns with limited traversing ability.

By the 1890s the turret had become the standard form of gun mounting. The guns themselves were also changing, and gunnery systems were becoming increasingly complex, with accuracy improved by visual range finders. Modern breech-loaders capable of firing 11- or 12-inch

1854–56	1854	1856	c.1860	1861–65	1862	1869	1870–71
The Crimean War.	English cavalry wiped out in the charge of the Light Brigade.	Louis Pasteur demonstrates that disease is spread by germs.	Ironclad warships are introduced, replacing wooden vessels.	The American Civil War.	Date of the *USS Monitor* wreck, an ironclad warship.	Leo Tolstoy publishes *War and Peace.*	The Franco-Prussian War.

diameter shells were mounted in the world's largest battleships.

During the Spanish-American War of 1898, the damage wrought by the American battleships' guns was particularly devastating. In the naval engagement of Santiago (July 3, 1898), a Spanish fleet including modern cruisers such as the *Cristobal Colon* was reduced to flaming wrecks in little over an hour (*pages 184–185*). Similarly, during the Russo-Japanese war of 1904–5, the Japanese fleet annihilated their Russian opponents in an impressive demonstration of the art of naval gunnery. The power of turn-of-the-century warship armament was ably demonstrated, and naval designers realized that speed and armor were lagging behind armament technology.

British naval designers produced an entirely new type of warship in October, 1906. *HMS Dreadnought* gave her name to an entire ship type, the heavily armed and armored battleships of the First World War. The *Dreadnought* was a revolutionary vessel, and like the *Monitor* before her, she made all existing warships obsolete. She carried ten immense 12-inch guns, mounted in five twin turrets. An armored belt protected her bridge, lower hull, and turrets could resist all but the most powerful shells.

Two further developments made *HMS Dreadnought* extraordinary. A new optical range finder allowed her main guns to be aimed accurately. She could steam at 21 knots and had a large coal capacity. The *Dreadnought* was able to outpace, outshoot, and outclass all other warships.

above: *Unrestricted submarine attacks widened the scope of naval warfare in the 20th century. "The San Demetrio, 5th November 1940." Oil painting by Norman Wilkinson.*

below: *The large steam ironclads of the mid-18th century still retained masts and sails for reasons of economy and cleanliness. "The turret ship HMS Captain." Oil painting by Demenico.*

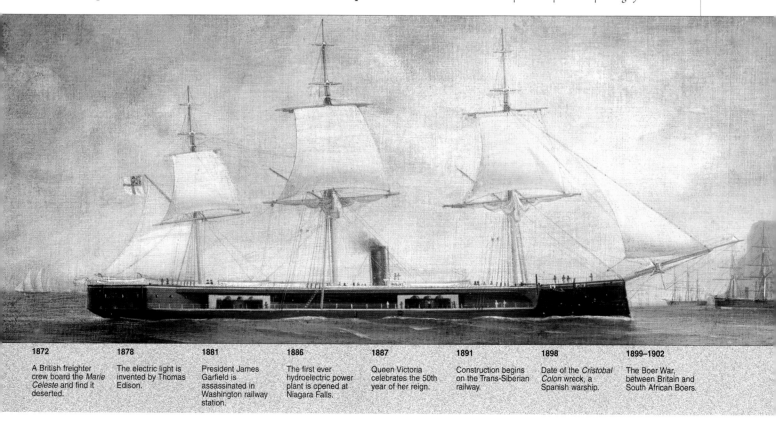

1872	1878	1881	1886	1887	1891	1898	1899–1902
A British freighter crew board the *Marie Celeste* and find it deserted.	The electric light is invented by Thomas Edison.	President James Garfield is assassinated in Washington railway station.	The first ever hydroelectric power plant is opened at Niagara Falls.	Queen Victoria celebrates the 50th year of her reign.	Construction begins on the Trans-Siberian railway.	Date of the *Cristobal Colon* wreck, a Spanish warship.	The Boer War, between Britain and South African Boers.

A World at War

The underdogs strike back

Other countries quickly followed Britain's lead—a German dreadnought was launched in 1907, and America was not far behind. By the outbreak of the First World War in 1914, the *Dreadnought* was already considered obsolete, and the British navy had 20 dreadnought or super-dreadnought vessels against Germany's 15 such ships.

Employing greater armor and large guns, super dreadnoughts were a development of the dreadnought, but still maintained a high speed. For example, the super-dreadnought battleship *HMS Iron Duke* carried ten 13.5-inch guns, larger weapons than anything afloat during the war. German super-dreadnoughts favored slightly smaller guns but employed better protection (*pages 186–187*).

Battleships weren't the only naval ship type. Cruisers were used as scout ships; battlecruisers were a hybrid design that combined the armament of battleships with the speed of cruisers at the expense of armor. Other comparatively new warship types were the destroyer and the submarine, both designed to use torpedoes.

Originally, a torpedo was an underwater explosive charge, often tethered to a stake, with a contact mechanism—Admiral Farragut's Civil War quote "Damn the torpedoes" referred to these early mines. The true torpedo was designed in the 1880s, and its first delivery system was the torpedo boat, small, fast craft that could dart in, fire at enemy capital ships, then speed away. This was unsettling for late 19th century major naval powers, such as Britain—small ships from small navies could now attack large ships. The answer was to produce the torpedo boat destroyer, a slightly larger vessel, equipped with rapid-firing guns, that could protect the capital ships from attack by torpedo boats.

By the time of the First World War, torpedo boats and destroyers were beginning to merge into one ship class, with a combined role. In a naval battle, it was envisaged that destroyer screens would clash, and the victorious side would press on to attack the enemy capital ships. Of course, while getting within torpedo range of a target, the attacking destroyer would bear the full brunt of the larger vessel's firepower. One hit could blow a destroyer out of the water, so a more stealthy approach was considered less costly.

Stealth craft of the seas

The stealth vehicle was the submarine. Early submarines were extremely limited in their range, endurance, and ability, but then anti-submarine tactics were also in their infancy. During the First World War, submarines came into their own, and German U-boats caused severe disruption to the

below: *The First World War marked the heyday of the battleship in naval warfare.*
"The Fifth Battle Squadron at the Battle of Jutland, 31st May, 1916." Oil painting by Arthur Douglas Wales-Smith.

1900	1904-5	1910	1911	1914–18	1915	1916	1919
The Commonwealth of Australia is established.	Japan wins the Russo-Japanese War.	Korea is annexed by Japan.	The Manchu dynasty is overthrown and the Chinese Republic formed.	The First World War.	A German U-boat sinks the *Lusitania*.	Albert Einstein publishes his *General Theoery of Relativity*.	Date of the High Seas fleet wrecks, German warships.

Allied war effort, and inadvertently brought the United States into the Allied camp when a U-boat sank the *Lusitania* in 1915.

In the period between the World Wars, both airpower and submarines were growing in ascendancy, although the old battleship advocates refused to relinquish their position at the pinnacle of the naval hierarchy. Experiments with carrier-borne aircraft at the tail end of the First World War resulted in the first true aircraft carriers, and when a second war broke out in September 1939, their abilities were demonstrated.

Germany was unable to build a fleet strong enough to protect carriers, and hence could not rival British control of seapower. Instead, it placed its emphasis on U-boats, and the substantial German fleet almost brought Britain to her knees through unacceptably high mercantile losses. Anti-submarine combat was an unspectacular but vital form of warfare, and Germany's strategic use of submarines was her only real naval tool in the Second World War.

Two actions in the early war years forced the advocates of battleships to finally sit up and take notice. The sinking of the British battleship *Royal Oak* in her home port by a German U-boat showed just how vulnerable capital ships were to torpedo attack (*pages 188–189*). In 1940, the British raid on Taranto in Italy by carrier-borne bi-planes resulted in the sinking or crippling of several Italian battleships. Naval warfare would be dominated by aircraft and submarines for the rest of the century.

The lesson was absorbed too slowly by American admirals to save them learning the hard way at Pearl Harbor. It is difficult to believe that the Japanese raid came a mere 80 years after the duel between the *Virginia* and the *Monitor*. As America was plunged into the horrors of a new World War, few had time to marvel at the progress of the revolution that had transformed naval warfare.

above: *A Royal Sovereign-class battleship of the British Royal Navy at anchor at the start of the Second World War. Aircraft and submarines would soon end the dominance of the battleship.*

1922	1929	1931	1936	1939–45	1939	1941	1943
Bolsheviks form the USSR. Benito Mussolini comes to power in Italy.	The Great Depression begins when Wall Street stock exchange crashes.	The Empire State Building is opened by President Hoover.	R. Watson-Watt and A.F. Wilkins invent radar in England.	Second World War; English liners brought into service as supply ships.	Date of the HMS Royal Oak wreck, a British warship.	The Japanese attack United States' vessels at Pearl Harbor.	French diver Jacques Cousteau invents the Aqua-lung.

USS MONITOR

1862 The ironclad remains of a revolutionary warship

The Confederate ironclad *CSS Virginia* steamed out of Norfolk, Virginia, on March 9, 1862, to do battle with the Union fleet. The *USS Monitor* was waiting for her, and the ensuing duel was the first battle between ironclads, one of the most famous engagements of the American Civil War.

The *Virginia* resembled an upturned bathtub, her iron superstructure pierced with gunports. The *Monitor* looked like a "cheesebox on a raft," the box being the turret that housed her two 11-inch guns. The ironclads battled for four hours, but the engagement ended in stalemate. Overnight, the wooden warship had become obsolete, and ironclad ships would form the backbone of the world's navies.

The *USS Monitor* was the prototype for a fleet of ironclad turret ships, designed and built by Swedish-born inventor John Ericsson. She was commissioned at the Brooklyn Navy Yard barely two weeks before her battle with the *CSS Virginia* (often erroneously referred to by her former name, the *Merrimac*).

The *Monitor's* hull was almost completely submerged, with no superstructure except the turret and a pilot house. Her hull was iron, although portions such as the lower hull and deck were constructed from wood covered with iron armor-plating. Her most innovative feature was her turret, the two smoothbore Dahlgren guns sited in tandem inside the circular armor-plated turret. A traversing mechanism allowed the turret to train slowly, although poor visibility meant that aiming was difficult. The guns were drawn into the turret to reload, and the gun aperture covered by an armored mantelet.

After the battle, both sides seemed wary to renew the conflict. The *USS Monitor* never saw action again. Two months after the battle, Norfolk was attacked by the Union and the *Virginia* was destroyed to prevent her falling into enemy hands. For the rest of 1862, the *Monitor* cruised the James river in support of the Union Army's peninsular campaign.

On the brink of collapse

In late December 1862 the *Monitor* was ordered to Charleston, South Carolina. While being towed south, she was caught in a storm off Cape Hatteras. The ironclad was swamped and sank at 1:30am on December 31.

Location: Off Cape Hatteras, N. Carolina
USA – Atlantic Ocean
35° 14' N, 75° 12' W
Depth: Deep (100–175ft)

While most of her crew were rescued, 16 sailors went down with their ship.

In August 1972 a scientific team supported by National Geographic Society searched for the wreck, locating her in 230 feet of water on August 18. Video images confirmed her identity after being compared with the vessel's original plans. Two years later the same team returned to the wreck, and used remotely operated underwater cameras to map her. The ironclad lay upside down, and her turret had become detached, pinned beneath and slightly to the side of her hull.

In January 1975 the site was designated as the First National Marine Sanctuary by the National Oceanic and Atmospheric Administration (NOAA). During the late 1970s further surveys were conducted using ROVs and mixed-gas divers, who physically examined the remains.

The divers were also able to examine the interior of the shipwreck. Although the metal had deteriorated significantly, a number of artifacts were recovered from the crew's quarters, and the internal plan of the ship was recorded. The finds included shoes, tableware, glasses, and weapons. An examination of the engine room revealed the main engine, displaced boilers, and the remains of the coal carried in her bunkers. The archæologists were unable to enter the turret, probably the most evocative part of the ship.

Further survey work in the 1980s revealed signs of deterioration—unless NOAA archæologists intervene, the hull will eventually collapse. The government agency is trying to determine a way to halt the deterioration and plans a stabilization project for the wreck and select recovery of her major components, assisted by the US Navy. The NOAA intends to enter the turret and examine its contents. Work on the project is expected to continue well into the new millennium. One can only hope that they succeed in preserving this unique legacy from the age of the ironclad.

above: *Medicine bottles recovered from the wreck of the USS Monitor's crew quarters. A representative sample of everyday items were recovered from the ironclad during the late 1970s.*

opposite: *A diver examines the overgrown remains of the USS Monitor's stern. The vessel lies upside down, revealing her exposed propeller shaft and mount.*

below: *The crew of the USS Monitor relax on deck after her battle with the CSS Virginia. An awning screens the ventilation grating on the top of her single gun turret.*

CRISTOBAL COLON

1898

A grim reminder of "a splendid little war"

above: *American warships wreak havoc on the lightly armed Spanish cruisers during the one-sided battle. "Action off Santiago de Cuba, May 3rd, 1898." Oil painting by Arthur Dugmore.*

Location: Off Southeastern coast of Cuba – Caribbean Sea
20° 0' N, 75° 58' W
Depth: Medium (30–100ft)

When America declared war on Spain in 1898, a jingoistic American diplomat declared it "A splendid little war." Fought over Spanish control of Cuba, the conflict embraced campaigns in the Philippines and Puerto Rico. By its close, the war had turned the United States into a world power and Spain into a minor one.

The war in Cuba centered around the activities of a small Spanish naval squadron commanded by Admiral Cervera. His force consisted of four modern cruisers: the *Cristobal Colon*, *Almirante Oquendo*, *Vizcaya*, and Cervera's flagship, the *Infanta Maria Teresa*, plus two small destroyers. Cervera's force was sent from Spain and reached Santiago in southeastern Cuba without loss, but within days the Americans had established a tight naval blockade of the port. Santiago de Cuba became the focus of the Cuban campaign, and an American expeditionary force landed at nearby Daiquiri on June 22, 1898.

The land campaign reached its climax with a charge up San Juan Hill, on July 1. The resultant capture of the San Juan heights allowed American troops to overlook the city, making the Spanish position untenable. Cervera could surrender his ships or try to break out. Honor forced the latter choice upon him, but the resulting battle was to be short, brutal, and one-sided.

The Spanish fleet sortied early in the morning of Sunday, July 3. At 9:35am, the American lookouts saw the leading Spanish ship appear at the harbor entrance. The officer in charge, Admiral Schley, ordered them to open fire. As the Spanish ships emerged, they turned hard to starboard and followed the shore, but each was subjected to the concentrated fire of four American battleships. The Spaniards returned fire with their lighter guns, but the heavy American shells had already begun to find their mark.

Santiago de Cuba massacre

The *Infanta Maria Teresa* was the first to be knocked out of the fight; Admiral Cervera ordered her beached on the Cuban shore. Within an hour, two other cruisers were destroyed, as were both of the destroyers. The only survivor of the once-proud Spanish fleet was the cruiser *Cristobal Colon*. Steaming at 15 knots, only the fast battleship *USS Oregon* and cruisers *USS New York* and *Brooklyn* were able to keep up with the *Colon*. The cruisers slowly managed to overhaul her.

By 12:20pm they opened fire, and after 20 minutes they scored a hit, slowing the Spanish ship. The *Colon* returned fire but failed to score a telling hit. Once the battleship came within range, the contest was all but over. By 1:30, the *Cristobal Colon* was forced to beach herself, her hull ablaze from bow to stern. The American victory was complete.

The wreck of the cruiser was located in a shallow bay, 50 miles west of Santiago. Surrounded by the Sierra Maestra mountains, the remoteness of the wreck made access difficult for divers. Following the Cuban revolution in 1956, only Cuban divers or those with government approval were allowed to dive on Cuba's shipwrecks.

In the 1980s the wreck was examined and found to be completely submerged and partly broken up. During the early 1990s the Cuban underwater archæology agency, CariSub, decided to conduct an extensive survey.

The *Cristobal Colon* still carried the scars of her final battle, with buckled armor plates and splintered decks. There was evidence that she had been consumed by a white-hot fire as she settled in the shallow water off the beach; metal artifacts were fused together and human remains were completely charred. Skulls pierced by shrapnel bore testimony to the ferocity of battle, while china tableware bearing the crown of Spain hinted at past glories.

The remains of the *Cristobal Colon* are covered by coral growth and draped by weed, and the hull is slowly disintegrating. The wreck of the once-elegant Spanish cruiser serves as a tomb for her crew as much as a reminder of the carnage wrought in the inappropriately labeled conflict fought just over a century ago.

above: *A Cuban archæologist examines a scatter of coal remaining from the now-collapsed bunkers of the Cristobal Colon.*

below: *Buckled plates and shell holes testify to the pounding inflicted on the Spanish ships by the US Navy. The hull has slowly collapsed over the past century.*

THE GERMAN HIGH SEAS FLEET

1919

The grand scuttle of Scapa Flow

above: *The German fleet enters captivity in Scapa Flow in November 1918.*

During the First World War, Scapa Flow in the Orkney Islands was the main base of the Royal Navy. The islands of the north of Scotland were strategically placed to prevent a sortie of the German High Seas Fleet and to protect the convoys sailing between Britain and her colonies. It was from here that Admiral Jellicoe's Grand fleet set sail to fight the Germans at the Battle of Jutland (1916). It was also the scene of the last naval act of the war.

By 1918, Germany was on her knees, and her admirals decided on one final Wagnerian sortie against the superior British fleet. Faced with certain death, the sailors mutinied and hoisted the red flag over the German fleet. Following the armistice of November 1918, a large portion of the German fleet was interned at Scapa Flow while the Versailles Peace Conference decided its fate.

Within a week, 74 disarmed ships of the former Imperial German Navy were steaming toward Britain's main naval base. The scene was almost unique in naval history, a dangerous foe vanquished without fighting a decisive battle emphasized "the silence and majesty with which seapower attains its ends." On Thursday November 21, the German fleet was safely and neatly interned in Scapa Flow.

The vanquished fleet included 11 battleships, five battlecruisers, and 50 destroyers. Morale was low among the German skeleton crews. Forced to remain aboard their ships, they longed to return home. As the ships were interned rather than captured, the British could not board the vessels, but had to guard them from a distance.

A marvelous display

Seven months later, the German fleet was still there. With the armistice period drawing to a close, Rear-Admiral von Reuter feared that hostilities would break out again. He would not let his ships fall into British hands, so plans were laid to scuttle the fleet. On June 21, 1919, the entire Grand fleet left Scapa Flow to conduct exercises, leaving two destroyers to guard the Germans. Von Reuter seized the chance and gave the command to scuttle.

Around noon, the British guardships noticed that the battleship *Friedrich der Grosse* was settling in the water. As they investigated, they

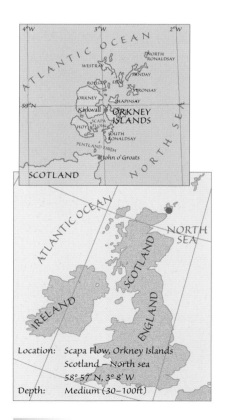

Location: Scapa Flow, Orkney Islands
Scotland – North sea
58° 57' N, 3° 8' W
Depth: Medium (30–100ft)

saw the rest of the German ships follow her lead. The ships had been rigged so that the process was irreversible. There was nothing the British could do but watch the spectacle. Some of the craft, like the battleship *Bayern*, capsized in deep water, while others, like the battlecruiser *Hindenburg*, settled on an even keel. As the boats sank, oil and debris floated to the surface amid boatloads of German sailors.

A party of local schoolchildren witnessed the scene, one calling it "a marvelous display, as the German ships sank all around us." The British boarded and beached some of the cruisers and smaller ships, but by evening over 50 warships lay on the bottom, including all the capital ships. The crews were imprisoned but later repatriated to Germany.

In the 20 years between the scuttling and the outbreak of the Second World War, most of the ships were removed for scrap, many by the salvage firm of Cox and Danks. This operation of raising and removing almost 40 ships was probably one of the largest diving and salvage projects ever undertaken. With the smaller ships, divers passed chains under the wreck; with the help of a floating dock, the craft could be lifted and moved onto the beach. For the battleships, divers patched holes in the hulls, which were then filled with air. Once on the surface the battleships were towed to the scrapyard.

For various reasons, several of the vessels were never salvaged, including three capital ships (the battleships *König*, *Markgraf* and *Kronprinz Wilhelm*), four cruisers, and three destroyers. Today, the wrecks of the German fleet are a diving attraction of international importance. They are protected by a strict no-recovery policy, but divers can still experience the majesty of these dreadnoughts in what amounts to Europe's largest underwater naval history museum.

below: *The crew of a Royal Naval tug examine a partially sunk and beached German destroyer after the scuttling of the High Seas fleet in June 1919.*

HMS ROYAL OAK

1939 Disaster in an invulnerable anchorage

above: *HMS Royal Oak at anchor in Scapa Flow soon before she was sunk by U-47. The attack, which caught the crew completely unprepared below decks, resulted in a very high death toll.*

Location: Scapa Flow, Orkney Islands
Scotland – North sea
58° 58' N, 2° 59' W
Depth: Medium (30–100ft)

When Britain entered the Second World War on September 13, 1939, the Royal Navy considered itself prepared for the conflict. The fleet reestablished itself in its old anchorage at Scapa Flow, a large, naturally protected body of water in the Orkney Islands, off the north of Scotland. It allowed easy access to the North Sea and the Atlantic—well placed to intercept any German maneuver. Access was restricted to a half-dozen entrances, which were closed using blockships or bridged by anti-submarine nets and patrolling warships. The base was deemed invulnerable to submarine attack.

At the outbreak of war, Commodore Karl Dönitz, commander of the German U-boat fleet, decided a daring commander could find a way into the anchorage. He chose Kapitänleutnant Günther Prien, commander of *U-47*. On October 8, 1939, the U-boat slipped out of Kiel. Four days later, she lay off Orkney as Prien decided how to enter Scapa Flow.

Near midnight, the U-boat surfaced and approached Kirk Sound, between the Orkney mainland and the island of Lambs Holm. Carried by the current and running on her silent electric motors, the boat managed to dodge the blockships and the headlights of a passing car. The U-boat was past the obstructions and loose in the anchorage!

Prien headed for the west side of the anchorage but found it empty of large warships. The U-boat turned toward the north of Scapa Flow, where reconnaissance flights reported seeing battleships at anchor. Prien crept along the eastern shore, hardly believing his bad luck at finding the anchorage deserted. Suddenly, the lookouts detected the shape of battleship, which they identified as Royal Sovereign class. It was *HMS Royal Oak*.

An unexpected assault

The *Royal Oak* was commissioned in May 1916, in time to participate in the Battle of Jutland. She was 614 feet long, had a fully loaded displacement of 35,000 tons (31,751 tonnes), and carried a crew of 1,198. She was armed with eight 15-inch guns, capable of firing a shell over

15 miles, and a secondary battery of 6-inch) guns. She was modernized three years before the war, and was considered a valuable part of the Royal Navy. On the night of October 13–14, she lay peacefully at anchor in the northeast corner of Scapa Flow.

At 1:00am, *U-47* fired three torpedoes from her bow tubes at the *Royal Oak*, 3,000 yards away. A fourth torpedo failed to launch. Prien swung his craft around and fired two torpedoes from his stern tubes. Four minutes later, the Germans heard a single muffled explosion. There was no apparent reaction from the *Royal Oak*, so Prien fired his reloaded bow tubes. Three minutes later the silence was broken by three huge explosions. The *U-47* was already away to safety; on October 17, Prien sailed into Kiel to a hero's welcome.

The crew of the *Royal Oak* thought the first muffled explosion was caused by an explosion in a paint store. Damage control parties tried to control the resulting fires. The second salvo ripped out her bottom and side 20 minutes later, and the ship listed heavily to starboard. By 1:30pm she capsized and sank, taking 833 sailors down with her.

Today, *HMS Royal Oak* lies in 98 feet of water, lying as she settled 60 years ago. Nets were placed over her to prevent bodies floating to the surface, and Naval divers recently removed her propellers to form part of a war memorial. Otherwise, she remains untouched, her status as a war grave preventing the attention of divers and souvenir hunters.

Her upturned hull can be seen from the surface through a diving mask, while the superstructure pinned beneath the hull is intact, save for a covering of marine growth. On the surface of Scapa Flow, a wreck buoy marks the site of her grave, and every year a wreath is cast into the sea over the *Royal Oak*'s remains, a tribute to the hundreds of dead souls beneath the waves.

above: *A wreck buoy marks the last resting place of the once-proud battleship and over 800 of her crew.*

below: *The beautiful and tranquil anchorage of Scapa Flow in the Orkney Islands was deemed to be secure against attack by German U-boats.*

INDEX